Measuring the Value of a Postsecondary Education

Edited by

KEN NORRIE *and* **MARY CATHARINE LENNON**

Queen's Policy Studies Series
School of Policy Studies, Queen's University
McGill-Queen's University Press
Montreal & Kingston • London • Ithaca

Copyright © 2013

SCHOOL OF
Policy Studies

Publications Unit
Robert Sutherland Hall
138 Union Street
Kingston, ON, Canada
K7L 3N6
www.queensu.ca/sps/

The preferred citation for this book is:
Norrie, K., and M.C. Lennon, eds. 2013. *Measuring the Value of a Postsecondary Education.*
Montreal and Kingston: Queen's Policy Studies Series, McGill-Queen's University Press.

Library and Archives Canada Cataloguing in Publication

  Measuring the value of a postsecondary education / edited by Ken Norrie, Mary Catharine Lennon.

(Queen's policy studies series)
Based on papers presented at a conference organized by the Higher Education Quality Council of Ontario, May 19-20, 2011:
Includes bibliographical references.
ISBN 978-1-55339-325-2

  1. Education, Higher—Aims and objectives—Congresses. 2. Education, Higher—Evaluation—Congresses. 3. Educational tests and measurements—Congresses. 4. Educational change—Congresses. I. Norrie, K. H. (Kenneth Harold), 1946- II. Lennon, Mary Catharine III. Queen's University (Kingston, Ont.). School of Policy Studies IV. Higher Education Quality Council of Ontario V. Series: Queen's policy studies series

LB2322.2.M42 2013   378   C2013-900037-2

CONTENTS

ABOUT THE AUTHORS

JEANA ABROMEIT is Professor of Sociology and Chair of the Council for Student Assessment at Alverno College in Milwaukee, Wisconsin. In August 2013 she became Associate Vice President of Academic Affairs. Abromeit received her doctorate from the University of Colorado at Boulder. In addition to her teaching, she has served as a consultant with faculty and institutions in the United States and internationally on teaching, learning, assessment, program/institutional assessment and cultural diversity. She is a consultant/trainer/mentor for the Higher Learning Commission, an accrediting institution and part of the North Central Association of Colleges and Schools. Since 1976, the Alverno College Educational Research and Evaluation Office has been conducting research on student learning outcomes, tracking entire classes of students from entry to graduation and up to five years afterward. Alverno College studies examine relationships among teaching, learning and assessment in general education and across different major fields.

ROGER BENJAMIN is President and CEO of the New York-based Council for Aid to Education, developers of the Collegiate Learning Assessment, which is considered the gold standard for measuring postsecondary learning outcomes. He was a senior research scientist at the RAND Corporation from 1990 to 2005 and director of RAND Education from 1994–1999. Previously, at the University of Minnesota, he was a member of the political science department, associate dean and executive officer for the College of Liberal Arts and vice president for academic affairs and provost. He also served as senior vice chancellor for academic affairs and provost at the University of Pittsburgh. Benjamin is the author or co-author of numerous monographs and articles on institutional design-related questions in political economy and education policy. He directs a program to introduce performance assessment throughout the K–16 education system in the United States and the member countries of the Organisation for Economic Co-operation and Development (OECD) as part of its Assessment of Higher Education Learning Outcomes (AHELO) project. The **Council for Aid to Education (CAE)** is a national non-profit organization initially established in 1952 to advance corporate support of education and to conduct policy research on higher education. Today CAE is also focused on improving quality and access in higher education. The Collegiate Learning Assessment (CLA) is central to that focus, a national effort to assess the quality of undergraduate education by directly measuring student learning outcomes.

KEN DRYDEN is a Canadian politician, lawyer, businessman, author, and former NHL goaltender. First elected to the House of Commons as a Member of Parliament in 2004, he was re-elected in 2006 and 2008. From 2004 to 2006, he was Minister of Social Development. A member of the Hockey Hall of Fame, the Canadian Sports Hall of Fame and the International Scholar-Athlete Hall of Fame, he was a goaltender for the Montreal Canadiens from 1971 to 1979, during which time the team won six Stanley Cups. His community and charitable work has focused largely on children, youth and education. He created the Ken Dryden Scholarships, awarded to young people currently or formerly in the care of the Canadian child welfare system. He holds a degree in history from Cornell University, a degree in law from McGill University and seven honorary degrees. He is the author of five books: *The Game, Home Game, The Moved and the Shaken, In School* and *Becoming Canada*.

MICHAEL GALLAGHER is Executive Director, Group of Eight, Australia. This group comprises the eight leading research-intensive universities in Australia, which demonstrate innovation in learning quality and evaluation.

Gallagher's previous positions include director of policy and planning at The Australian National University; head of Australian Education International within the Department of Education, Science and Training; head of the Commonwealth administration of higher education; and head of the Department of Employment Education and Training Corporate Services. He has a long history in the education industry including teacher and lecturer and a member of the Wran Committee on Higher Education Financing. He has worked overseas for the World Bank and also continues to undertake work for the Organisation for Economic Co-operation and Development on higher education issues.

VIRGINIA HATCHETTE is CEO, Postsecondary Education Quality Assessment Board (PEQAB), which is the Ontario agency charged with evaluating the quality of postsecondary programs and assessing whether students meet learning outcomes. Hatchette has worked in the Ontario public service for 10 years, and has held positions related to degree quality assurance, and university governance and accountability. With PEQAB colleagues, she co-authored Ontario's degree qualifications framework, and with provincial partners, the pan-Canadian degree quality framework. Prior to joining the Ontario public service, she was a faculty member in the department of psychology at St. Mary's University in Halifax. She has published in the area of student achievement and created educational shareware. Established in 2000 under the *Post-secondary Education Choice and Excellence Act*, PEQAB reviews the quality of degree programs offered pursuant to the consent of the Minister of Training, Colleges and Universities, and the capacity of institutions to provide them.

JILLIAN KINZIE is Associate Director, Indiana University Center for Postsecondary Research and the NSSE Institute. Kinzie conducts research and leads project activities on effective use of student engagement data to improve educational quality, and is currently co-principal investigator on the Spencer Foundation-funded project, Learning to Improve: A Study of Evidence-Based Improvement in Higher Education. She managed the Documenting Effective Education Practices project and Building Engagement and Attainment of Minority Students, and is a research associate on the National Institute for Learning Outcomes Assessment project, an initiative to assist institutions and others in discovering and adopting promising practices in the assessment of college student learning outcomes. She received her doctorate in higher education from Indiana University Bloomington. Prior to this, she was a faculty member at Indiana University and worked as a researcher and administrator in academic and student affairs at several institutions, including Miami University and Case Western Reserve University. She has co-authored numerous publications including *Student Success in College: Creating Conditions that Matter*. The **National Survey of Student Engagement (NSSE)** is one of the most widely used instruments for measuring postsecondary student engagement. Established in 1998, NSSE annually collects information at hundreds of four-year colleges and universities in the United States and Canada about student participation in programs and activities that institutions provide for their learning and personal development. The results provide an estimate of how undergraduates spend their time and what they gain from attending college.

DIANE LALANCETTE is an assessment analyst at the Organisation for Economic Co-operation and Development's Directorate for Education and its Assessment of Higher Education Learning Outcomes (AHELO) project, which will test what students in higher education know and can do upon graduation. She has worked as a specialist in measurement and evaluation for the past 20 years and has held positions in three different Canadian provinces responsible for policy, marking, and reporting of student assessment results. She was also responsible for the implementation and administration of national and international assessment programs as well as the analysis, interpretation and reporting of those assessments. Lalancette has worked with national and international education assessment experts and senior government officials in the development and implementation of public policies and new programs, developing and monitoring performance measures and other education indicators. She holds a master's in education, measurement and evaluation from Université de Montréal, where she also lectured. OECD's Assessment of Higher Education Learning Outcomes project is a direct evaluation of student performance and will provide data on the relevance and quality of teaching and learning in higher education. The test aims to be global and valid across diverse cultures, languages and different types of institutions as a tool for universities to assess and improve their teaching; for students to make better choices in selecting institutions; for policy-makers toward greater accountability; and for employers to know if the skills of the graduates entering the job market match their needs.

MARY CATHARINE LENNON is a Senior Research Analyst at the Higher Education Quality Council of Ontario (HEQCO), an arms-length research agency of the Ontario government, where she is currently leading projects on establishing and measuring learning outcomes.

Her understanding of higher education research and policy comes from both academic research and professional experiences. She has been involved in higher education policy development, advice and research in institutional, provincial, inter-provincial and international educational agencies including the Council of Ministers of Education, Canada, and the Association of Commonwealth Universities. She also studied comparative and international higher education issues and policies in both her Masters and Doctoral programs. Currently a PhD Candidate in Higher Education at OISE/University of Toronto, she also holds degrees from Simon Fraser University (MA, Educational Leadership) and Queen's University (BA, Psychology).

With this background, the majority of her work extends towards international and comparative system level policy issues including System Design, Accountability, Quality Assurance and Governance. She is currently responsible for HEQCO's suite of student learning outcomes projects including piloting the Collegiate Learning Assessment across the province, facilitating Tuning projects with three sectors of academic disciplines, and acting as the Canadian National Project Manager for the OECD's AHELO feasibility study.

HOLIDAY HART MCKIERNAN is General Counsel and Vice President of Operations for the Indianapolis, Indiana-based Lumina Foundation, the largest foundation in the United States dedicated exclusively to increasing students' access to, and success in, postsecondary education. McKiernan directs the foundation's legal affairs and also leads Lumina's exploration of the Bologna Process—the European Union's project to harmonize higher education programs and degrees by defining curricula learning outcomes by subject area. She speaks frequently on legal, governance and policy issues concerning non-profit organizations and higher education institutions. Prior to joining Lumina in 2003, she was executive director and counsel for Alpha Chi Omega and advised universities on approaches to high-risk student behaviour. She has co-authored several journal articles on institutional change and learning assessment. She serves on numerous boards including the Board of Visitors for DePauw University, from which she received her BA. She received her law degree from Indiana University. **Lumina Foundation for Education** is a private, independent foundation based in Indianapolis and founded in 2000. Lumina is committed to enrolling and graduating more students from college, and pursues this goal by identifying and supporting effective practice, encouraging effective public policy, and using its communications and convening capacity to build public will for change.

KEN NORRIE earned a BA (Honours) in economics from the University of Saskatchewan in 1967 and a PhD from Yale University in 1971. He joined the University of Alberta in 1971, was Chair of Economics 1997–99 and Dean of Arts 1999–2001. He joined McMaster University in 2002 as Professor of Economics and, until October 2006, as Provost and Vice-President (Academic). He was Vice-President (Research) for the Higher Education Quality Council of Ontario (HEQCO) from February 2007 until January 2012. He retired from McMaster University with the rank of Professor Emeritus.

Professor Norrie was seconded to the Royal Commission on the Economic Union and Development Prospects for Canada 1983–85. In 1990–91, he was Clifford Clark Visiting Economist at the Department of Finance, Government of Canada. He was the editor of *Canadian Public Policy/Analyse de Politique* 1986–90 and has served on several editorial boards.

Professor Norrie's teaching and research interests lie in the areas of Canadian economic history, higher education, regional economics, and economic policy. He is the author or co-author of five monographs and numerous journal articles, book chapters, conference proceedings and HEQCO reports.

ROBERT WAGENAAR is Historian, Director of Undergraduate and Graduate Studies at the Faculty of Arts of the University of Groningen in the Netherlands and joint coordinator of Tuning Educational Structures in the World, projects to design and implement curricula on the basis of a student-centred approach and learning outcomes. Wagenaar is an external higher education expert for the European Commission and has been involved in initiatives to harmonize European higher education, including the development of a European Credit Transfer and Accumulation System and the Qualifications Framework for the European Higher Education Area. He chairs the Dutch team of experts for the implementation of the Bologna Process in Dutch higher education institutions. He is coordinator of the Erasmus Mundus Master Programme of Excellence Euroculture: Europe in the Wider World, and joint coordinator of the Erasmus Mundus External Cooperation Windows for Mexico and Central America. Tuning methodology has been tested in some 60 countries, including Russia, 19 countries in Latin America and the USA. Most recent Tuning initiatives are the development of Sectoral Qualifications Frameworks for Social Sciences (2008–2010) and Humanities and the (performing and Creative) Arts (2010–) and Tuning Australia, Tuning USA and a Tuning feasibility study for Africa, commissioned by the European Commission (2010–2011). As part of the OECD AHELO project, Tuning designed Conceptual Frameworks of Expected/Desired Learning Outcomes in Economics and Engineering.

LORNE A. WHITEHEAD, Professor and NSERC/3M Chair, Physics and Astronomy, University of British Columbia, leads the Carl Weiman Science Education Initiative—a five-year project to improve undergraduate science education through defining and measuring learning outcomes. Whitehead received his doctorate in applied optics from UBC and has substantial experience in technological, business and administrative innovation. He received his BA, master's and doctoral degrees in physics from UBC and has extensive private industry experience, both in collaboration with major multinational firms and in the founding of several UBC spin-off companies. He has held a number of administrative positions at UBC including associate dean, dean pro tem, vice-president academic and leader of education innovation. In these roles he has worked to apply the methodology of innovation to the improvement of teaching and learning. Currently, in collaboration with the Carnegie Foundation for the Advancement of Teaching, he is helping to organize a network of universities studying the influence that senior leadership can have on accelerating the adoption of evidence-based improvements of teaching and learning in higher education. The **Carl Wieman Science Education Initiative** was conceived to reshape science education at UBC. Its primary mission is to support science departments in their efforts to provide a superior education for all undergraduate students enrolled. The program explores useful and efficient ways to incorporate research on learning science and measuring the learning of science into the standard educational practices of departments and faculty, and identifies (or develops as needed) effective, reliable, and easily used educational technology.

FOREWORD

Harvey P. Weingarten

The legislated mandate of the Higher Education Quality Council of Ontario (HEQCO) is to provide advice to the provincial government to improve the accessibility, quality, and accountability of Ontario's public postsecondary system. The advice we provide is based on research we commission or conduct, examination and assessment of international best practices or distillation of advice we get from experts.

The issue of quality dominates HEQCO's current agenda. There are several reasons for this. First, the quality of the education provided by a postsecondary system (and, therefore, the quality of its graduates) is rightfully the currency by which a higher education system is judged and ranked. Second, the dominant expectation imposed by students, the public, and governments on its public higher education system is the responsibility to prepare students for successful, meaningful, and contributing personal and professional lives. Third, there is reason to be concerned about the quality of higher education in light of the significant increases of enrolment that have taken place without a commensurate increase in resources. This problem is particularly acute in Ontario because of the success its system has had in accommodating the large number of students desiring a postsecondary education, even in financially difficult times.

We appreciate the significant literature that has attempted to define what is meant by "quality" in higher education and how it should be measured. Our strategy at HEQCO was not to get deeply involved in these important, but often theoretical, debates. Rather, we have adopted the pragmatic approach, as have others, of examining quality by asking the question of what it is graduates should know and be able to do upon completion of their programs and the allied question of how these desired learning outcomes could be measured. To that end, we are sponsoring research evaluating presumed effective teaching methods in large classes or the ways learning technologies can be used to promote better learning. In addition, we are leading the Ontario participation in an international assessment of learning outcomes [as part of the Organisation for Economic Co-operation and Development's Assessment of Higher Education Learning Outcomes (AHELO) project], employing the Tuning method to our discipline "sectors," and piloting the Collegiate Learning Assessment (a measure of the acquisition and development of critical thinking skills) in universities and colleges. I invite you to visit our website (www.heqco. ca) to get more details on these various projects and their current status.

Prior to starting these projects, we thought it would be a good idea to hear from experts around the world who were already deeply engaged in the articulation and measurement of learning outcomes. So, in May 2011, we convened an international group of experts in Toronto to speak about the approaches they have taken to the articulation and measurement of learning outcomes. This monograph presents their contributions to the conference. We thank the speakers for their participation and for their willingness to share their insights and best thinking with us. We hope that their contributions help you, as they did for us, better appreciate how the adoption of a learning outcomes perspective can improve quality in higher education and contribute to the resolution of a variety of vexing challenges, such as the creation of a more robust transfer credit system, that now face public postsecondary systems.

Harvey P. Weingarten
President and CEO
Higher Education Quality Council of Ontario
Toronto, Ontario

Introduction and Overview

Ken Norrie and Mary Catharine Lennon

The quality of higher education has received increasing attention internationally in recent years. There are a number of reasons for this focus. Fiscal considerations are one obvious factor. Years of underfunding in the face of rising enrolments have meant higher student–faculty ratios, larger average class sizes, increasing reliance on contract professors, and more online course delivery. While firm evidence is still lacking, there is a widespread presumption that these changes have meant diminished educational quality. Higher education is widely viewed as a key input to success in the new economy, so there is a noticeable interest in testing this presumption.

Those paying for higher education are demanding more accountability from the sector. Incremental revenue in many jurisdictions has come disproportionately from tuition and other fees, causing students and their families to pay closer attention to what they are getting for their higher education investment. Governments, too, are seeking evidence of educational quality as they are faced with allocating increasingly scarce public funds among competing priorities.

Globalization has also played a major role. Increasing numbers of students travel abroad to study and growing numbers of colleges and universities compete to attract them, creating both a demand for information on educational quality and an incentive to supply it. Graduates are also more mobile internationally, leading to a need among employers for better information on the knowledge and skills embodied in credentials from unfamiliar higher education systems.

The rise of new higher education providers is another factor. Colleges are offering university credit courses and new universities—public and private, domestic and foreign—are springing up in many jurisdictions. To generate enrolment, these institutions need to provide a clear indication

Measuring the Value of a Postsecondary Education, ed. K. Norrie and M.C. Lennon. Montreal and Kingston: Queen's Policy Studies Series, McGill-Queen's University Press. © 2013 All rights reserved.

about the quality of their programs to potential entering students, graduate and professional school admission officers, and potential employers.

Finally, and not to be underestimated, there is real concern about the potential distorting effects of university rankings. These exercises have proliferated in recent years and receive considerable media and public attention. The variables that enter into the calculations differ among rankings, but most rely heavily on input indicators and reputational surveys. The concern is that institutions will respond to the rankings by focusing on indicators that are, at best, only loosely associated with learning quality.

There has been a flurry of activity in recent decades responding to these challenges. There is a discernible sequence in the response, although developments did not proceed in neat chronological order. The first step in the new focus on quality was to shift from viewing educational attainment as a set of inputs, such as credits completed, to viewing it as a set of learning outcomes and abilities. Europe was the epicentre of this activity, although the approach was quickly adopted and adapted in other jurisdictions.

As the shift to learning outcomes and abilities spread, the logical next step was to determine if these outcomes were actually being achieved. This task meant developing credible tools to measure something as complex and multi-dimensional as higher education. There has been considerable progress in developing and disseminating measurement tools, but observers agree that much work remains.

Having the tools to measure and evaluate outcomes and competencies is only valuable if institutions are willing and able to use the information effectively in their academic planning. Hence, the third step was to incorporate evidence on learning quality outcomes into academic planning exercises. Here, progress is lagging. The culture of measurement and continuous improvement is often lacking in higher education institutions. And, even when it is present, they do not always have the skills and experience to use data effectively.

The Higher Education Quality Council of Ontario (HEQCO) convened a conference in Toronto on 19–20 May 2011 at which educational leaders from around the world were invited to report on efforts to enhance educational quality and to share their insights on next steps. This volume contains the papers presented at the conference. The order follows the sequence noted above. Section I details the efforts to define higher education quality in terms of learning outcomes. Section II deals with measurement issues: why we should measure, how we might measure, and why measurement still encounters such resistance. Section III addresses the challenge of bringing about culture change in higher education institutions and provides examples where significant change has been achieved.

REDEFINING EDUCATIONAL QUALITY

As noted, Europe was the epicentre of the shift to learning outcomes in postsecondary education. These education initiatives were part of a larger set of policy responses to European economic integration and the goal of increased labour mobility. Officials understood that the patchwork set of higher education frameworks in place acted as a barrier to the international movement of skilled labour, and that some degree of harmonization was required.

The result was the Bologna Declaration of 1999 and its subsequent refinements. This process, ultimately agreed to by 47 European ministers of education, was to create an integrated European Higher Education Area (EHEA) by 2010. The process had a number of complementary goals and activities, but three elements are key to the present discussion:

- establish a common system of degree types,
- achieve the harmonization of degree types through Qualifications Frameworks that set out expected learning outcomes, and
- extend the curriculum and performance criteria to the discipline level.

The first element required the replacement of a patchwork set of degree types with the Anglo-Saxon model of cycles: defined as short cycle (generally equivalent to the Canadian college diploma or US associate's degree), first cycle (first undergraduate degree) and second cycle (i.e., master's degree). Later, the third cycle (doctoral education) was included. The structure is now commonly known as the 3+2+3, indicating the length of time of each first, second, and third cycle. For some countries, such as the United Kingdom, Ireland, and France, this system was generally in place and required limited systemic modification. For others, such as Germany, and those using the post-soviet model of longer first degrees, this required a full overhaul of the existing system.

Harmonization of degree length and structure began with the development of the Dublin Descriptors, which set out expected learning outcomes for the three initial cycles. Briefly, learning outcomes are statements of what a learner is expected to know, to understand, and/or be able to demonstrate after completion of learning. They are formulated or expressed in terms of abilities, or, as they are more commonly known in Europe, competences, that the learner is expected to develop over the course of study. That is, this approach conceives of educational quality as a set of learning outcomes, rather than as a set of inputs, and encourages course and curriculum designers to consider what students can do with what they have learned.

The Dublin Descriptors were the foundation of the postsecondary section of the European Qualifications Framework (EQF), a document agreed to in 2008 which describes learning outcomes at eight levels of education (from basic to advanced education). The General Qualifications for Credentials in the European Higher Education Area (specific to postsecondary education) outlines the qualifications upon completion of a "cycle." The transnational document has three areas of what they describe as Learning Outcomes: knowledge, skills, and competences. The intent is that all higher education systems in Europe will align with the criteria and structures in order to ease student credit transfer, mobility, and recognition.

The EQF is the basis of National Qualifications Frameworks (NQFs) in each country. NQFs are meant to align with the EQF but allow for local variation. NQFs have developed at different speeds in different countries, but they all relate back to, and are in line with, the EQF. The result is that most European nations now have national frameworks that outline degree level expectations.

National qualifications frameworks are still quite general, however, focusing as they do on credential levels. The obvious challenge was to extend the concept of expected learning outcomes determined by international bodies and national governments into the institutions and into the programs themselves. This required a different way of thinking to ensure that there was agreement across Europe in what knowledge and skills do graduates of, say, chemical engineering or history programs have, and what can they do with their education.

The Tuning process described in the paper by Robert Wagenaar is the response to the challenge of implementing system-wide changes in institutions that are fundamentally autonomous. Wagenaar is co-director of the International Tuning Academy and Director of undergraduate and graduate studies at the University of Groningen in the Netherlands. He has been an instrumental player in the Tuning project from its inception.

The Tuning project was intended to support the Bologna Process by supporting dialogue on the transformation of the system at the university level by enhancing understanding, transparency, and agreement in the description of higher education programs.

Tuning complements the Bologna Process in two important ways. First, as noted, it extends the idea of learning outcomes and competencies to the program level. Tuning has spurred the development of benchmark statements for a growing number of subject areas. Initially, these were for traditional subject areas, such as chemistry or history, but they have now been extended to professional degrees and interdisciplinary programs. A key feature of this extension is to identify and articulate both generic and subject-specific components. Wagenaar stresses that these learning outcomes and competencies are meant to be points of reference only, and that there is ample room for diversity and autonomy.

The other unique feature of Tuning is that it is a bottom-up rather than top-down process. Subject area groups of approximately 15 academics from a range of nations draw up conceptual frameworks for their respective disciplines. These program profiles are developed through extensive consultation and feedback from faculty, students, alumni, employers, and professional organizations.

Tuning also pays attention to the need to identify the best approaches and methodologies to achieve the learning outcomes. The list of possible learning activities is extensive, ranging from lectures and seminars to work-based practice and online/distance courses. Best practices will vary among programs, but Tuning stresses that the actual choice should be reflected in course manuals. Wagenaar acknowledges that this step is still very much a work in progress.

In sum, the Tuning methodology is a dynamic, multi-step process: determine the need and potential of a degree program; define the program learning outcomes and key competencies; identify these for each module or course unit; identify the approach to teaching, learning, and assessment; and implement, monitor, and improve.

Tuning has had wide international dissemination: 19 Latin American countries, seven US states, Australia, Russia, Africa and (now) Ontario have all undertaken Tuning projects. Each jurisdiction has adapted the framework to suit its own purposes, but the fundamental notion of academics and experts collaborating on suitable learning outcomes that compliment and support the existing, or developing, Qualifications Frameworks is widespread.

The bold European initiative of a harmonized European Higher Education Area was repeatedly met with fear of standardization, concerns with implementation, and reluctance to change. However, after a decade of efforts, the Bologna Process is considered to be a significant success. Not only has the Bologna Process increased integration, transparency, and mobility in Europe, it has provided inspiration to other jurisdictions, where the concepts and activities were adopted and also adapted to suit the local higher education environments.

The United States of America is one such jurisdiction. Holiday Hart McKiernan, Vice President Strategic Operations and Chief of Staff, traces the development of activities at the Lumina Foundation, primarily focusing on Tuning USA and the Degree Qualifications Profile. Lumina is a US-based independent foundation with the primary goal of supporting postsecondary participation in the United States of America. More specifically, they have proposed a target of a 60 percent attainment rate by the year 2025. Founded on principles of the economic and civic benefits of education, Lumina believes clearly articulated educational outcomes are vital to ensuring labour market success of its citizens, ultimately improving national productivity. Hence, their primary work is to focus on establishing ways to define and articulate quality.

Their first activity in this area was to examine the work of the European Tuning activities and adapt them into the Tuning USA project. Based on the European model, Lumina worked in six disciplines across institutions in a number of states to clarify the value of a credential. While the results of tuning various disciplines across institutional types are still coming in, its initial findings suggested that faculty engagement is key to the process, as is recognizing that what is valuable has not always been measured.

Stemming from the Tuning activities of establishing commonalities at the discipline level, it became apparent that the United States of America required a common Degree Qualifications Profile. The Degree Profile is intended to be a roadmap that sets out reference points that articulate and benchmark the skills and knowledge gained in an associate's, bachelor's and master's degree. It classifies learning outcomes into the area of broad, integrative knowledge; specialized knowledge; intellectual skills; applied learning; and civic learning.

Hart McKiernan notes that the presence of clear and trusted learning outcomes allows the Degree Profiles to serve a number of purposes. First, it can aid students in better understanding the pathways available to them. Also, it can be seen as a powerful economic tool which demonstrates the skills and abilities of graduates, and with feedback from employers, there can be greater alignment between education and the labour market. The common understanding of Degree Profiles may also assist institutions in developing their curriculum, as it provides a reference framework. Currently, Degree Profiles are being piloted in some institutions to determine how this might take place.

Finally, in the decentralized US system, the Profiles may aid a common understanding of a credential while still respecting institutional autonomy. Furthermore, they may be a powerful tool for accreditors, by supporting consistent and transparent expectations and quality assurance processes. In providing a common framework for describing learning outcomes, Lumina hopes to influence the conversation towards accurately measuring quality. This, in turn, should aid the education to labour market alignment, ultimately improving the productivity of the nation.

The next chapter in this section is by Michael Gallagher, Executive Director of the Group of Eight (universities) in Australia. Gallagher focuses on the series of higher education reforms undertaken in Australia in the period since 2008 aimed at making Australia one of the most highly educated and skilled nations in the world. He covers eight major policy initiatives, three of which deal specifically with learning outcomes and competencies.

One initiative was to revise the *Australian Qualifications Framework* (AQF), first introduced in the mid-1990s. The new AQF identifies ten qualification types and titles (e.g., bachelor's degree) and for each describes learning outcomes in terms of knowledge, skills, and application of knowledge and skills. The appendices to the paper present the range of descriptors for the higher education qualification types (levels six to ten) and more specific descriptors for three types of master's degrees.

Gallagher describes the new framework as being stronger and more coherent than the former.

A second initiative was the creation of a new national body for regulation and quality, the Tertiary Education Quality and Standards Agency (TEQSA), which began operations in spring 2012. This body will ultimately have a wide range of powers, such as accrediting providers, evaluating the performance of institutions and programs, encouraging best practices, simplifying regulatory arrangements, and providing greater national consistency. The agency will establish minimum acceptable standards and will require higher education providers to meet or exceed these standards to remain registered.

TEQSA provides an interesting example of the struggle between government regulation of higher education and institutional autonomy. The initial bill met considerable resistance from university leaders and was subsequently redrafted to take some of these concerns into account. As of yet, there are no guidelines on teaching and learning standards, research standards, or information standards, although these are expected in 2012.

A third initiative was increased attention to the articulation of academic standards, and measurement issues in particular. Australia is participating in the engineering strand of Assessment of Higher Education Learning Outcomes (AHELO) (see below), and the Australian Council for Educational Research (ACER) is actively involved in developing and piloting tests for the AHELO initiative.

The Australian government also supported a one-year demonstration project to investigate teaching and learning standards. The idea was to develop threshold learning outcomes for subject areas. Outcomes were generated for a number of disciplines, with more expected by the end of 2012. The descriptions take the form of expected graduate capabilities and vary in the degree of detail. Interestingly, TEQSA will not use these statements in its quality assurance role.

Gallagher assesses these recent Australian initiatives in light of a specific set of higher-education criteria including improving national coherence; moving to the forefront of international practice; and addressing public concerns such as effectiveness, transparency, and comparability. He concludes that there is greater policy and regulatory consistency on a national basis and that Australia's new regulatory framework is "internationally advanced." But, tensions remain. He argues that the government's policy initiatives and underfunding are putting downward pressure on quality and calls for a more nuanced policy framework and a more mutual process of policy development.

The final chapter in this section is by Virginia Hatchette who was, at the time of the conference, CEO of the Postsecondary Education Quality Assurance Board (PEQAB).

Education is a provincial responsibility in Canada, and regulatory processes vary markedly across the country. Ontario is the largest province and has the greatest concentration of higher education institutions. There are 20 public universities offering degrees; 24 public colleges offering certificates, diplomas, and degrees; a smattering of private and out-of-province institutions offering various credentials; and a large number of private career colleges providing occupational training.

Ontario has three sets of quality assurance processes. The Council of Ontario Universities (COU) is responsible for quality assurance for under-graduate and graduate programs at the province's public universities. The Ontario College Quality Assurance Service (OCQAS) oversees diplomas and certificates issued by the colleges. PEQAB is responsible for quality assurance for degrees by colleges and by out-of-province providers.

Hatchette notes that Ontario was a relatively early adopter of qualification frameworks. The reasons for the shift are the familiar ones: new higher education providers, new types of credentials, and new technologies for delivery. The first framework was introduced in Canada in 2003, and a pan-Canadian framework was in place by 2007. Ontario worked with stakeholders to produce the Ontario Qualifications Framework (OQF), which encompasses expected learning outcomes for the full range of credentials from apprenticeship certificates to doctoral degrees.

The OQF has six general categories of competencies that the graduate is meant to achieve: (i) depth and breadth of knowledge, (ii) conceptual and methodological awareness, (iii) communication skills, (iv) application of knowledge, (v) professional capacity / autonomy, and (vi) awareness of the limits of knowledge. These expectations are expressed most generally at the credential level, in more detail at the discipline level, and in most detail for a specific discipline at a specific institution. Hatchette illustrates this principle with the example of an honours bachelor of science degree in psychology. As is the norm, expectations increase with the level of the credential.

Ontario institutions are also expected to be able to demonstrate that expected learning outcomes are being achieved. Methods for doing so vary. For PEQAB experts review a random sample of work by students in the terminal stages of their programs that are deemed by the institution to be exemplary, average, and minimally acceptable. Hatchette notes that direct review of student work is a necessary measure of program quality and, if conducted appropriately, may be a sufficient condition.

APPROACHES TO MEASUREMENT

There is a long history of trying to measure and evaluate educational quality. Traditional approaches fall into three categories. The first is measuring inputs, such as the calibre of students applying and registering, graduation rates, student–faculty ratios, library budgets, proportion of faculty tenured or tenure-track, etc. A second approach is to track labour market outcomes, such as employment rates or average salaries. The third approach is to rely on student and employer surveys. These traditional measures, or at least some of them, are useful for planning purposes but have well-known limitations as quality indicators.

Researchers responded to the need for more credible indicators with a number of new quality measures. The chapters in Section II present the most prominent examples.

The first chapter in this section is by Jillian Kinzie, Associate Director of the Indiana Center for Postsecondary Research. Kinzie writes from her long involvement with the National Survey of Student Engagement (NSSE) and her more recent association with the National Institute for Learning Outcomes Assessment (NILOA).

Kinzie begins by noting that the two purposes of assessment—accountability and improvement—do not rest comfortably together. The accountability paradigm is characterized by external influence, summative judgment, compliance, and a reporting ethos. The products are standardized and comparative measures, and they are meant to be publicly reported. By comparison, the improvement paradigm is internally-motivated, features formative feedbacks, employs multiple instruments, and stresses internal communication.

Kinzie notes that there are two types of measures of educational quality: indirect or process and direct or outcome. The National Survey of Student Engagement (NSSE) is a prominent example of an indirect measure. It is based on research that shows that student engagement is a good proxy measure for desirable learning outcomes. Since 2000, nearly 1,500 universities in the United States of America and Canada have participated in NSSE, and many have incorporated NSSE into their academic planning. More recently, institutions across Australia and New Zealand have participated in the AUSSE (an adapted version of NSSE), along with many other countries, including South Africa.

Direct measures are standardized performance tests designed to demonstrate what students have learned and can do. Prominent examples of direct tests include CAE's Collegiate Learning Assessment (CLA), ACT's Collegiate Assessment of Academic Proficiency, and the ETS® Proficiency Profile.

Kinzie argues that direct and indirect measures can be used effectively together for academic planning purposes. Outcome measures provide evidence of achievement of learning goals while process measures help identify what contributes to outcomes.

The first step in quality enhancement—that of articulating learning outcomes—is now common in the United States of America. A NILOA survey of provosts revealed that three-quarters have adopted common learning outcomes for all undergraduate students. A second NILOA survey at the program or department level revealed that 80 percent had established intended learning outcomes. Special questions on the 2010 NSSE survey indicated that three-quarters of students believed their institution had a common set of learning goals.

The NILOA surveys revealed a wide range of approaches to gathering evidence on learning outcomes. At the institution level, the most common measures are national surveys, such as NSSE and standardized measures of knowledge and skills, such as the Collegiate Learning Assessment (CLA). At the program level, the most common measures are student portfolios and other measures of specialized knowledge.

Kinzie concludes by considering what is stalling progress. She questions the common perception that there is not sufficient, high-quality data available. The challenge, rather, is using the data available to improve student learning for many institutions lack the necessary expertise or experience.

The second chapter in this section is by Roger Benjamin, President of the Council for Aid to Education. Benjamin begins by contrasting the evaluation activities of the two core functions of higher education: undergraduate education and research. There are clear metrics for research, well understood and accepted evaluation processes, and an explicit reward system. Nothing comparable exists for evaluating undergraduate education or even teaching performance.

Benjamin stresses the importance of higher education to future US prosperity, and contrasts this need with the reality of underfunding of recent times, resulting in low participation and completion rates. He sees this underfunding as resulting from confusion over public and private responsibilities for higher education. He urges for a debate on higher education and recognizes that this debate will result in increasing demands for transparency, accountability and restructuring, particularly with respect to the quality and growth of student learning.

He argues that faculty must be central to this process, and for faculty to be involved, the assessment instruments must be seen to be valid and reliable and of direct use in the classroom. He addresses what he terms seven red herrings about assessment in higher education and identifies institutional inertia and risk aversion as the reason these common perceptions are not more widely debunked.

Benjamin argues that credible measurement tools are available. He refers to NSSE and the academic planning initiatives it has spawned and to the standardized tests that Kinzie also references. Benjamin was instrumental in the development of the CLA and offers more detail on this measure. The CLA is designed to gauge generic skills: critical thinking, analytical reasoning, problem solving, quantitative reasoning, and written communication ability. It is generally administered at the institution level and employs a "value-added" approach. Importantly, it allows for differing student abilities by standardizing test results by SAT scores.

The CLA can be longitudinal or cross-sectional in implementation. If longitudinal, students write the test when they enter into their first year of a program and again just before graduating. The results demonstrate (hopefully) the gain in critical thinking acquired over the course of their postsecondary education (be it a two-year diploma or bachelor's degree). The alternative is a cross-sectional design wherein a sample of first- and fourth-year students write the test, with the difference in average scores taken as the measure of institutional value added.

The CLA has a performance task and two writing tasks. The performance task requires students to apply what they have learned to solve problems and make recommendations. They are given access to a document library that contains relevant and useful information as well as some irrelevant material, forcing them to evaluate sources. The writing tasks involve making an argument and breaking an argument.

The final chapter in this section is by Diane Lalancette, Assessment Analyst at the Organisation for Economic Co-operation and Development's (OECD) Directorate for Education. As with other authors, she begins by noting that higher education is a critical factor in success and sustainability of the knowledge economy. Thus, there is a greater need to pay attention to quality and relevance. Yet, there is an information gap as we are not able to make comparative judgments about the capabilities of students in different jurisdictions or the quality of teaching and learning. Without adequate information on these elements, international rankings and comparisons have been largely based on reputation and research.

The AHELO feasibility study initiated by the OECD is an attempt to fill this gap by determining alternate measures of an institution's success. The international organization is well versed at running international assessments including the Programme for International Student Assessment (PISA) and the Programme for the International Assessment of Adult Competencies (PIAAC).

The study's objectives are to test the science of assessment and to test the practicality of implementation. It asks: Is it possible to devise and implement standard tests that can be used by countries with very different languages and cultures and postsecondary systems to measure what final-year undergraduate students know and can do?

AHELO has four strands of research: a generic strand, two discipline-specific strands, and a value-added strand. Additionally, there is data collection on contextual dimensions. There are a minimum of seven jurisdictions in each strand, representing diverse languages and cultures, and all jurisdictions complete the contextual surveys. The tests will be in the field in the spring 2012.

The first strand focuses on generic skills, such as critical thinking, problem solving, etc. AHELO is attempting to use a modified version of the CLA to determine international agreement on generic skills. The second strand focuses on specific disciplines and has designed assessments to test the ability of students to apply knowledge in new situations. The disciplines chosen for the pilot project are economics and civil engineering. The value-added strand seeks to determine if there is a gain in knowledge and skills from the point of entry to the point of exit—similar to the value-added idea of the CLA.

Finally, the context dimension seeks to understand the environments in which the students learn, which includes student background characteristics, faculty characteristics, and institutional characteristics. This information will support a more holistic understanding of student learning.

Lalancette reports that OECD officials are encouraged by the degree of success to date. The pilots have demonstrated that it is possible to reach international agreement on articulating and measuring expected learning outcomes in diverse national and cultural settings and for a range of disciplines, and to provide alternatives to common rankings.

Bringing About Change

The final section deals with the challenges of bringing about the change suggested by the evidence on enhancing educational quality. There are two chapters in this section, although others in the book are also relevant.

The first is by Lorne Whitehead, Professor of Physics and Astronomy at the University of British Columbia. Whitehead begins by asking why we might wish to measure quality and provides two general answers. The first is to ensure "fair value" to students and the public more generally. The second is to guide improvement. He argues that both are important, although his paper relates more to the second motivation.

Whitehead warns of the dangers of measurement in such a complex sector. He argues that it is best to view measurement as a necessary condition for improving quality but not a sufficient one. He also warns of the dangers if we measure the wrong things, the same point made strongly by Ken Dryden in his after-dinner address at the HEQCO conference. Whitehead lists seven common concerns with measurement and elaborates on one in particular: that measurement sometimes "just feels wrong."

The core of Whitehead's chapter is a simple model depicting a hierarchy of factors related to learning. He sees four basic levels. The base level is learning outcomes, i.e., what we want students to obtain from education. The next level up is educational experiences, which can also be thought of as teaching in the broadest sense of that term. The third level comprises factors directly influencing educators, such as knowledge about teaching and the reward structure for effective performance. The top level contains the factors that can influence culture within institutions. He includes leadership in this category, but acknowledges that it is not always easy for leaders to change academic culture significantly.

He notes that evaluation is common at the first level, but that most measures are not useful for long-term retention. Recent tools for gauging student learning are important, but they are slow and expensive guides to improving teaching. Measurement at the second level generally involves student surveys and peer reviews of teaching. These provide shorter feedback loops and are less expensive. Measurement at the third level is very general and ill-defined, although he argues it is possible to gauge specific aspects of culture, such as attitudes about teaching responsibilities, confidence in the reward system, and perception of policies and procedures.

Whitehead concludes by identifying two viewpoints regarding measurement in higher education that, he believes, are holding back progress. One view, common within the sector, is that measurement-based approaches are overly simplistic and are therefore harmful. For many outside the higher education system, this skepticism is seen as an attempt to avoid being accountable. He argues for a middle ground. Measurement is necessary for evaluation and improvement. But, it must be pursued with due diligence and attention to its proper use.

He refers briefly to two initiatives that are attempting this middle ground. The first is the Carl Wieman Science Education Initiative at the University of British Columbia and the University of Colorado Boulder, which he describes as an experimental attempt to enhance the culture of a few academic departments in order to improve teaching and learning. The second is the network program organized by the Carnegie Foundation for the Advancement of Teaching, which uses the techniques of networked improvement communities.

The second chapter in Section IV is by Jeana Abromeit, Professor of Sociology and Chair of the Council for Student Assessment at Alverno College in Milwaukee. Alverno College is widely recognized as a leader and innovator in higher education. The college's very early use of expected learning outcomes, measurement, and evaluation is of particular note for this book.

Abromeit provides a brief history of outcomes and assessment at Alverno. The initiative began in 1970–1971 when the president asked four questions of academic departments that probed the idea of outcomes-based education, and distinguishing between general education and disciplinary knowledge. The responses to the questions produced four institution-wide learning outcomes: (i) communication, (ii) problem solving, (iii) valuing, and (iv) involvement. These outcomes were subsequently extended to eight in number and referred to as abilities. The curriculum has been continuously revised and refined to ensure that students can demonstrate these core abilities.

The principles underlying the Alverno approach illustrate its early adoption of ideas that are now common: educators are responsible for making learning more available by articulating outcomes and making them public; education goes beyond knowing to being able to do what one knows; and abilities need to be defined in a way that our teaching of them features increasing expectations over levels.

Alverno set learning outcomes at three levels—institution, program, and course—which then went into creating an integrated curriculum. She describes the process as follows. First, they specified institution-wide abilities. Then, each department created student learning outcomes for each of its programs, i.e., what a student in a particular major can do with what she knows upon graduation as a result of a set of learning experiences. Next, they formulated learning outcomes for each course. Finally, they developed assessment plans for each program as part of a dynamic process for teaching and learning improvement.

Alverno relies on a number of indicators of student learning: capstone experiences, portfolios, scores and pass rates of licensure/certification exams, substantial course assignments, and group projects. They also rely on indirect indicators, such as student and alumni surveys, exit interviews, focus groups, course evaluations, and NSSE scores.

Ken Dryden's Presentation

The conference dinner speaker was Ken Dryden who can be described variously as former NHL star goalie and member of the Hockey Hall of Fame, former federal politician and cabinet member, as well as author and commentator. He generously agreed to provide a copy of his remarks for inclusion in this book.

He begins by noting the pressures for measurement: the high cost of education and growing student debt levels, uncertain job prospects for graduates, and the trend to measurement in general.

If we are going to measure, as we must, it is important to measure the right things. He illustrates this point with an example from the NHL. A formula ostensibly designed to evaluate players turned out, upon inspection, to work in the opposite direction. The trainer had identified the best player in the game in his (and, to be fair, virtually everyone's) opinion, and then used this profile—his strengths—to decide what were important measures of success. Dryden suggests that this approach sounds a lot like university ranking exercises.

What are the right things to measure? Dryden's response is to talk about what a university or college is and what is its value. It is a place where students realize that learning matters and come to believe that they *can* learn. It is where students develop the capacity and the instinct to "think the future." This is what we need to be able to measure. Because if we can measure these things, we will do them. But if we can only measure the wrong things, he warns, "don't bother."

SUMMARY

This book is intended to provide readers with an overview of key learning outcomes, activities of development, implementation, and assessment taking place worldwide. It is apparent that the activities range significantly. They cover arenas of international, regional, political, and institutional settings. The examples of activities range from large-scale student assessments of engagement or knowledge to small groups of faculty establishing common languages and expectations.

The chapters also demonstrate how learning outcomes can serve different purposes in the landscape of postsecondary education. Some, such as Kinzie, Benjamin, Whitehead, and Abromeit, consider how these activities can be used for institutional change and planning. Others, such as Gallagher, McKiernan, and Hatchette, reflect on how learning outcomes can support accountability and transparency at the system level. Furthermore, the chapters from Wagenaar and Lalancette demonstrate how learning outcomes can contribute to regional and international accountability and transparency.

Despite the dramatically different approaches and purposes of the activities, the work described in each of the chapters in this book demonstrates the emerging trends and similar goals of translating postsecondary education study into a set of understandable and measurable elements.

SECTION I

REDEFINING EDUCATIONAL QUALITY

1

MODERNIZATION OF HIGHER EDUCATION PROGRAMS IN EUROPE: STUDENT-CENTRED AND LEARNING OUTCOMES-BASED

Robert Wagenaar

INTRODUCTION

Until a decade ago, I used to ask new graduates whether they were able to describe—in a number of convincing statements—the (relevant) competences they had developed during their studies for a future employer. The vast majority of students looked completely puzzled. They had never asked this question of themselves, although they were in the process of applying for a job. In class the issue also never arose. Without a doubt, students built up knowledge and skills in a range of modules, but not many raised the question about whether there was consistency in the learning—or should we say teaching—process and whether what was learned / taught was relevant for their employment. Academic staff were convinced they did a good job because it was transferring their know-how to a future generation of graduates and employees. In many cases students took a long time to finish their studies, but who bothered? Much has changed since I first raised my question; a lot has not (yet). Considerable progress has been made to describe programs in terms of their profile and desired outcomes. And as important: serious steps have been made regarding the measuring of the value of postsecondary education both in terms of learning outcomes achieved and employment possibilities. This chapter will describe the activities of the Tuning project over the past ten years as a key element to reach the objective of establishing one European Higher Education Area.

Measuring the Value of a Postsecondary Education, ed. K. Norrie and M.C. Lennon. Montreal and Kingston: Queen's Policy Studies Series, McGill-Queen's University Press. © 2013 All rights reserved.

Harmonizing Systems and Structures

Since 1999 Europe has made tremendous progress in reforming and harmonizing its postsecondary education area. Drivers have been the Bologna Process, based on a Declaration (1999) which has been signed by 47 countries as of 2011, as well as—for the European Union—the Lisbon Strategy, now called Europe 2020. The latter strategy aims to make the European Union a knowledge-based, highly competitive economy in the global arena.

Countries have agreed to implement comparable and compatible student-centred, outcome-based, and transparent higher educational programs. It is imperative that comparability and compatibility be understood against the background of the importance of mobility and transnational education in Europe. Student and staff mobility are viewed as an important means to develop a European Higher Education Area. Additionally, the reforms should be seen in the context of high drop-out rates, which may signify the ineffectiveness of teaching, learning, and assessment that existed in continental European higher education institutions.

In the early stages of the Bologna Process, its initiators concluded that not only systems and structures were required to be harmonized (based on the three cycle model of bachelor, master, and doctorate) but also, clear indicators were needed to measure the outcomes of the learning process at every level. Therefore, an informal group of ministry representatives and higher education quality assurance experts, who dubbed themselves the Joint Quality Initiative (JQI), took the lead defining standalone descriptors for the bachelor, the master, and the doctorate levels. These became known as the Dublin Descriptors and were officially adopted by the Bergen Ministerial Bologna Process follow-up summit of 2005 as part of the Qualifications Framework for the European Higher Education Area.[1]

The Dublin Descriptors provide general statements of typical expectations of achievements and abilities associated with awards that represent the outcomes of learning of a Bologna cycle. The descriptors are phrased in competence levels in such a way that bachelor, master, and doctorate are clearly distinguished from each other. The following five sets of criteria are applied:

- acquiring knowledge and understanding,
- applying knowledge and understanding,
- making informed judgments and choices,
- communicating knowledge and understanding, and
- capacities to continue learning.

At present, all higher education programs in Europe, new and old, are (or should be) assessed within the framework of an external peer review and/or accreditation process, against these criteria.

TUNING PROJECT

At the same time the JQI started its activities, a group of around 100 selected and renowned universities in Europe, supported morally and financially by the European Commission, set up the so-called Tuning Educational Structures in Europe Project, which, since 2000, gradually developed into a process itself. The faculty-based project was a direct response to European governments' policy and activities to develop one European Higher Education Area. For obvious reasons, the stakeholders in higher education—management, faculty and students—wondered whether well thought through reforms would be possible without their (in)direct involvement. This concern was real given the fact that the Bologna Process was mainly steered by government officials.

Tuning "began and developed in the wider context of the constant reflection within higher education, demanded by the rapid pace of change in society (…) The need for compatibility, comparability and competitiveness of higher education in Europe has arisen from the need of students, whose increasing mobility requires reliable and objective information about educational programmes on offer. But besides this, (future) employers in (and outside) Europe require reliable information about what a qualification, a degree stands for in practice" (González and Wagenaar 2003). From the beginning, the Joint Quality Initiative and the Tuning project were considered complementary. This was formally concluded at the official Bologna seminar "Working on the European Dimension of Quality," held in Amsterdam in 2002. It was named the Amsterdam "Consensus," reflected in a report which was published on the official Bologna website (Westerheijden and Leegwater 2003).[2]

The ambitious program drawn up by Tuning can be summarized as follows. The development of:

- a transparent way to (re-)design degree programs based on the concept of student-centred learning: learning outcomes and workload based credits;
- a language understood by all stakeholders (employers, professionals and academics): generic and subject specific competences;
- an approach respecting and allowing for differentiation/diversity;
- an approach for developing flexible and diverse degree programs in a Lifelong Learning context;
- shared reference points at subject area level; and
- methodology for high standard degree programs in terms of process and outcomes.

The Tuning agenda was directly copied into the Berlin Communiqué of 2003: "Ministers encourage the member states to elaborate a framework of comparable and compatible qualifications for their higher education systems, which should seek to describe qualifications in terms of workload, level, learning outcomes, competences, and profile." Since the publication of the Bologna Declaration in 1999, the ministers of the signatory countries have met every two years to reflect on the progress made in the Bologna Process as well as to set new targets for it, expressed in communiqués.[3]

The Tuning methodology, which is described in detail in a number of Tuning publications (Gilpin and Wagenaar 2008) and can also be found on the Tuning website[4], is based on a ten step approach: (i) determine need and potential of a degree program; (ii) define its profile and its key competences; (iii) formulate the program learning outcomes; (iv) decide whether to "modularize" or not: allocate credits to its units / modules; (v) identify competences and formulate learning outcomes for each module or course unit; (vi) determine the approach to teaching, learning, and assessment; (vii) check whether the key generic and subject specific competences are covered; (viii) describe the program and the course units (modules); (ix) check balance and feasibility; and (x) implement, monitor, and improve. This approach is visualized below in Figure 1.

This approach takes into account the opinions of all stakeholders involved; that is, academic staff, students, alumni, (potential) employers, and professional organizations. It has raised awareness about making a distinction between generic or transversal skills or competences on the one hand and subject specific ones on the other.

FIGURE 1
Tuning Dynamic Quality Development Circle

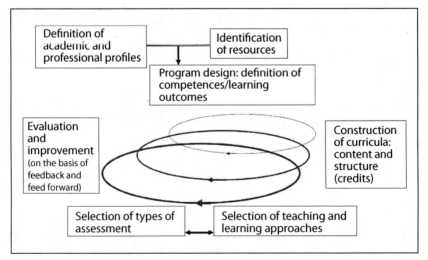

Source: González and Wagenaar (2008).

When designing this methodology, it was concluded that the only reasonable way forward would be to change the paradigm of teaching, learning, and assessment from an input and staff-centred approach into an output and student-oriented one. Student-centred programs are defined here as having "an approach or system that supports the design of learning programs which focus on learners' achievements, accommodate different learners' priorities, and are consistent with reasonable students' workload (i.e., workload that is feasible within the duration of the learning program). It accommodates for learners' greater involvement in the choice of content, mode, pace, and place of learning."[5] The European ministers of education followed this line of thinking by stipulating it in their Berlin Communiqué (2003).[6] This decision had far reaching consequences because it implied a change of mindset of the academic staff responsible for designing and delivering degree programs, at all three credential cycles involved.

As has already been mentioned, Tuning introduced new language to develop a better understanding of the learning process and its outcomes. It made the distinction between competences and learning outcomes to give credit to the different roles of students/learners and academic staff. Although being aware that in the Anglo-Saxon world interpretations of competences are understood mainly in the context of vocational education, it was concluded that this term offers the best opportunity to align with the world outside academia. The argument runs as follows: the aim of a learning process is to make the learner more competent. This is done by developing (further) subject specific competences and generic competences or transferable skills. It is important to separate specific competences from generic competences/transferable skills although they will be taught in conjunction. In job descriptions employers use competences as an expression to identify the knowledge, skills, attributes, attitudes, and values required. In continental Europe competences are understood as encompassing knowledge, understanding, and skills. Fostering competences is the objective of any educational program. These competences are developed and obtained by the learner. The level of competence achieved in a program is expressed in terms of the learning outcomes, which are statements of what a learner is expected to know, to understand, and be able to demonstrate after the completion of a period of learning. These learning outcomes are formulated by the academic staff. This concept can be visualised as follows:

Respecting Diversity by Profiling

The motto of Tuning is to tune educational structures and programs on the basis of diversity and autonomy. The name Tuning was chosen to reflect the idea that postsecondary educational institutions do not look

FIGURE 2.   Competences Formed in Different Course Units/Modules and Assessed at Different Stages

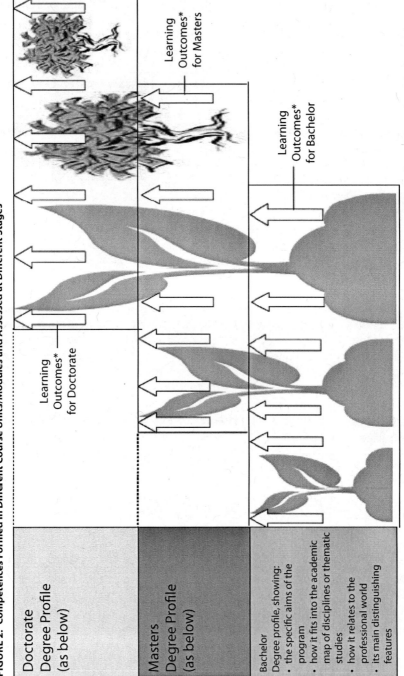

Note: *Statements formulated by academic staff of what a learner is expected to know, understand and be able to demonstrate after completion of a process of learning.

Source: González and Wagenaar (2010).

for uniformity in their missions and in their degree programs. They do not aim for a unified, prescriptive or definitive curriculum. However, points of reference, convergence and common understanding are needed. These points are required to measure quality and performance and act as a sort of yardstick. That is why Tuning focused from the very start on profiling and introduced a model, an approach, which respects and allows for flexible and diverse degree programs in a Lifelong Learning (LLL) context. It introduced the concept of a degree program profile, using the following definition: "A degree profile is a description of the *character of a degree program* or qualification. This description gives the main features of the program, which are based on the specific aims of the program, how it fits into the academic map of disciplines or thematic studies, and how it relates to the professional world" (González and Wagenaar 2003, 151).

The degree profile is an important instrument for transparency. It allows for comparison and understanding and serves different stakeholders' needs: (potential) students and graduates, academics, professional organizations, employers, and society as a whole. Tuning, together with recognition experts of the European Network of Information Centres (ENIC) and the National Academic Recognition and Information Centres in the European Union (NARIC), have developed a template for defining a degree program profile. The degree program profile contains the following elements: (i) mission statement or aim; (ii) characteristics, including orientation and distinctive features; (iii) its relevance to the professional world; (iv) possibilities for further education; (v) education style; (vi) program competences; and (vii) program learning outcomes. Such a profile is also an important tool to distinguish more research-oriented programs from applied- or vocational-oriented ones. It shows the diversity and autonomy of a particular program in relation to similar programs. The template for a degree program profile has a stand-alone function but can also be included in another European feature: the Diploma Supplement. This document accompanies a higher education diploma, providing a standardized description of the nature, level, context, content, and status of the studies completed by its holder. It should be offered to every graduate free of charge.[7]

In addition to the profile, another important element for flexibility of degrees and pathways/specializations within a program should be mentioned, which is the European Credit Transfer and Accumulation System (ECTS). ECTS has been accepted by European countries as their standard. Originally launched as a credit transfer system in 1989, Tuning has played a major role in developing ECTS into a credit accumulation system as well, by linking learning outcomes to the concept of student workload-based and time related credits. This approach is reflected in the present ECTS Users' Guide, which has been written by a group of international experts under the supervision of the European Commission.[8] In ECTS, credits are only awarded when the learning outcomes have been achieved. Tuning has also showed how these credits can be calculated in an objective and reliable way (González and Wagenaar 2003, 82-89).

INTERNATIONAL SUBJECT AREA REFERENCE POINTS

A major contribution to the educational debate has been the development of sets of international reference points or benchmark statements for a growing number of subject areas. These reference points, which are known as standards in some educational systems, offer descriptors in terms of key competences and learning outcomes statements of what can be expected of a learner in a particular field after finishing his or her studies. In this respect, the work done by the Quality Assurance Agency (QAA) in the United Kingdom has been very inspirational. Starting in 2000 the QAA has published more than 50 honours degree subject benchmark statements—drawn up by groups of academic experts—covering even more disciplines. At the beginning these were mainly UK-focused, but in revised and later published statements, more account has been taken of international work like Tuning.[9]

The strategy used to implement this part of the project was accomplished by installing "subject area groups." The term subject area group was chosen because it was perceived as being broader than the term discipline group. In 2000, when designing the first Tuning project, after long consideration, the choice was made for traditional subject areas: earth sciences, business, chemistry, educational sciences, history, mathematics, and physics. The argument for doing so was that if these "traditional disciplines" would be open for reform, others—including multi-disciplinary and interdisciplinary ones—would more easily follow. After two years of experience, other subject areas were included, such as nursing, representing the health sector, as well as regulated degrees, and European studies, representing a complex interdisciplinary degree program. For each subject area group, approximately 15 academics were brought together representing their respective nations. Each subject area group completed a template, later named conceptual frameworks, for their subject area. These were also used at a later stage by the Thematic Networks Programs (TNPs)—large scale programs granted by the European Commission, like medicine, music, art and design, dance and theatre, and gender studies. In 2009, this template was also applied to develop for the Organisation for Economic Co-operation and Development (OECD) the Tuning-AHELO Conceptual Frameworks of Expected/Desired Learning Outcomes in Economics and Engineering. AHELO stands for Assessment of Higher Education Learning Outcomes and aims to determine whether it is possible to develop a measurement instrument to meaningfully compare the level of learning worldwide at the end of the first cycle.[10]

The OECD initiative shows that the work established by Tuning has worldwide relevance. This is also proven by the fact that in many parts of the world, learning outcomes-based national frameworks of qualifications have been or are being developed. A qualifications framework can be defined as a single description at the national level or level of an educational system, which is internationally understood. The framework describes all qualifications awarded in the system considered and related to each other in a coherent way.[11] At the European level, two so-called overarching qualifications frameworks have been developed. The first, discussed earlier, is the Qualifications Framework for the European Higher Education Area, which has been adopted by 47 governments. The second qualifications framework, covering all learning in a Lifelong Learning (LLL) context, has been drawn-up by the European Commission, and agreed upon in 2008 by the European Parliament and other relevant European institutions. The EQF for LLL is based on eight levels of which level 5 covers the short cycle degree of two years, level 6 the bachelor, level 7 the master, and level 8 the doctorate. Within this framework three types of descriptors are distinguished: knowledge, skills, and competences. In the context of the EQF for LLL, competence is described in terms of responsibility and autonomy.[12]

Recently, the European Commission has stimulated the development of sectoral qualifications frameworks, either to cover a particular employment sector like information and communication technology or a domain or sector of related fields of studies like natural sciences. This last type of framework should act as an intermediary between general descriptors and subject specific ones. Tuning has started to develop sectoral frameworks as well. The first completed was social sciences. Sectoral frameworks for the humanities and creative and performing arts are projected to follow soon.[13] Figure 3 shows the relationship between the different types of frameworks. It is obvious that the internationally established Tuning subject areas reference points are an indispensable element.

In an important recent publication by Paul L. Gaston, entitled *The Challenge of Bologna*, Tuning is criticized for being too traditional by focusing on mono-disciplinary studies (Gaston 2010).[14] During the ten years of its existence, Tuning has gradually concluded that in practice mono-disciplinary studies are developing in the direction of multi- and sometimes interdisciplinary ones by broadening both their theoretical and methodological framework and scope. This is reflected in the templates. Practice demonstrates that the Tuning approach can effectually be used to develop and enhance all types of educational programs, whether mono-, multi- or interdisciplinary. The basic idea of Tuning is that each degree program is designed in such a way that learners will develop the particular mix of competences that are considered useful and necessary for the academic, professional, and/or vocational area. This is reflected

FIGURE 3
Qualifications Frameworks and Reference Points/Standards

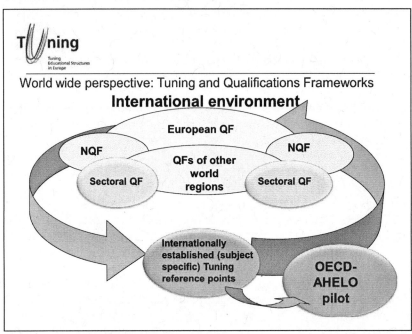

Source: González and Wagenaar (2008).

in the key competences identified and the formulated set of learning outcomes. It seems fair to state that Tuning represents the spirit of the times as is illustrated by the outcomes of an important seminar on the Bologna Process, held in Ghent, Belgium, in May 2008. "In the last decade the Bologna Process has been focusing on structural reforms. In the next stage, the focus will shift to the learning process itself. The approach must become more 'student-centred' and the attention to discipline-specific outcomes should be accomplished by a blurring [of the] boundaries between disciplines."[15]

The above is best illustrated by the following concrete example: the Erasmus Mundus Master of Excellence Euroculture: Europe in the Wider World.[16] The EU European Union Erasmus Mundus Program offers very competitive student grants for European and mainly non-European students for a selected number of master's degree programs (and since 2009 also for PhD programs). These programs are chosen by the European Union in a highly competitive procedure. Their purpose is to serve as examples for the development of transnational integrated degree programs leading to a joint degree offered by two or more consortium universities. The Tuning methodology was applied when designing the Euroculture program. This exemplary program is interdisciplinary by definition, which is reflected in its aim and formulated according to the three types of descriptors applied in the EQF for LLL: The mission of the program is to provide graduates with the following:

- Knowledge: An analytical understanding of European identity, civil society, the ongoing European unification process in itself, its cultural and social dynamics, and the consequences for its citizens and the wider world;
- Skills: The ability to identify and problematize what Europe and the European Union represent for its citizens and for the wider world; and
- Competences: The ability to translate analysis of current turmoil regarding the handling of multicultural society issues into feasible solutions.

These statements have been translated into three sets of learning outcomes. The first one, outlined below, focuses on knowledge and understanding:
Graduates will have *achieved* the following Euroculture program learning outcomes at graduation:

KNOWLEDGE

- Highly specialized knowledge, some of which is at the forefront of knowledge in a field of work or study, as the basis for original thinking and/or research

- Critical awareness of knowledge issues in a field and at the interface between different fields

(EQF-LLL descriptor level 7)

Analytical understanding of European identity/ies, civil society/ies, the ongoing European unification process in itself, its cultural and social dynamics and the consequences for its citizens and the wider world:

- Thorough knowledge and understanding of the phenomena of multiculturalism, national and European identity, current political governance, and evolving social-political processes on the basis of four concepts, namely: Communication, Co-operation, Mobility of Citizens, and Active Citizenship;

- Thorough (historical) understanding of the European integration process in a global perspective;

- Thorough knowledge and understanding of theoretical and methodological approaches, in particular comparativism and constructivism, which allow for independent research in the academic field involved;

- Experienced knowledge and understanding of different regional and national perceptions of the European integration process from a cultural-social perspective including awareness of the push and pull factors in the process of European identity formation and in relation to other countries;

- High level of sensitiveness based on knowledge and insight regarding cultural-social differences and similarities at group, local, regional, national, European, and global level; and

- Performing and presentation of the outcomes (in oral and written form) of independent research by making efficient use of primary and secondary sources (e.g., libraries, computerized material, bibliographical material).

This information offers a very clear picture of what can be expected of a graduate, but also identifies employment possibilities.

This current transnational and interdisciplinary MA program is a clear example disproving Paul Gaston's criticism of Tuning that it focuses too much on traditional mono-disciplinary degree programs. Other examples are found in the *Tuning publications Reference Points for the Design and Delivery of Degree Programmes in Gender Studies,* and *Reference Points for the Design and Delivery of Degree Programmes in European Studies.*[17]

Measuring Quality of Outcomes

The last item discussed in this chapter concerns approaches that articulate and capture the intended learning outcomes as well as the instruments to measure whether these have been achieved at graduation. According to Tuning, outcomes of a degree program cannot be separated from the quality of the process to design and deliver it. Much has already been said about the designing phase. The actual implementation process in terms of what the best strategies are to develop the identified key competences of a degree program and achieving the learning outcomes defined, have not been addressed yet. Identifying the best approaches and methodologies is a serious challenge and a crucial part of the paradigm change required. This change from staff-centred to student-centred will take time and commitment, because current approaches are probably not sufficient. Important to stipulate here, is that the quality of a learning outcome statement is a crucial factor. It should not only be measurable, but formulated in such a way that it can be learned and taught. The implication is that every learning outcome statement should meet a set of characteristics and key components.

Characteristics of good, verifiable, comprehensive, and observable program and module/course unit learning outcomes are: sufficiently specific, objective (neutral), achievable, useful, relevant, and standard-setting. But, this is not sufficient. When formulating learning outcomes, five criteria should be respected: (i) it should contain an active verb, (ii) there should be a clear indication of the type of learning sought, (iii) the topic area should be identified, (iv) it should have a clear indication of the standard or level intended/to be achieved, and (v) it should hold information about scope and context. The model described here was developed in the framework of the EU-supported Competences in Education and Recognition Project (CoRe). As part of the project meta profiles, including sets of key competences and their related learning outcomes statements were developed for the bachelor, master and doctorate for history, nursing and physics. The CoRe project showed its participants the difficulty of writing strong and reliable learning outcomes statements. The publication *A Tuning Guide to Formulating Degree Programme Profiles Including Programme Competences and Programme Learning Outcomes,* which is the outcome of the project, should also serve as a resource for other subject areas.[18] The guide has attracted a lot of interest from all over the world, which can be seen as proof of its usefulness for the design and updating of degree programs.

Assessment methods and approaches regarding learning and teaching are intricately related. In many cases it might be preferable to first decide the way to assess the set of intended learning outcomes for a module or course unit before developing the learning and teaching strategy. The mode of learning is related. Tuning identified the following main modes of learning: lecture, seminar, tutorials, research seminar, exercise classes or courses, workshops, problem-solving sessions, laboratory teaching, demonstration classes, placement, work-based practice, fieldwork, and online/distance learning or e-learning. This list is far from complete. Tuning also made a list of learning activities and an overview of modes of assessment (Gilpin and Wagenaar 2008). It goes without saying that each mode requires its own combination. Ideally this should be reflected in the course manual of every module or course unit. Such a manual should contain—besides basic information about the course unit   a list of competences for the course unit which are derived from the program's key competences, a set of learning outcomes, indicating the level of competence to be developed, learning and teaching style (for example problem-oriented), content description, literature to be used, position of the unit in the progression route of competence development in the program, a weekly program of activities, calculation of student workload, assessment criteria, and procedure. The manual should be distributed and discussed at the start of the first meeting and evaluated in the final one.

Despite its successes, the Tuning project still requires more improvements in order to guarantee the quality of procedure and outcome. It is thought useful to develop a list of indicators and descriptors at every indicated level of competence—formulated as an achievable learning outcome. Regarding generic competences, serious work has been done by a team of educational experts at the University of Deusto, Bilbao coordinated by Aurelio Villa Sánchez and Manuel Poblete Ruiz. Making the distinction between instrumental, interpersonal, and systemic generic competences, they have identified and described 35 competences. These competences range from analytical thinking, decision-making, problem-solving, writing skills, oral communication, teamwork, conflict management, negotiation, creativity, project management, and leadership.

For each of the competences, three levels of mastery have been identified, which allow for developing progression levels within a degree program and between degree programs. These levels have been related to five indicators and five descriptors each. The descriptors indicate an increasing level of complexity and therefore mastery. Both indicators and descriptors offer an excellent base for designing the course unit or module in terms of teaching, learning, and assessment. It is also a good instrument for grading. All material can be found in the Tuning publication *Competence-based learning: A proposal for the assessment of generic competences* (Sánchez and Ruiz 2008). An example of this approach is offered below in the generic competence *Teamwork: capacity for working in a team and for assuming responsibility of tasks*. The following levels of achievement can be defined:

First level: Actively participates and collaborates in team tasks and encourages trust, friendliness, and focus on the common goal through the attitudes he/she conveys.

Second level: Contributes to the consolidation and development of the team, encouraging communication, fair distribution of tasks, a pleasant atmosphere, and cohesion.

Third level: Runs work groups, guaranteeing the integration of all group members, and their focus on an excellent level of work achieved.

Table 1 offers an impression of the subdivision of level three in indicators and descriptors. We give the first three indicators only:

What can be established for generic competences or transferable skills can also be done for subject area related knowledge, understanding, and skills (in terms of methodologies and techniques). This type of work should be teamwork-based, which fits the student-centred approach, by requiring that degree programs are designed and delivered as a collaborative effort. It also implies that the implementation of the degree program—including its units—is a shared responsibility. Sharing also means collegial peer reviewing with respect to course outlines (as reflected in the course manual) and assessment tasks.

CONCLUDING REMARKS

After more than ten years of "Bologna," it can be concluded that the main features of an overall structure to establish a European Higher Education Area are in place in most of the signatory countries. This can be seen in the stocktaking reports which are published as part of Ministerial Bologna follow-up meetings every two years.[19] The three cycle system, a quality assurance system and the ECTS credit system have become part of the national legislations of the 47 countries involved in the Bologna Process. Instruments have been developed for the implementation of ECTS, the establishing of a reliable quality assurance system based on clear standards and guidelines[20], and a methodology for designing and delivering competence and learning outcomes-based, student-centred degree programs, based on agreed descriptors included in overarching qualifications frameworks.

TABLE 1
Teamwork: Third Level of Achievement

TEAMWORK: THIRD LEVEL OF ACHIEVEMENT (1/2)

DESCRIPTIONS

Levels of Achievement	Indicators	1	2	3	4	5
THIRD LEVEL: Is capable of running work groups, guaranteeing the integration of all group members, and their focus on an excellent level of work achieved.	Actively co-operates in the planning of group work, the distribution of tasks, and deadlines.	Does things without any prior planning.	Makes last minute plans, and leaves loose ends. Unrealistic deadlines.	Makes concrete suggestions for the distribution of tasks, and sets reasonable deadlines.	Stimulates the participation of other group members, coordinating their contributions.	Distributes feasible tasks to members, along with clear aims, in time-pressured situations when there are many elements to be dealt with.
	Efficiently manages meetings.	Is not capable of coordinating a meeting for which he/she is responsible.	Attempts to manage the meeting but is not in control of the timetable, commitments made, nor the results.	Efficiently manages meetings, and achieves objectives.	Efficiently manages meetings, achieving balanced participation from all those present.	Achieves balanced participation and commitment from all team members.
	Suggests ambitious and well-defined goals for the group.	Is incapable of forming clear objectives for the group.	Suggests "fuzzy" goals that confuse the group.	Suggests attractive goals for the group, and defines them clearly.	Encourages the team, defining achievable goals and a clear vision for the future.	Energizes the team so that they take on group objectives as their own.

Source: Sánchez and Ruiz (2008, 244).

The latter, a consistent methodology for designing and delivering degree programs, that is the Tuning approach which was validated by renowned academics in 2008, is gradually finding its way to higher education institutions and groups of academics in and outside Europe. Its products are well received and known by organizations responsible for quality assurance and accreditation, as well as European-wide disciplinary organizations like, for example, the ones for engineering, physics, nursing, and music. In other parts of the world, the Tuning approach is developed and tested with full respect of the existing educational culture. Examples include the fully-fledged projects for Latin America and Russia. The Latin American project, which is in its third stage, involves 19 Latin American countries, their governments and rectors' conferences, and approximately 140 Latin American higher education institutions in 15 different subject areas.[21] Also, in the United States, a project has been implemented involving originally three and now seven states, organized by the Lumina Foundation and with the support of the US federal government.[22] Furthermore, Tuning is running a large-scale pilot project in Africa. A feasibility study has been implemented in Australia and another one is currently underway in Canada. The Canadian province of Ontario is also implementing "sector"-wide Tuning projects in social sciences, life and health sciences and physical sciences.

Although Tuning can boast success, it is also fair to state that the switch of paradigm described above is not easy to achieve because it requires the acceptance of individual academics. It will take time to win their hearts and minds. This can be done by showing them that the approach is in their best interest as teachers and researchers. Experience shows that the outcomes of Tuning makes education more attractive and transparent to students and influences their commitment and effort to succeed in a positive way. In the longer run, we also hope to prove the approach has a positive impact on employment chances and career perspectives.[23]

Higher education is like a mammoth tanker; it is not easy to change its course. In many European countries, faculty are still struggling to implement the three cycle system in an effective way and to base degree programs on the European credit system ECTS. Introducing the new paradigm of student-centred education based on the learning outcomes approach—although inevitable in the long run—is for many still a hard road to travel. It is expected, however, that in the next decade, with new generations of academics entering the field, this will change. To help departments and their faculty, the International Tuning Academy was established in 2010 as a joint venture of the Universities of Deusto and Groningen. Its main objective is to distribute the Tuning material and to assist academic staff in using it in practice. It will also serve as a platform for reflection among academics. It has become clear over the years that change requires tailored training and support which will be offered by the Academy as well.

The pressure for accountability will force higher education institutions to prove that their degree programs are up to standard and that there is a demonstrated need for their graduates in the labour market. This, in particular, applies to continental Europe where higher education is still perceived as a public responsibility. This means that the (vast) majority of funding of higher education institutions comes from taxpayers. They want to have the assurance that this money is spent wisely and effectively. It is therefore higher education's obligation to society to meet its expectations. The Tuning initiative is at their service, by offering a clear-cut methodology not only for Europe but worldwide.

NOTES

[1] See official Bologna Process website for the period January 2004–June 2005: http://www.bolognabergen2005.no/. See also *A Framework for Qualifications of the European Higher Education Area. Bologna Working Group on Qualifications Frameworks* 2005.

[2] See for the consensus document: http://www.bologna-berlin2003.de/en/bologna_seminars/quality_assurance.htm.

[3] See http://www.bologna-berlin2003.de/pdf/Communique1.pdf.

[4] See http://www.unideusto.org/tuningeu/.

[5] This definition is included in *A Tuning Guide to Formulating Degree Programme Profiles. Including Programme Competences and Programme Learning Outcomes* (Lokhoff and Wagenaar 2010). In the glossary of this publication many more relevant definitions used in the Tuning and European Higher Education Area framework can be found.

[6] See http://www.bologna-berlin2003.de/en/aktuell/haupt.htm.

[7] For further information about the Diploma Supplement, see the website of the European Commission: http://ec.europa.eu/education/lifelong-learning-policy/doc1239_en.htm.

[8] See ECTS Users' Guide.

[9] See QAA for the UK benchmark statements. The page also contains a reference to Tuning. The QAA is an independent body funded through subscriptions from higher education institutions and through contracts with the major UK funding councils, and has a mission to safeguard standards and improve the quality of UK higher education. The benchmark statements have been well received in the past and serve now as a backbone to the UK quality assurance system.

[10] For a general description of the project see: http://www.oecd.org/document/22/0,3746,en_2649_35961291_40624662_1_1_1_1,00.html. For the Tuning-AHELO conceptual frameworks see: http://www.oecd.org/document/51/0,3746,en_2649_35961291_42295603_1_1_1_1,00.html.

[11] This definition is applied in *A Framework for Qualifications of the European Higher Education Area. Bologna Working Group on Qualifications Frameworks* (2005, 30).

[12] See http://ec.europa.eu/education/lifelong-learning-policy/doc44_en.htm.

[13] See http://www.unideusto.org/tuningeu/.

[14] For more information, see *The Bologna Process for U.S. Eyes: Re-learning Higher Education in the Age of Convergence.* (Adelman 2009). Adelman devotes a large part of his publication to Tuning.

[15] See http://www.ond.vlaanderen.be/hogeronderwijs/bologna/Bologna Seminars/documents/Ghent/Summary_concluding_debate.pdf.

[16] See http://www.euroculturemaster.org/. The two year MA Euroculture is offered by a consortium of European and non-European universities: Groningen (The Netherlands) (coordinator), Deusto-Bilbao (Spain), Göttingen (Germany), Krakow (Poland), Olomouc, (Czech Republic), Strasbourg (France), Udine (Italy), Uppsala (Sweden), Indiana University (US), University of Pune (India), Osaka University (Japan) and UNAM (Mexico).

[17] See http://www.unideusto.org/tuningeu/publications.html.

[18] See http://www.core-project.eu/.

[19] See http://www.ond.vlaanderen.be/hogeronderwijs/bologna/actionlines/stocktaking.htm.

[20] See the publication of the European Association for Quality Assurance in Higher Education (ENQA): http://www.enqa.eu/files/ESG_3edition%20%282%29.pdf.

[21] http://www.tuningal.org/.

[22] See http://www.luminafoundation.org/newsroom/news_releases/2009-04-08-tuning.html, http://www.luminafoundation.org/tag/tuning/ and http://tuningusa.org/Projects.aspx.

[23] For this purpose *A study to produce a robust methodology to evaluate the application of the Tuning approach* was designed, which is co-financed by the Lumina Foundation based in Indianapolis USA and the European Commission.

REFERENCES

Adelman, C. 2009. The Bologna Process for U.S. Eyes: Re-learning Higher Education in the Age of Convergence. Washington.

A Framework for Qualifications of the European Higher Education Area. Bologna Working Group on Qualifications Frameworks. 2005. Copenhagen: Danish Ministry of Science, Technology and Innovation.

ECTS Users' Guide. 2009. http://ec.europa.eu/education/lifelong-learning-policy/doc48 en.htm.

Gaston, P.L. 2010. *The Challenge of Bologna: What the United States Higher Education Has to Learn From Europe, and Why It Matters That We Learn It,* 7 and 154-156. Sterling: Stylus Publishing.

Gilpin, A. and R. Wagenaar. 2008. Approaches to Teaching, Learning and Assessment in Competence-Based Degree Programmes. In *Universities' Contribution to the Bologna Process: An Introduction,* edited by J. González and R. Wagenaar, 91-118. 2nd ed. Bilbao: University of Deusto.

González, J. and R. Wagenaar, ed. 2003. *Tuning Educational Structures in Europe: Final Report. Pilot Project – Phase One.* Bilbao: University of Deusto.

——. 2008. *Universities' Contribution to the Bologna Process: An Introduction,* 2nd ed. Bilbao: University of Deusto.

González, J. and R. Wagenaar. 2010. Tuning Educational Structures in the World: What is Tuning Offering Our World Partners? Powerpoint presentation to the Department of Education and Culture, European Commission, Brussels.

Lokhoff, J. and R. Wagenaar, a.o. eds. 2010. A Tuning Guide to Formulating Degree Programme Profiles. Including Programme Competences and Programme Learning Outcomes. Bilbao, Groningen and The Hague. http://www.unideusto.org/tuningeu/news/289-recently-published-degree-programme-profiles.html.

Quality Assurance Agency for Higher Education (QAA). n.d. UK benchmark statements. Accessed 5 December 2012. http://www.qaa.ac.uk/AssuringStandardsAndQuality/subject-guidance/Pages/Subject-benchmark-statements.aspx.

Sánchez, A.V. and M.P. Ruiz, ed. 2008. *Competence-Based Learning: A Proposal for the Assessment of Generic Competences*. Bilbao: University of Deusto.

Westerheijden, D. and M. Leegwater, ed. 2003. Working on the European Dimension of Quality: Report of the Conference on Quality Assurance in Higher Education as a Part of the Bologna Process, Amsterdam, 12-13 March 2002. The Hague: Ministry of Education, Culture and Science.

2

Increasing Attainment in the United States: Quality is about Learning—What Students Know, Understand and Are Able to Do

Holiday Hart McKiernan

Introduction

In just two decades, the number of Canadian jobs filled by university graduates has doubled to 4.4 million. The government projects that nearly 75 percent of new jobs created by 2017 will require a degree, not to mention jobs vacated by baby boomers, 70 percent of which will call for postsecondary graduates (Davidson 2011).

Canada, of course, is not alone. These daunting statistics reflect a global shift to a new knowledge economy; an economy that requires demonstrable, employable skills of its workforce, skills that increasingly rely on training beyond high school. The United States joins Canada in facing this challenge and opportunity: how to supply a new economy with highly-skilled workers. Rising to this is impossible without a shared, clear definition of "highly-skilled." That definition—and successful re-invigoration of higher education to serve students and the marketplace better—hinges on one concept: quality learning.

Simply put, success will require a seismic shift from what is taught to what is learned. Our economic growth and social stability depend on it.

That explains why we at Lumina Foundation care about shifting the national conversation, but it is also important to understand the Foundation's agenda and how it fits into the broader educational attainment

Measuring the Value of a Postsecondary Education, ed. K. Norrie and M.C. Lennon. Montreal and Kingston: Queen's Policy Studies Series, McGill-Queen's University Press. © 2013 All rights reserved.

goal in the United States. Lumina Foundation is a private, independent American foundation established in Indianapolis, Indiana in August 2000 and is exclusively committed to enrolling and graduating more students from college. As the nation's largest foundation dedicated to increasing students' access to and success in postsecondary education, Lumina is focused on a singular goal: to increase the percentage of Americans who hold high-quality degrees and credentials to 60 percent by 2025. To reach this goal, Lumina commits over USD$40 million each year to identify and support effective practice, encourage effective public policy, and use our communications and convening capacity to build public will for change.[1]

Lumina's goal, coupled with the Obama administration's vision that by 2020, 55 percent of Americans will have at least an associate degree, signals an audacious national college attainment movement in the United States. This movement must begin by reframing the role of higher education in the 21st century: to generate quality learning outcomes that are relevant to demands of the current marketplace but adaptable for the marketplace of the future.

HIGHER EDUCATION TO WHAT END?

"By 2018, we will need 22 million new workers with college degrees—but will fall short of that number by at least 3 million postsecondary degrees ... At a time when every job is precious, this shortfall will mean lost economic opportunity for millions of American workers."

"Help Wanted," a report by the Georgetown Center on Education and the Workforce

Just as Canada is watching its workforce shift to one dominated by the need for workers with postsecondary credentials, the United States is facing a deficit of workers with the college-level learning required to succeed in the new economy. This is complicated by a higher education system structured to better serve a 19th century student than 21st century student. The 21st century student runs the gamut—racially, ethnically, and socially. They are recent high school graduates and second-career retirees. They are part-time distance learners and full-time resident students, GED completers, certificate seekers, and evening MBA students. They are not, however, the target audience of the current system.

In addition to being designed to serve a small minority of students, the business model of American higher education is outmoded. As opposed to explicit, transparent, transferrable, and workforce-relevant learning outcomes, it is designed around units, such as hours spent in traditional courses.

Reconciling this mis-match is not merely an exercise in rhetoric, it is an economic imperative. As the United States struggles to rebound from a global economy in flux, experts agree that persistently low rates of college attainment are slowing the recovery. And because workers without college-level learning are ill-equipped to fully participate or succeed in a complex, global knowledge economy, it becomes a matter not only of sluggish recovery but also of long-term economic detriment.

Labour economist Tony Carnevale of the Georgetown University Center on Education and the Workforce has helped spur urgency in our national debate by underlining this point. Carnevale estimates that by 2018, 63 percent of all of the nation's jobs will require some form of postsecondary education or training. Furthermore, industrial shifts are pointing to a downward trajectory of employability and earning power. On average, in industries that are growing the fastest—healthcare and various service industries—about seven in ten workers have at least some college. On the other side of the ledger, in the industries that are declining in terms of their relative share of jobs, only four in ten workers have attended college. The message is clear: in the coming years and decades, fewer and fewer jobs will be available to those who lack postsecondary education.

Even in a recession, college graduates are employed at much higher rates than are non-college graduates. Today, while overall unemployment rates in the United States hover near 10 percent, only 4.5 percent of college graduates are unemployed. It has become clear, not just to economists, but to employers and to millions of Americans that completing some form of higher education is the best insurance against job loss.

The data on wages are equally compelling. Yes, people with two- and four-year college degrees earn more than high school graduates. It is a natural assumption. But did you know that in the new global economy the earnings gap between the credentialed and non-credentialed in the United States is growing at an accelerated rate? This gap—what economists refer to as the wage premium—is growing. Individuals with a bachelor's degree, for example, make an average of 84 percent more over their lifetimes than those with just a high school diploma. This is an increase even since the late 1990s, when the differential was about 75 percent. This increasing wage premium suggests that labour markets are undersupplied with postsecondary graduates. Even in this job market, employers are willing to pay an increasing premium for college graduates.

Our long-term economic security as a nation relies on a mobile, educated, well-trained workforce, yes. It also relies on an engaged, informed, and empowered citizenry. College graduates vote and volunteer at a greater rate than those with only a high school degree. Postsecondary attainment has also been positively linked to self-sufficiency: in the United States, college graduates are less likely to rely on public assistance funding to survive, less likely to commit a crime, and less likely to live in poverty. What at one time may have been an argument of humanity is now blended with enlightened self-interest: in order to have—and for our children and their children to have—a peaceful, stable, and prosperous nation, we need to reduce equity gaps and improve attainment rates in higher education.

So the motivating economic and civic factors behind the big goal are clear. What we are often asked is why 60 percent and why the year 2025? Our goal is based on careful calculations of the likely gains under the current modus operandi and the potential gains by a thorough and actionable review of the system as it stands. Based on workforce, labour market, census, and OECD data, we believe a 60 percent attainment rate is necessary but also attainable and more closely aligns with emerging workforce needs.

But how can we map the path to the goal? By beginning with the end in mind first: Reviewing data on workforce needs against the skills and knowledge delivered by curricula across US institutions, and then reviewing the opportunities for improved and integrated student experiences. In short, we reach the goal by totally changing the game and without ever sacrificing the core elements of a high quality education.

ON QUALITY

Quality learning outcomes are, as one might imagine, in the eye of the beholder. So, when Lumina and its partners began exploring ways to define and articulate quality, we turned to the "beholders." We first observed the successes and challenges faced by Europe during the Bologna Process, the systematic effort to harmonize degree cycles and institutions. At the centre of some of Bologna's most important work, we found ourselves drawn to the idea of "Tuning." Tuning involves creating a framework that sets forth clear responsibilities for institutions and establishes clear learning expectations for students in each subject area while balancing the need among programs to retain their academic autonomy and flexibility. The objective is not to standardize programs offered by different institutions but to better establish the quality and relevance of degrees in various academic disciplines.

In 2002, Europe completed the first round of Tuning, involving nine subject areas at 137 universities in 16 countries. Through last year, at least 145 universities in 33 countries had participated. Faculty members have applied Tuning to business administration, chemistry, education sciences, European studies, history, earth sciences, mathematics, nursing, and physics. Outside of Europe, the most noted adaptation of Tuning occurred in Latin America with 12 disciplines at 182 universities in 18 countries.

In the United States, efforts to benchmark learning outcomes at the discipline level have neither happened systematically nor on any significant scale. Widely applied to a range of disciplines, the Tuning platform could shift the focus in American higher education from consideration of generalized notions of what is indirectly taught at the associate's, bachelor's, and other levels to specific knowledge and skills that students need to learn and apply, making the value of specific degrees more readily apparent, said Clifford Adelman,[2] an American expert on the Bologna Process and a senior associate at the Institute for Higher Education Policy[3] in Washington, DC.

The Lumina Foundation decided to test whether the Tuning process that was being employed in Europe and beyond would have applicability and effectiveness in the diverse, complex context of American higher education. Lumina collaborated with university faculty across six disciplines—biology, chemistry, education, graphic design, history, and physics—in the higher education systems of Indiana, Utah, and Texas.

The objective of Tuning USA was to look for ways to articulate the common skills and knowledge developed among and across disciplines, regardless of institution. The lessons are still emerging but among key early takeaways one may discover two key principles: (i) faculty engagement matters and (ii) what is valuable has not always been measured.

Despite these important insights yielded by Tuning USA, an important question persists. Once one determines that curricular elements are worth measuring, how does one measure them? And if one solves for that, how does one then address what matters most: What have students learned about how to apply the knowledge gained? This daunting question led directly to a movement to articulate what associate's, bachelor's, and master's degrees truly mean.

Also, in looking back on the potential gains we foresaw by introducing Tuning to the United States, we considered that Tuning alone could not produce the student-centred element of the following benefits:

- making higher education more responsive to changes in knowledge and its application;
- establishing the relevance of postsecondary programs to societal needs and workforce demands;
- aligning the roles of higher education institutions;
- facilitating retention, especially among students from underserved groups, by creating clear pathways to degree completion;
- simplifying the process for students transferring credits between institutions;
- increasing the emphases on lifelong learning and important-but-often-undervalued transferable skills; and
- increasing student engagement in the learning process.

The important dialogue begun by Tuning needed to go one level deeper: What could students truly demonstrate and do after graduating from a postsecondary program but, more importantly, how could a student navigate his/her entire educational career with that knowledge being transparently presented to him/her?

So began the development of a Degree Qualifications Profile[4] (DQP). The Degree Profile, currently being tested by a select group of regional accreditors and associations, is designed to assist institutions in illustrating clearly what students should be expected to know and be able to do with the degrees they earn. The Degree Profile was developed in consultation with Cliff Adelman, Senior Associate at the Institute for Higher Education Policy (IHEP); Peter Ewell, Vice President at National Center for Higher Education Management Systems; Paul Gaston, Trustees Professor at Kent State University and author of *The Challenge of Bologna*; and Carol Geary Schneider, President of the Association of American Colleges and Universities.

The Degree Profile provides a roadmap by which higher education can more efficiently produce adaptable workers who possess high level skills and relevant knowledge. Students who, DQP co-author Carol Geary Schneider explains, "[are equipped to] thrive in every sphere of life—personal, economic, civic, democratic, environmental, and global."

This draft aspires to create a common vocabulary for sharing good practice; a foundation for better public understanding of the function, necessity, and relevance of higher education; and reference points for accountability stronger than test scores, graduation rates, research dollars, student satisfaction ratings, or patents alone. Furthermore, the Degree Profile creates an environment in which students can make more informed decisions, navigate an integrated system, and transfer prior learning credits, all with the confidence of knowing that their degrees represent valuable and marketable skills.

The Degree Profile proposes a set of reference points that benchmark what it should take for students to earn a degree at each of the three levels addressed, in addition to whatever an institution requires in terms of credits, grades, and specific course completions. Beyond encouraging thoughtful discussion and evolution of those reference points, the Degree Profile can serve other purposes either lacking or imperfectly realized in American higher education today. While it is difficult to anticipate all of the purposes that the Degree Profile can serve, there are several obvious applications that deserve mention.

At the curriculum and classroom level, instructors and students can refer to the Degree Profile as a common source of understanding and as a point of departure for agreement on more detailed and specific expectations regarding the development of programs, courses, assignments, and assessments. At the college and university level, the Degree Profile provides reference points that allow faculty members to articulate and better align institutional student learning outcomes with departmental objectives.

The Degree Profile also should offer students and advisers reference points for degree planning. In addition, institutions can use the Degree Profile to help align their expectations with those of other institutions and to give prospective students a clear statement of the outcomes they seek to assure. Regional accreditors should find that the Degree Profile prompts them to reach the consensus on learning outcomes that is being sought by many leaders and opinion makers. And, specialized accreditors can use the Degree Profile as a platform for relating disciplinary expectations to institutional ones.

In addition, the focus on student learning embodied in the Degree Profile and its clear demarcation of increasing levels of challenge as a student progresses from one degree level to the next should enable:

- a continuing and sustainable emphasis on learning as the proper determinant for the quality and value of degrees, which should help correct the tendency to view the credential as an end in itself, independent of the learning it should represent;
- refinement and further elaboration of points of alignment between and among secondary schools and postsecondary institutions regarding achievement levels in specific knowledge, skill, and application areas;
- guidance (a) for students on what to expect at the next degree level, (b) for students who intend to transfer from one institution to another, and (c) for students returning to higher education after a period of absence;
- expansion and elaboration of connections between school-based learning and out-of-school learning, including creditable prior learning (e.g., from employment) by adult students; and
- development of reference points to assess students' progress and levels of achievement in relation to specific learning outcomes.

We appreciate, though, that an entirely new dialogue about what is taught versus what is learned cannot succeed in a vacuum. It must be relatable and connected to current pedagogy related to learning outcomes in higher education. The Degree Profile provides a framework for higher learning and a set of common benchmarks at each degree level, describing the student performance that should be expected at each. It does not attempt to standardize degrees or to define what should be taught and how it should be taught. But, it does define desired learning outcomes in five basic areas of learning: (i) broad, integrative knowledge; (ii) specialized knowledge; (iii) intellectual skills; (iv) applied learning, and (v) civic learning.

Specialized Knowledge

Across all fields or majors, learning must be deep enough to assure mastery of a chosen subject. In all fields there are common learning outcomes involving terminology, theory, methods, tools, literature, complex programs or applications, and understanding the limits of the field.

Broad, Integrative Knowledge

While learning must be deep, it also must be wide in order to support inquiry into different subjects and to help students appreciate how all subjects connect. The DQP provides that students should be engaged in practices of core fields from the sciences through humanities and the arts and that they should develop global and cultural perspectives. The DQP says that learning should be integrated and furthered at all degree levels and provides a cumulative context for specialized studies.

Intellectual Skills

The DQP defines these as "manifestations of well-defined cognitive capacities and operations." Five cross-cutting intellectual skills, which overlap and interact, should transcend disciplinary boundaries. They are analytic inquiry, use of information resources, engaging diverse perspectives, quantitative fluency, and communication fluency.

Applied Learning

Although typically not stressed in discussions of higher education outcomes, applied learning is actually the most critical outcome of all. What students can actually do with what they have learned is the ultimate benchmark of learning. Connecting all degrees and areas of learning, applied learning emphasizes a commitment to analytical inquiry, active learning, and real-world problem solving.

Civic Learning

This kind of learning prepares students to be responsible citizens of their democracy. Civic inquiry requires that students combine knowledge and skills in both broad and specialized fields. But, it also demands engagement—actually applying these skills to relevant questions and problems. Students realize these objectives largely through experiences outside of class and by reflecting on and analyzing those experiences.

While sample outcomes for each area are described independently, in practice there should be considerable overlap and integration. For example students gain conceptual understanding and sophistication both by exercising their intellectual skills and by applying their learning to complex questions and challenges in academic and non-college settings. Still, for the sake of clarity, the Degree Profile treats each of the basic areas of learning separately even when the language of the student learning outcomes is similar.

Here are a few guidelines for understanding the learning outcomes as presented in the Degree Profile:

- They are intended to be summative for each degree addressed. Students can attain these outcomes at any point in the course of their academic journeys. Just as learning is cumulative, but rarely follows a rigid sequence, evidence for learning is cumulative and reflects programmatic and individual differences.
- The learning outcomes are presented as illustrations. While they indicate a range of performance, the implied forms of assessment are illustrative as well—not exhaustive.
- The descriptions of learning outcomes are presented through active verbs that tell all parties—students, faculty, employers, policy-makers, and the general public—what students actually should do to demonstrate their mastery. These active verbs are deliberately cast at different levels of sophistication as the Degree Profile moves up the degree ladder. The Degree Profile avoids terms, such as "critical thinking," "appreciation," "ability," or "awareness," because these do not describe discrete activities that lead directly to assessments.
- The learning outcomes do not prescribe *how well* a student must demonstrate mastery; they are intended to define the achievement of competence. Standards for quality necessarily embody local judgments based on explicit criteria for performance.
- The document does not invoke illustrations from specific disciplines, occupational fields, institutions, or associations. Those illustrations should emerge through use of the Degree Profile and will, over time, enrich it.
- The five broad areas of learning are not presented as necessarily of equal value for all providers of higher education. However, the integration of these areas should represent a widely shared curricular goal.
- Finally, although some learning outcomes are reiterated for the sake of emphasis, in practical terms, all outcomes identified for the bachelor's degree assume those listed for the associate's degree, and outcomes stated specifically for the master's degree include those for the associate's and bachelor's degrees. Each section of the Degree Profile thus demonstrates the principle of incremental challenge and accomplishment from one degree level to the next.

The Degree Qualifications Profile is a potentially powerful tool and one that could spur a cultural shift. Clear and informed advising. Reduced cost and time to degree. Improved credits transfer. Clear and trusted learning outcomes. Increased interplay of higher education with employers. It is an exciting menu of potential gains. More than 100 institutions and 30 states are testing the Degree Profile under the auspices of several partner organizations: the Western Association of Schools and Colleges, the Higher Learning Commission, the Council of Independent Colleges, the American Association of State Colleges and Universities, and the Association of American Colleges and Universities. We have already learned that the implementation of such a tool reveals the diversity and autonomy of the US education system. This is both a challenging backdrop and a major strength.

MOBILIZING THE MARKET FOR CHANGE

Canada's Knowledge Infrastructure Program's investment in the enhancement of institutions' ability to attract, support, and prepare students as the highly-skilled workers of tomorrow elevated the role of stakeholders beyond educators in reforming education. The work to define quality learning outcomes affords the same opportunity—and brings with it the same imperative—for reformers in the United States.

Quite simply, the Degree Profile and related efforts to reinvent the business model of higher education cannot succeed without the engagement of the marketplace. For one, higher education must demonstrate that it is a stable, productive, and efficient enterprise aligned with the needs of students and their eventual employers. By extension, higher education will demonstrate that it is, perhaps, the most important economic development tool of our time. But, to be able to effectively demonstrate this, students and employers must share with faculty and administrators the understanding of what degrees truly represent.

The Degree Profile was designed with this shared sense of quality outcomes in mind. Focused on five learning areas (specialized knowledge, broad/integrative knowledge, intellectual skills, applied learning, and civic learning), it is meant to help employers better understand what graduates bring to the table. In turn, as it is tested and tweaked, employers could conceivably help inform institutions of gaps in skills and knowledge among degree-holders.

In addition to offering greater alignment of needs, expectations, and outcomes through work such as the Degree Profile, the national attainment movement is challenging higher education to think more carefully about how it delivers degrees. The for-profit sector can offer rich insight about ways to invest in good business practices and transformative change. Business is uniquely positioned to help higher education make the shift to a model that rewards completion, not enrolment.

A 2010 Lumina report *Navigating the New Normal*, which discusses the opportunities presented by economic constraints for thoughtful alignment of higher education spending with the goals of access, quality, and improved attainment, estimates that it will cost USD$33 billion for the nation to reach 60 percent attainment by 2025. A business-as-usual financing model will effectively guarantee further declines in attainment. And, a business model that produces unclear outcomes and varying quality will not rise to meet the challenges of the "new normal."

In the new normal, students must be able to demonstrate college level learning to thrive in the new knowledge economy. In the new normal, every nation must prioritize increasing attainment of high-quality degrees and credentials among its citizens in order to grow the global economy. Neither condition can be met without new thinking about how to better measure the value of an education. That value can only be determined by a transparent, intentional approach to defining quality learning outcomes, one that moves us from the new normal to new heights of widely accessible educational excellence.

A SHARED QUALITY ARCHITECTURE

In a system as decentralized and complex as the US higher education system (to say nothing of the equally crowded landscape of accreditors), the greatest challenge may not be the daunting charge of increasing access to quality education. The greatest challenge may be giving the process some teeth by which our institutions simultaneously feel ownership and accountability.

The best way would be for leaders of the higher education community, working co-operatively with students, employers, and others, to pilot a common degree framework and then to honour its demands. With the value American higher education places on institutional autonomy, the most desirable approach is to voluntarily build consensus around the concept. The second way in which a common degree framework could come about would be for accrediting agencies to shift from their current input-oriented assessment modalities to a vastly more output-oriented approach. Once they make that shift, they would be well on their way towards assessing quality with reference to a framework quite similar to the one described here.

Institutional Initiatives

A US overarching common degree framework consisting of general student learning outcomes at each degree level would ideally be developed and fostered through the voluntary, combined effort of higher education leaders, experts, and key stakeholders. The diversity of US higher education leadership provides for a wealth of expertise and experience that, if united towards the common purpose of establishing agreed-upon national student learning outcomes at each degree level, could create the ideal framework for the US higher education system. These stakeholders could reach a consensus that shared learning outcomes are a desirable and feasible solution to some of the problems plaguing higher education today, and then to discuss the best process for designing and implementing these learning outcomes in a manner that reflects the uniqueness and complexity of US higher education.

In *The Challenge of Bologna* (Gaston 2010), Professor Paul Gaston proposed uniting faculty members, students, university board members, administrators, and state higher education officers, members of the public, and higher education association representatives, a group which he terms the *Higher Educators' Congress*. The Higher Educators' Congress would carefully delineate the strengths and weaknesses within the current higher education system and distill an agenda for reform intended to address the current problems in US higher education. One focus might be creating a national framework of student learning outcomes for each degree. Through a collaborative voluntary effort, higher education leaders would "frame a strategy of reform that first recognizes and incorporates existing efforts and then identifies gaps and the means of addressing them." In the context of a framework discussion, this would entail recognizing those associations, institutions, disciplines, states, and individuals who have already begun to work towards remedying many of the issues that a qualifications framework would address. This stocktaking would prevent duplicative efforts, build upon already-established practices, and identify stakeholders who had not been involved in the process, but whose dedication to transforming US higher education would merit their inclusion. The stakeholders would collaborate, among other things, to identify general student learning outcomes at each higher education degree level.

The pilot projects that are testing the Degree Profile are considering an array of issues. The work is to provide Lumina and the authors with valuable input on the content of the DQP, such as what is missing and what needs to be changed. Second, the Lumina Foundation wants to know more about how institutions map their programs to the Degree Profile and what evidence of student learning they have to demonstrate to prove that students have mastered the competencies. The Lumina Foundation wants information about how institutions go about engaging faculty because it is Lumina's view that faculty participation is essential to this effort being effective. And, finally, the Lumina Foundation wants advice from those testing the Degree Profile about whether and how to imbed a shared understanding of what a degree means in terms of learning into the diverse American higher education landscape. In other words, how to bring this sea change about voluntarily by those who own and are responsible for our higher education system.

Initiatives by Accrediting Agencies

The traditional function of accreditation in the United States is to assess and make a judgment for the government and the public on the quality of higher education programs or institutions in relation to predetermined standards (Orlans 1975). The modern accreditation process has evolved into a comparison of an institution's programs and activities to its own stated mission and goals, rather than a comparison to uniform standards. While accrediting agencies are technically private associations comprising institutional members, they also possess an "involuntary and public character" because of the federal government's reliance upon accreditation to determine institutional eligibility for federal funding (Orlans 1975). Accreditation is not compulsory; an institution must apply to be reviewed by the relevant agency. In so doing, the institution signifies that it seeks to conform to the accrediting agency's standards so that it may reap the resulting benefits, most notably federal aid eligibility (Orlans 1975). The accreditation process involves peer review of an institution or program by higher education faculty, administrators, and members of the public (CHEA 2002). Thus, from the perspective of an institution, accreditation is essentially a seal of approval from its accredited institutional peers stating that the institution meets shared expectations of quality within higher education. In their capacity as warrantors of higher education institutions for the federal government, the public at large, and for the benefit of the accredited institutions, accrediting agencies have tremendous potential to initiate a movement for reform at the institutional level.

If a voluntary process of defining student outcomes results in a common degree framework, accrediting agencies can play a significant role in influencing the implementation and use of the common degree framework to drive accountability and provide assurance of quality. A collaborative effort by the regional and specialized accrediting agencies could reinvent modern accreditation to better address some of the issues facing higher education today. As accrediting agencies approach the issue of developing a common degree framework, they should turn to their existing accreditation process to build upon the quality-review elements that already work to promote quality and consistency, and to make changes to the process to better meet the original, fundamental goal of accreditation: accurately measuring quality.

THE ANCHOR TO CHANGE IN AMERICAN HIGHER EDUCATION: QUALITY IS LEARNING

To be able to increase the number of Americans with degrees to 60 percent, to be able to increase the productivity of US higher education institutions and systems, and to be able to focus on degree completion, there is one construct that must anchor all of these initiatives, and that anchor is quality. For too long quality has been based on input measures and perceptions of institutional prestige. Quality needs to be grounded in learning, in what students know and are able to demonstrate as a result of their studies. By focusing on learning, American higher education will be charting a system that is student-centred. Quality is learning—it is what students deserve and what the United States needs for its citizens to be able to actively participate in our democracy and for the country to be globally competitive in the 21st century.

NOTES

[1] See www.luminafoundation.org.

[2] See http://www.ihep.org/about/bio-detail.cfm?id=18.

[3] See http://www.ihep.org/.

[4] See http://www.luminafoundation.org/publications/The_Degree_Qualifications_Profile.pdf.

REFERENCES

Council for Higher Education Accreditation (CHEA). 2002. *The Fundamentals of Accreditation: What Do You Need to Know?* Washington, DC: Council for Higher Education Accreditation, 2. Accessed 4 July 2012. http://www.chea.org/pdf/fund_accred_20ques_02.pdf.

Davidson, P. 2011. Postsecondary Education Pays for Economic Growth. iPolitics.ca, 17 March 2011. Accessed 4 July 2012. http://www.ipolitics.ca/budget2011/?p=60118.

Gaston, P. 2010. *The Challenge of Bologna: What US Higher Education Has to Learn from Europe and Why It Matters That We Learn It.* 183-185. Sterling: Stylus Publishing.

Orlans, H. 1975. *Private Accreditation and Public Eligibility.* 2-3. Washington, DC: US Office of Education.

3

STANDARDS-BASED ACCOUNTABILITY IN HIGHER EDUCATION IN AUSTRALIA

Michael Gallagher[1]

INTRODUCTION

The chapter is in three parts: (i) a brief background on tertiary education in Australia, (ii) an outline of major current policy initiatives of the Australian government, and (iii) an appraisal of policy tendencies and their implications.

PART A: BACKGROUND ON THE AUSTRALIAN TERTIARY EDUCATION SYSTEM

Tertiary education in Australia is defined primarily according to the nature of qualifications offered and awarded. Several institutional types have been formed at various times, many initially designed to offer particular kinds and levels of qualification. Over time the institutional boundaries have blurred, except for doctoral degrees, which, with very few exceptions, are awarded exclusively by universities.

The original designation of institutional types by level of qualification encompassed three "sectors": *"vocational education and training"* (VET), offering mainly certificate and diploma level awards; *"higher education"* (HE), offering diplomas and bachelor's and higher degrees; and *"adult and community education"* (ACE), where formal awards are not offered. In this chapter *"higher education"* refers to all programs leading to diploma and degree qualifications regardless of the institutions or providers that offer them.

Measuring the Value of a Postsecondary Education, ed. K. Norrie and M.C. Lennon. Montreal and Kingston: Queen's Policy Studies Series, McGill-Queen's University Press. © 2013 All rights reserved.

Scale and Shape

The higher education sector up until 1987 was divided between universities and colleges of advanced education (CAEs), with only the former funded publicly to undertake research. The binary divide was closed over the period 1988–1991, with the CAEs becoming universities and eligible for research funding and able to confer doctoral awards.

There are public and private providers in all sectors. Public (government) VET providers are classified as technical and further education (TAFE) institutions, some of which operate as independent institutions while others are organized on a state or territory (provincial) or regional (sub-provincial) basis. Most of the private providers are established in the VET sector. Table 1 shows the estimated number of students and providers in the Australian tertiary education sector.

In some states, several public universities are dual-sector, in that they are funded by governments to offer VET and HE awards. Additionally, many institutions have "commercial arms" offering fee-paying foundation and pathway courses to international and domestic students across the schooling, VET, and HE sectors.

Altogether, there are some 185 institutions in Australia approved by the Australian government to deliver higher education courses. Some of these are established legally as higher education institutions (HEIs) while others are registered as VET providers with approval to offer higher education courses in some fields. Currently there are 44 "self-accrediting" institutions (that is, institutions authorized through their establishing legislation to accredit their own degrees and diplomas, including 37 public universities, two private universities, two foreign universities, and three private self-accrediting institutions). There are 141 "non-self-accrediting"

TABLE 1
Providers and Enrolments by Sector of Tertiary Education (Australia 2010)

	Providers	Enrolments	Enrolments Full-Time Equivalent
Higher Education—Public	38	1,111,352	803,741
Higher Education—Private	87	81,305	57,718
Vocational Education and Training—Public (a)	2,794	1,799,000	655,800
Vocational Education and Training—Private (b)	~3,000	~2,200,000	802,000

Sources: Government-subsidized providers, including government-established institutions and private providers receiving government subsidies; Harris (2006); DEEWR-selected Student Statistics (2011); NCVER Australian Vocational Education and Training Statistics (2011).

institutions (that is, institutions whose degrees and diplomas must be accredited by an agency of a state or territory government), including four private arms of public universities, 18 governmental instrumentalities (e.g., TAFE institutions or State TAFE systems), 14 institutions of professional associations, 34 faith-based institutions, and 71 private entities (Heaney, Heaney and Ryan 2010).

The non-self-accrediting institutions have some significance in the Australian system of higher education supply: 79 (56 percent) are approved to offer FEE-HELP loans[2] to their enrolled students; 83 (59 percent) are registered training organizations (RTOs) delivering VET programs as well as higher education courses; 81 (57 percent) offer postgraduate awards, 16 (11 percent) offer research degrees, and 94 (67 percent) are approved to provide courses for international students (Heaney, Heaney and Ryan 2010). Overall, the private higher education sector accounts for around 10 percent of international student enrolments.

In 2009, higher education students totaled 1,134,866, of which 28 percent were international students. Of the total enrolments, 66 percent were studying at bachelor's or sub-bachelor level, 29 percent were enrolled for non-research graduate degrees and five percent for graduate degrees by research. Whereas 75 percent of international students were fee-paying, only 10 percent of domestic students were enrolled on a fee-paying basis.

Governmental Roles and Responsibilities

Under the Australian Constitution, education is a responsibility of the states. Tertiary education institutions are typically established under statutes of state governments. Those statutes define the roles, powers, and governance structures of tertiary education institutions and their accountability requirements. Each university has its own establishment act.

The federal government has involved itself progressively in education since the late 1940s, through the provision of scholarships to war veterans, the provision of scholarships through development aid to students of other countries, the funding of scientific research, the funding of living allowances for eligible tertiary students, and the provision of financial assistance to non-government schools.

In the mid-1970s, the federal government undertook to provide free higher education and, by agreement with the states, assumed the primary responsibility for higher education financing. In 1994, the states referred their powers to the federal government to fund higher education institutions directly, on terms including structured inter-governmental consultations. In 2003, the federal government extended income-contingent loans to domestic students enrolled with accredited private higher education providers. Research is predominantly funded by the Australian government, although some states provide specific funds for research infrastructure.

For the calendar year 2011, the federal government provided AUD$9.7 billion in funding to higher education providers for teaching and learning (including loans to students). The bulk of government funding is provided through tuition subsidies (Commonwealth supported places or CSPs), mostly for undergraduate students. The funding rates vary by field of study but are common for all HEIs. Up until 2012 CSPs have been allocated to public HEIs for an agreed number of full-time equivalent student places. Penalties have been imposed normally when HEIs fail to meet their enrolment targets either by under or over enrolling.

The regulatory architecture prior to 2012 has included: (i) a national qualifications framework; (ii) registration procedures for the licensing of providers to offer programs leading to higher education qualifications; (iii) consumer protection for fee-paying international students; (iv) a range of internal institutional quality monitoring procedures; (v) independent external quality auditing; and (vi) public information about institutions, courses, graduate destinations, and satisfaction.

Since the early 1990s, Australia has adopted a standards-based approach, with a focus on inputs, with regard to the initial accreditation of higher education providers, and a fitness-for-purpose approach to quality auditing, with a focus on processes, with regard to established universities. Quality auditing in respect of other higher education providers has been more at arm's length via audit of state and territory licensing agencies.

PART B: HIGHER EDUCATION REFORM IN AUSTRALIA, 2008–2012

In 2008, the Australian government embarked on a program of higher education reform.[3] It framed its approach to reform in the following terms:

- To underpin its vision for Australia to be one of the most highly educated and skilled nations in the world.
- In a period of expansion, when higher education institutions are attracting students who have not traditionally considered going to university and student pathways are linked to funding, institutions will be required to demonstrate that their graduates have the capabilities that are required for successful engagement in today's complex world.
- The government will ensure that domestic and international students have better information about how our higher education institutions are performing.
- Taxpayers will be able to see whether value for money is being delivered and the national interest is being well served. (Australian Government 2009)

The reform program involves eight major initiatives of the Australian government: (i) student-driven funding of higher education;

(ii) developing mission-based funding compacts and performance funding, including measures of student learning; (iii) strengthening the Australian Qualifications Framework; (iv) establishing a new national regulator, the Tertiary Education Quality and Standards Agency; (v) articulating academic standards; (vi) strengthening consumer protection for international students; (vii) assessing the quality of research; and (viii) increasing public information about higher education capacity and performance.

1. Student-driven Funding of Higher Education

In 2009, the Australian government accepted the recommendation of the 2008 Review of Higher Education to "introduce a demand-driven entitlement system for domestic higher education students, in which recognized providers are free to enrol as many eligible students as they wish in eligible higher education courses and receive corresponding government subsidies for those students" (Bradley et al. 2008). The associated arrangements proposed by the Bradley panel included:

- apply initially to undergraduate courses but then be extended to postgraduate coursework level courses subject to further work on the balance of public and private benefits at that level of study;
- apply initially only to public universities (Table A providers under the *Higher Education Support Act 2003*), but would be extended to other approved providers when new regulatory arrangements are in place;
- set no time or dollar limit on the value of the entitlement;
- allow eligible providers to set their own entry standards, and determine which, and how many, students to enrol;
- allow providers to change the mix of student load by discipline cluster in response to demand; and
- allow the government to exclude a course of study from the demand-driven system if it wished to regulate student or graduate numbers.

The government has not extended the demand-driven funding model beyond public universities. Nor has it extended the arrangements to apply to postgraduate coursework. Rather, it has removed sub-bachelor's programs and postgraduate courses from the demand-driven system. Student places in these programs are to be allocated annually by the minister to particular institutions. Additionally, under the *Higher Education Support Amendment (Demand Driven Funding System and Other Measures) Act, 2011*, the minister will have reserve powers to restrict the scale and scope of the demand-driven model in order to contain fiscal costs and address imbalances in graduate output and labour market requirements. Thus there will be a demand-driven system for the bulk of bachelor's degree programs and a designated system for all other government subsidized programs.

Indexation of University Funding

In 2010, the government adopted a new formula for the indexation of payments to universities for teaching and research, and related purposes. The major change is to link movements in university salaries to those of professional occupations rather than to the minimum national wage. Over 2011–2015 the new indexation arrangements, which apply to the increased student participation, will add some AUD$550 million to university payments. Nevertheless, the value of the indexation relates to the adequacy of the base funding amount per student place, which falls short of identified delivery costs at least in several fields.

Review of Base Funding for Higher Education

A review of base funding was initiated in 2010 in response to the Bradley review's recommendation to "commission an independent triennial review of the base funding levels for learning and teaching in higher education to ensure that funding levels remain internationally competitive and appropriate for the sector."

The review, given to the government in October 2011, was released in December for consultation purposes, with the government reserving its response. The review found that universities need better funding and that some disciplines are more under-funded than others. It recommended that the government continue to control tuition prices for domestic undergraduate students and that the ratio of the government funding contribution to the student funding contribution per place should revert to 60:40 for all fields of study.

The review also suggested that CSPs could be allocated at a discounted rate to non-university providers that do not have research cost overheads. It also proposed that up to 5 percent of a university's enrolments might be eligible for premium funding in "flagship" courses.

The principal issues are not the cost relativities of disciplines but the adequacy of the total funding amount per enrolment and the share of the costs borne by government and students. The Australian government has indicated that additional funding will not be forthcoming in the current budgetary circumstances. If future government funding is directed primarily to expanding enrolments, higher education institutions will need increased tuition pricing flexibility if quality is not to deteriorate.

2. Mission-based Funding Compacts and Performance Funding

Universities were to have been rewarded for delivering agreed outcomes through performance funding arrangements. Facilitation funding of AUD$400 million over four years from 2011 was tied to agreement on strategies for achieving a university's teaching and learning mission and agreement to targets relating to specific Australian government attainment and equity goals. Reward funding of AUD$335 million over four years was to be available from 2012 for universities that meet their performance targets. The performance framework will proceed with seven indicators across the three performance categories (participation and social inclusion, student experience, and quality of learning outcomes). In its May 2011 budget, the Australian government announced its intention to further strengthen its quality agenda by developing, testing and implementing three new performance measurement tools: (i) the *University Experience Survey* (UES), (ii) the *Collegiate Learning Assessment* (CLA), and (iii) a composite *Teaching Quality Indicator*.

Performance targets will be set for the UES indicator in the second compact (commencing 2014). The government will give consideration to setting targets for the CLA indicator of "domestic undergraduate value added generic skills," in the following compact period. The Education Department will seek to work with Graduate Careers Australia to review the *Course Experience Questionnaire* (CEQ) so that benchmarks for the indicators that are measured through the CEQ can be established for the second compact period. In its May 2011 budget, the government cut performance funding for 2012 by AUD$95 million, and AUD$30 million was cut from funding for developing improved indicators, effectively deferring part of performance funding until better indicators are developed.

The development of the composite indicator of teaching quality has now been disbanded because it was found to be unworkable.

> Instead of rewarding universities for improvements on survey-based measures, the Government has decided to focus on the development of student experience and quality of learning outcomes measures for use in the *MyUniversity* website and to inform continuous improvement by universities. (Evans 2011)

3. Strengthened Australian Qualifications Framework

The inter-governmental Ministerial Council for Tertiary Education (MCTEE) at its meeting on 18 March 2011 adopted a revised Australian Qualifications Framework (AQF), subject to clarification of some matters relating to master's and doctoral degrees. The new AQF removes the sector classifications of the previous AQF which was developed in the mid-1990s. The revised AQF maps qualification types and titles to 10 "levels" each of which describe learning outcomes in terms of knowledge, skills, and the application of knowledge and skills. *Appendix 1* shows the range of descriptors for postsecondary qualifications. *Appendix 2* shows the level 9 descriptors for three types of master's degree.

The level 9 and level 10 types and titles reflect the result of a protracted struggle between the AQF Council (comprising ministerial appointments representing employers, trade unions and state government agencies) and universities over the preceding 12 months. The Ministerial Council struck a compromise which preserves the integrity of the AQF Council's levels model but with greater flexibility, including the recognition of internationally credible degrees at the master's level with the title of doctor (e.g., Juris Doctor) which the AQF Council tried initially to prohibit. The issuance and pathway policies also reflect compromises. Initially the AQF Council sought to mandate automatic credit transfer from one level to another, and to require its logo on university testamurs.

Nevertheless, the new AQF is not only stronger and more coherent than the previous version but has shifted from a descriptive to a prescriptive framework and is more firmly part of the regulatory arrangements governing tertiary education in Australia.

4. The Tertiary Education Quality and Standards Agency (TEQSA)

In 2009 the Australian government announced "a new era of Quality in Australian Tertiary Education" involving the establishment of a national body for regulation and quality assurance with a wide range of functions:

> The Tertiary Education Quality and Standards Agency (TEQSA) will enhance the overall quality of the Australian higher education system. It will accredit providers, evaluate the performance of institutions and programs, encourage best practice, simplify current regulatory arrangements and provide greater national consistency. TEQSA will take the lead in coordinating this work and establishing objective and comparable benchmarks of quality and performance. The agency will collect richer data and monitor performance in areas such as student selection, retention and exit standards, and graduate employment. (Australian Government 2009)

The appropriateness of placing these multiple responsibilities in a single agency may be questioned on grounds of role ambiguity. An agency empowered to de-license a provider is not obviously best placed to help it improve its deficiencies. Nevertheless, the government has pressed on, albeit unilaterally, relying on a head of power under the Constitution, viz. the corporation's power, which was interpreted broadly by the High Court in 2006. Because universities conduct trading and commercial activities, they may be regarded as corporations, even if such activities are not their core business and the universities are not-for-profit organizations. This matter may be contested in the court at some stage.

The Australian government's stated main concern is "to safeguard the quality of education provided, ensuring that it is not compromised as the sector expands." That is, the stronger standards and quality regimen is partly a consequence of the government's decision to fund universities for any number of domestic undergraduate students they decide to enrol and thus to relinquish any influence over the quantity of enrolments and student entry standards, such as through funding compact negotiations. The prudence of that policy may be questioned on grounds of merit-based access or the ability-to-benefit principle and on grounds of fiscal responsibility, especially as demographically-driven demand from school leavers and adult learners expands over the next decade. Additionally, employers may not regard it as efficient to base all future graduate output on the choices of students alone.

The initial Bill for an Act establishing TEQSA failed to reflect a risk-based and escalated approach and gave government ministers and TEQSA officers unprecedented intrusive and punitive powers. Pushback from the university sector led the government to redraft the Bill to enshrine and reflect three basic principles of regulation which underpin TEQSA's risk-based regulatory approach and with which TEQSA must act in accordance. Those principles are:

- *regulatory necessity*—TEQSA must not excessively burden higher education providers when exercising its powers;
- *reflecting risk*—TEQSA must take into account a range of factors in the context of each higher education provider, including their past compliance with the Act; history of scholarship, teaching and research; student experiences; and financial status and capacity; and
- *proportionate regulation*—TEQSA's powers must be exercised directly in proportion to any non-compliance, or risk of future non-compliance, by higher education providers.

TEQSA would pursue a standards-based approach to regulation and require higher education providers to meet or exceed these standards so as to remain registered. The "standards" would be determined by the responsible Australian government minister having regard to the advice of a standards drafting panel appointed by the minister. The "standards" include: (i) provider registration standards, (ii) provider category standards, (iii) course accreditation standards, (iv) qualifications standards, (v) teaching and learning standards, (vi) research standards, and (vii) information standards.

By dint of these principles being enshrined in the legislation, unreasonable actions of TEQSA will be appealable in the Federal Court and the Administrative Appeals Tribunal. The revised bill also requires TEQSA to obtain institutional consent to compliance assessments and thematic reviews. Additionally, it establishes institutional appeals mechanisms. The import is that TEQSA will have to take into account the diversity, missions, curriculum, and approach to delivery of established universities. TEQSA will be obliged also to adopt an escalating approach to enforcement.

There is also a separation of standards-setting power from monitoring and enforcement. The standards that TEQSA is to monitor and enforce are minimum acceptable (threshold) standards. The standards that may affect registration and accreditation are the provider and qualifications standards, and not the teaching and learning standards, research standards, information standards, or any "other" standards.

A revised (fourth) draft of the Provider Standards was issued for consultation in November 2011. They cover eight areas:

- *provider standing*, encompassing purpose, reputability and accountability of the provider;
- *financial viability and safeguards*, encompassing resources and management capacity, and tuition and financial safeguards for students;
- *Corporate and academic governance*, encompassing governance arrangements, strategic planning and risk management, review and quality assurance;
- *Primacy of academic quality and integrity*, encompassing open intellectual inquiry, integrity of student assessment, and compliance with codes of conduct, safety and ethical requirements for research;
- *Responsibilities to students*, encompassing provision of information, support and equitable treatment;
- *Management and human resources*, encompassing qualifications of personnel, sufficient staffing, effective management processes, and performance feedback mechanisms; and
- *Physical and electronic resources and infrastructure*, encompassing safe and well-maintained facilities, adequate IT hardware and software, and adequate security.

Draft provider category standards have also been issued. They cover the following categories: (i) *Australian University*, (ii) *Australian University College*, (iii) *Australian University of Specialisation*, (iv) *Overseas University*, (v) *Overseas University of Specialisation*, and (vi) other *Higher Education Provider*. The categories make no explicit provision for polytechnics, liberal arts colleges, or community colleges. Such providers would be expected to fall within the higher education provider category.

Of particular interest is the set of standards for the Australian university category, which includes two requirements relating to the conduct of research:

- the provider self-accredits and delivers qualifications that meet the qualification standards across a range of broad fields of study (including master's (research) and doctoral degrees in at least three broad fields of study; and
- the provider undertakes research that leads to the creation of new knowledge and original creative endeavour at least in those broad fields of study in which master's (research) and doctoral degrees are offered.

The standards for the Australian university college category set the research requirement for master's (research) and doctoral degrees to be "in one broad field of study." The Australian university of specialization category sets the research requirement to be "in one or two broad fields of study only." Thus, the title *university* requires research to be undertaken, and *research* is defined in terms of "new knowledge and original creative endeavour." By this definition *research* is distinguished from scholarship and from translation of existing knowledge into business innovation or community problem solving. Under the new registration provisions, it would not be possible to be a *university* with a focus on teaching and community service through knowledge translation—even though that is what several existing Australian universities are in practice. The provider category standards as proposed would impede the structural differentiation that is necessary for the Australian higher education system to meet the diversity of learner needs cost-effectively.

Interestingly, the draft provider and provider category standards differ from those proposed in the 2008 Higher Education Review report, where *universities* were seen as being required to "deliver higher education qualifications including research higher degrees in at least three broad fields of education and a larger number over time" and "undertake sufficient research in all narrow fields in which research higher degrees are offered." The requirement relating to sufficiency has been removed and "narrow" fields have been replaced with "broad" fields. This is a curious dilution. The broad field of "natural and physical sciences" includes geophysics and biology. The broad field of "society and culture" includes law and sport and recreation. There is no obvious sense to the requirement that in order to be registered as a university to offer a PhD in one of the biosciences, it suffices to be undertaking research in geophysics.

At this stage there are no drafts of teaching and learning standards, research standards, or information standards in the public domain. TEQSA commissioners and members of the TEQSA standards panel have the power to draft such standards, and these are expected to be issued throughout 2012.

5. The Articulation of Academic Standards

Australia is a participant in the engineering strand of the OECD's Assessment of Higher Education Learning Outcomes (AHELO) project. The Australian Council for Educational Research (ACER), a non-government body, is extensively involved in the various AHELO strands. These include an economics discipline strand and a generic skills strand, involving modification of the Collegiate Learning Assessment (CLA). The Australian government is interested in using the CLA for measuring "value added" in higher education. However, value added is not yet included in the AHELO work program.

Additionally, the Australian government, through its Education Ministry (the Department of Education, Employment, and Workplace Relations) contracted the then Australian Learning and Teaching Council (ALTC) to undertake a one-year demonstration project to inform the further development of learning and teaching academic standards. The project aimed to define and describe "threshold learning outcomes" encompassed within the expectation that bachelor degree graduates have "broad and coherent knowledge and skills for professional work and/or further learning" (ALTC 2011).

The Final Report of the Learning and Teaching Academic Standards Project was released on 18 March 2011 (ALTC 2011). The AUD$4.1 million project produced threshold learning outcomes for history, geography, creative arts, engineering and ICT, health, medicine and veterinary science, accounting, and law. Work on science, architecture, and building is expected to be finished by the end of the year when the ALTC itself is abolished.

The products of the demonstration project typically contextualize statements of expected graduate capabilities within disciplinary and professional practice frameworks. For geography threshold learning outcomes statements were expressed at a high level with regard to "knowing," "thinking," "investigating and problem solving," "communicating," and "self-directing and collaborating." For engineering and ICT, the statements are more precise.

The ALTC academic standards statements will not be taken up by TEQSA, although TEQSA itself has yet to indicate how it proposes to address academic standards. The ALTC project was generally seen by its participants to be worthwhile in re-engaging conversations within disciplinary communities. Threshold learning outcomes were developed through structured discussion involving professional bodies, accreditation bodies, employers, and graduates as well as academic institutions and teachers. They are regarded as useful inputs to curriculum design at the institutional level. They do not suggest ways and means of teaching or assessment.

6. Consumer Protection for International Students

Since the mid-1990s, Australia has had a reasonably robust system of consumer protection and quality assurance in place with respect to providers of educational services to international students. However, inconsistent monitoring and compliance enforcement across the states and territories, in the context of rogue providers and education agents emerging in the mid-2000s when Australia's student migration laws were relaxed, exposed weaknesses and led to revised arrangements. TEQSA now provides for tighter and nationally consistent regulation of all providers. Additionally, the *Education Services for Overseas students Act* has been strengthened, with more exacting requirements for registration on the Commonwealth Register of International Courses for Overseas Students (CRICOS). A new National Tuition Protection Service (TPS) is to be established, encompassing all providers including the public universities, which were previously not caught by its requirements to offer alternative placements for students whose original provider could no longer deliver the course in which they enrolled. It is yet to be determined how the TPS will operate across different providers with very different student profiles. It is intended that the new arrangements will accommodate risk-based student admissions and visa compliance checks—removal of country risk levels and associated financial capacity and English language proficiency (IELTS) requirements.

7. Assessing the Quality of Research

The Australian government has set a range of goals for university research: (i) increasing the number of research groups performing at world-class levels, (ii) increasing collaboration between universities, (iii) increasing the research capacity of smaller and regional universities, (iv) reducing the gap in funding for the indirect costs of research, and (v) increasing the number of students completing higher degrees by research.

The legislation establishing TEQSA requires that higher education institutions with the title of *university* must meet threshold "provider standards" including the requirement that universities deliver master's (research) and doctoral degrees in at least three broad fields of study and undertake research in those fields. It is not yet clear how the research standards will relate to the research quality assessment exercise (ERA).

The 2010 Excellence in Research for Australia (ERA) initiative has involved the Australian Research Council organizing an independent assessment of the quality of research outputs of the research, and research and teaching academic staff of Australian universities. The assessments have been applied to research works produced over the period 2003 to 2008, using a mix of academic peer review and available metrics (e.g., publications, citations, and other measures). A five-point rating scale was applied by field of research classification at four-digit and two-digit levels, where a rating of three was equivalent to world standard, four was above world standard and five well above. The indicators employed were:

- *Indicators of research quality:* Ranked outlets, citation analyses, ERA peer review, and peer-reviewed Australian and international research income.
- *Indicators of research volume and activity:* Total research outputs and income.
- *Indicators of research application:* Research commercialization and other applied measures.
- *Indicators of recognition:* A range of esteem measures.

The results of the 2010 exercise were mixed. According to the ARC's national report on ERA 2010, some two out of three (65 percent) of the units of evaluation assessed in ERA were rated at world standard or above (i.e., received 3s, 4s or 5s). Of the 2,435 units of evaluation that were assessed from 40 institutions (697 at the broad two-digit level, 1,738 at the four-digit discipline level), the following ratings were received:

- 308 units of evaluation rated at five or "well above world standard" (69 at the broad two-digit level, 239 the four-digit discipline level);
- 508 units of evaluation rated at four or "above world standard" (115 at the broad two-digit level, 393 the four-digit discipline level); and
- 776 units of evaluation rated at three or "at world standard" (229 at the broad two-digit level, 547 at the four-digit discipline level).

Ratings of four and five were concentrated in nine universities. A further eight universities achieved a rating of five for just one two-digit field. There was a long tail. At the bottom end, two universities failed to achieve a rating of three in any field. Another two did not rate above three, and one of them achieved three in only two fields. If the research standard threshold for university provider category registration were set at world average performance in three broad fields, then five of Australia's current universities would not meet that criterion.

The Australian government is preparing for consultations over the use of the 2011 ERA for resource allocation, including for research infrastructure block grants, through the Sustainable Research Excellence (SRE) program, and for the funding of research training places through the research Training Scheme (RTS) formula. The SRE program fund is being progressively increased to raise the indirect cost rate to 50 percent on average of nationally competitive research grants. Universities have been engaged in a "transparent costing" exercise to help identify the range of indirect costs in the sector.

8. Increasing Public Information about Higher Education Capacity and Performance

The government is intending to set up a "My University" website in 2012, which will include information about universities' performance against their compact performance targets, along with other information about course offerings, services, and prices. The initial set of information to be provided includes: (i) student applications data, (ii) student to staff ratio, (iii) degree completion, (iv) student retention and attrition, (v) student satisfaction (CEQ), and (vi) graduate destinations.

Part C: An Assessment of the Policy Direction in Australia

Improving National Coherence in Tertiary Education

A particular interest of the Australian government is to achieve greater policy and regulatory consistency on a national basis for tertiary education. The government has been able to move ahead in respect of higher education because of its dominant funding role. In vocational education and training, where financing responsibilities are more divided between the federal and state governments, progress has been more protracted. Nevertheless, the government is putting together frameworks that can function on a nationally consistent basis across the whole tertiary sector eventually, such as the revised Australian Qualifications Framework (AQF) and TEQSA, while leaving open for further development the issues of student-driven funding and structural diversification of provision.

Moving to the Forefront of International Practice

As noted during the development of the new AQF, a preoccupation with national neatness led to some parochial proposals, which were eventually modified, such as the prohibition on offering qualifications of international reputability. Nevertheless, when the several elements are taken together, Australia's new regulatory framework for higher education is internationally advanced. It sets a foundational level of provision quality below which providers will be unable to operate. It has strength in legislation to deal with future growth of private local and foreign for-profit providers, global consortia, and mixed mode providers.

Addressing Emerging Concerns among the Broader Community

We can understand the factors driving governments to be more exacting in respect of higher education quality, even if the ways and means they choose may not always be consistent with the interests of universities. There are compelling grounds for governments to ensure that the community can have confidence in higher education institutions and the programs and qualifications they provide. The four principal grounds are probity, effectiveness, transparency, and comparability.

The probity threshold: In the interests of students, and graduates and their employers, it is important that governments take appropriate action to weed out rogue and low-quality providers and expose fraudulent qualifications on offer within their jurisdictions. Accordingly, for the purpose of consumer protection, governments around the world are tightening provider licensing criteria to ensure that only bona fide operators are eligible for registration, and undertaking closer and more frequent monitoring of providers' continuing compliance with their entry registration conditions.

The effectiveness imperative: Modern economies must have more highly educated and skilled workforces to be globally competitive. This requires effective action not only to ensure the availability of high-level expertise but also to raise human capital capacity across a wider base. The education and training system must actually produce the output quality that is required: students must be learning, teaching must develop learning, and assessment must identify how much learning takes place. If it fails to do so, the economy will be less productive than it needs to be and an unacceptable number of people will fail to find rewarding work. Postsecondary qualifications must have meaning in testifying to the possession of understandings and skills. A major challenge is to achieve better learning outcomes for groups of people participating in higher education who have not been well served by prior schooling.

The transparency requirement: With increasing diversity in forms of higher education, there is a call to clarify the meaning of qualifications in testifying to sets of graduate capabilities. In view of the multiple entry paths to higher education, the diversity of learning modes, and the varying destinations of graduates, there is a call to make more explicit the implicit judgments which have been made traditionally within the confines of universities, for instance, about assessment grades and credit for prior learning. The criteria for decisions need to be open for those outside the academy to see and understand, and challenge where necessary, such as in instances of inconsistency and arbitrariness in the grading of student work.

The comparability challenge: Potential participants in tertiary education want to make sense of what is available and make informed decisions about where and what to study. The increasing international mobility of higher education students and graduates and the proliferation of providers of higher education services and qualifications challenge governments to find new ways and means of safeguarding credential integrity and improving the authentication and equivalence of educational qualifications. Students want to know the worth of their degrees, reflecting their efforts and achievements, without being limited by preconceptions of institutional prestige. Employers seek to have a reasonable basis on which to compare graduate applicants for jobs. They want to know the similarities and dissimilarities of qualifications, including those with the same titles awarded by different providers.

There is not necessarily any single best way of responding to these imperatives but rather a variety of ways. However, there appears to be some convergence internationally around a number of ways that are preferred by governments, and these are typically simple, quantifiable measures, notwithstanding the complexity of the issues and the multiplicity of drivers.

Drivers of the New Approach

The causes for reform are driven by a range of changes in the economic and social functions of higher education and the operating circumstances of postsecondary institutions, especially in the role of universities. A paradoxical common thread among the various drivers is that of higher expectations of higher education but lower public spending on it and lower public trust in academic judgment.

Wider expectations of higher education and university research: Contemporary universities have enlarged roles through accumulation over time of multiple functions from their own initiatives, state directives, market opportunities, and social expectations. Because universities have become more integral to the knowledge society, they are more roundly subject to scrutiny. As society becomes more knowledgeable, universities come under pressure to expand the kinds of knowledge they provide and to diversify the criteria by which they are judged (Bleiklie and Byrkjeflot 2002). As higher education seeks to serve a greater proportion of the population and to meet the need for an increasingly well-educated, economically competitive, and socially responsible citizenry, the public becomes more interested in the results being achieved from the extensive investment. There is a sharper focus on cost-effectiveness: How well are students learning and how efficiently do postsecondary institutions operate?

The rise of the evaluative regulatory state: Higher education is no less subject than other areas of education and other areas of social activity to the regulatory predispositions of governments. In higher education, as in relation to the financial sector, light-touch regulation is giving way to more hands-on regulation. Additionally, the more intrusive role of the state in relation to academic affairs is a product of a firm belief in human capital investment as a key source of productivity improvement, innovation, and economic competitiveness. It also coincides, at least in the advanced western economies, with relatively lower levels of government investment in higher education, in comparison with private sources of funding and national economic capacity. As they become more parsimonious, governments demand greater accountability of the institutions they continue to fund and give themselves the heightened role of safeguarding the interests of private consumers and investors.

The shift from pre-mass to mass and to post-mass higher education participation: With the majority of workforce entrants now having postsecondary qualifications, governments and employers regard postsecondary education as no less important for them to influence as schooling:

> … as an undergraduate degree comes to replace the high school diploma as a gateway to even basic levels of sustainable employment, distrust increases in the professional authority of the professoriate. With increasing influence

and declining trust, the focal point of professional accountability shifts from members of the profession to the clients and their representatives. (Borden 2010)

Governments are driven to step in as the bases of trust in the worth of educational qualifications are called into question. The traditional bases of trust, whether prior knowledge of the awarding institution or confidence in the processes of external verification by peers, have been challenged for their subjectivity, exclusivity, and narrowness. This problem is exacerbated by the breakdown in post-mass systems of the informal cultural induction of academic assessors in pre-mass systems when academic careers were relatively stable. The changing pattern of academic staffing, including greater use of casual or sessional personnel in teaching, tutoring, and marking, makes the transfer of implicit understanding very difficult. In response a model of "trust-free" specification of criteria has emerged but not without its own difficulties resulting from a tendency to over-specification with a consequential trivialization of outcomes and lowering of standards (Wolf 1995) and tension between educational purposes and accountability requirements (Young 2007).

The changing nature of higher education demand and supply: The enlarged and more diverse student body generates a wider range of education providers and greater variety of, and ways and means of, learning. The expansion and diversification of higher education requires new forms of information and channels of communication about the orientation and quality of different higher education institutions and programs, so that potential participants can make sense of what is available and make informed decisions, and employers can have a reasonable basis on which to compare graduate applicants:

> the old forms of trust, appropriate to an elite system, are insufficient when confronted with millions of students, hundreds of thousands of courses, thousands of universities and with the demands of millions of employers. (Floud 2006)

Indicators of quality erosion in higher education: Community attention has been drawn to the risks to quality in higher education as indicated by increasing student/teacher ratios and class sizes, growing concern about plagiarism, unfamiliarity with new methods of continuous and online assessment, and the increasing use of group learning activities. Additionally, changing patterns of *student engagement* in university life, including reduced campus attendance and longer hours in employment, raise questions about depth of learning (James, Krause and Jennings 2010).

Disaffection with conventional quality assurance and performance reporting: Four particular areas of disaffection with the application of quality auditing to higher education may be discerned: (i) the failure of quality assurance mechanisms to rid the system of low-quality providers; (ii) a burdensome process for institutions that induces compliance and is subject to gaming; (iii) the tendency of quality assurance to reduce diversity and quality; and (iv) deficiencies in the quality of information available to students, employers, and others.

The democratization of access and seamlessness agenda, and the assault on provider capture: Education providers, through their control over qualifications and the routes to achieving them, can be seen to have "captured" the market, thereby creating inefficiencies and blockages for learners (Raggat and Williams 1999). The trend towards learner-centred education and generic criteria for all qualifications is presented as fairer for all and supports widening participation and lifelong learning, on the assumption that anyone can reach the highest levels when freed from the restrictive constraints of institutions. Comprehensive (whether linked or integrated) national qualifications systems, which define qualifications in terms of learning outcomes independently of where and how they are attained, are seen by advocates of lifelong learning as a reform tool. Seamless qualifications pathways remove barriers between institutions and subsystems of education and training (for example, vocational education and training, general education, higher education and adult learning) and facilitate access, transfer, and progression (Grm and Bjornavold 2010; Walls and Pardy 2010).

Approaches to Reform

In response to these drivers, the accountability for quality in the higher education agenda involves four relatively new approaches to system reform: (i) assuring acceptable threshold standards, (ii) validating quality beyond the threshold, (iii) achieving productivity improvements, and (iv) accounting for learning additionally.

Assuring acceptable threshold standards: With growth and diversification of student numbers and postsecondary providers, the need is seen to safeguard consumers and the reputability of qualifications by requiring providers to meet specified minimally acceptable or *threshold standards.* These *provider standards* determine the criteria for providers to be licensed to operate and for them and/or their students to be eligible for public funding. Typically, they cover inputs and processes seen to be necessary for adequate capacity (e.g., sufficiency of human resources and physical facilities to serve the volume of activity), financial viability, sound governance, academic quality, and reliability.

The most difficult of these are *academic standards* relating to the quality of teaching, learning, and scholarship. Typically, threshold *academic standards* relate to *entry standards* for student admissions and teaching faculty appointments. Contemporary practice in accreditation and quality assurance contexts also involves *process standards*, including curriculum design, teaching methods, student engagement, and assessment policies and practices. In diverse, post-mass systems of postsecondary education, where students learn in various modes, the notion of threshold standards for the academic processes of delivery is problematic but not impractical.

A more recent and controversial approach to threshold standards relates to the expected outputs and outcomes of educational processes. These *outcomes standards* may be expressed as demonstrable capabilities of graduates related to the learning attainment expected for a given level of educational qualification, such as those expressed in national qualifications frameworks or by regional accrediting bodies, or by individual postsecondary institutions.

The framing questions are: (i) *How can we be confident that all accredited providers can deliver good quality education?* and (ii) *How can we be sure that all graduates are capable of performing at an acceptable level?*

There are significant issues involved in relating institution-specific goals to national or even international expectations of comparability of learning outcomes standards. The notion of comparable standards for learning outcomes from postsecondary education, even at the threshold level, is conceptually difficult and academically contested. It is also a significant challenge to realize in practice because there are so many variable factors that have to be taken into account. There is also the profound risk that acceptance of threshold learning outcomes standards will promote sameness in assessment, reduce diversity in educational offerings, and limit improvements in learning (Craddock and Mathias 2009).

Validating quality beyond the threshold: Even if it were possible to verify attainment of threshold learning standards, it would be insufficient for higher education institutions that aim higher and seek to stretch students to perform at their best. Indeed for a higher education system aspiring beyond mediocrity, it is necessary to be able to distinguish excellence amid diversity and to validate the claims of institutions about the quality of their performance. This challenge necessarily involves a customized, rather than a common, approach to standards validation.

The framing questions are: (i) *How good are we?* and (ii) *How do we know?*

Three approaches to quality validation can be identified: (i) intra-institutional validation, (ii) inter-institutional validation, and (iii) external validation. Each of these approaches may be applied at the whole-of-institution level or on a discipline basis. Arguably, each approach should have a role. The main policy issue for institutions is to determine the appropriate balance among the approaches and their inter-relationships.

Intra-institutional validation may involve internal monitoring, audits, and reviews of alignment between program objectives, learning experiences, assessment processes and student outcomes, and comparisons across programs within an institution, such as the distribution of grades. Inter-institutional validation may involve benchmarking institutional practices not only against national average standards but against peer institutions, including international peers. External validation may involve independent audits and reviews by professional bodies and international experts.

A key question is whether governments should be involved directly in arranging external validation processes and prescribing any particular measures, as distinct from setting policy expectations that institutions should themselves arrange for their claims to be verified in appropriate and transparent ways.

Achieving productivity improvements: The need for productivity improvement in postsecondary education derives, on the one hand, from the expectation of governments who seek greater and more cost-effective participation, and on the other hand, from the necessity for postsecondary institutions to produce more graduates at lower unit costs without loss of quality. New technologies for teaching and learning offer both efficiency gains and improvements in teaching and learning effectiveness. However, productivity involves quality as well as efficiency; and as participation increases and government funding per student falls, an interesting reciprocity of responsibilities arises between governments and institutions.

Governments want to be able to assure the community that expansion does not come at a cost to quality, that students are obtaining value for money, and that taxpayers' funds are being well spent. In a post-mass system of higher education participation, what matters to governments is the absolute growth of annual budget outlays, even if, as matters to higher education institutions, the per student funding rate is declining. Postsecondary institutions want to be able to indicate tipping points of funding levels, beyond which it is unreasonable to expect quality to be maintained. Such indicators may include student/teacher ratios, degrees of student engagement with teachers, expressions of student satisfaction with teaching, rates of student progress and completion, graduate employment and income returns, and other learning process and outcome indicators.

Three approaches to productivity may be identified: (i) increasing the productivity of administration, (ii) improving the productivity of teaching, and (iii) improving the productivity of learning. The former may involve process efficiency reviews and re-engineering, joint procurement, shared services with other institutions, and outsourcing of administrative processing.

Improving the productivity of teaching may involve strategies for increasing the intensity of utilization of space and infrastructure and the use of new teaching technologies. Increasing the productivity of learning may involve strategies for reducing student dropout rates, especially in first year, through readiness programs, buddy systems, and structured student support. Some segmentation of approaches may be required for different students, such as between those who can benefit from less teaching and more independent learning, and those who require more intensive learning support.

The framing questions are: (i) *How can we achieve greater student through-put at lower unit costs and with enhanced quality of learning?* (ii) *Where can we make cost savings?* and (iii) *What are the priorities for the most expensive educational interventions?*

Accounting for learning additionality: The contemporary conversation in postsecondary education across several countries also refers to accounting for *learning additionality*. This approach strives to integrate improvement goals with accountability purposes, with a focus on *value added*.

The framing questions are: (i) *How well do higher education institutions extend the knowledge and skills of their students?* and (ii) *How do they and the wider community know?*

This approach necessarily involves institutional purpose-specific and cohort-specific as well as individualized measures, rather than a common testing framework. However, the current international tendency is to conflate the purpose of student learning improvement with that of assuring threshold standards through standardized tests. The rationale appears to be that mean performance on a test defines the threshold standard and that institutions and even national systems of higher education can be compared reliably according to changes over time in their mean scores and the spread of attainment within the groups tested. There are considerable questions to be asked about these various assumptions, and they are being posed in the context of the OECD's AHELO project, the US experience with the CLA, and Australia's consideration of the CLA and other measures.

Tensions in the Policy Framework

However, there are various tensions to be dealt with as the new framework is refined and matures.

The fundamental problem is that the Australian government's policy and financing settings are putting downward pressure on quality, and all the new regulatory and performance accountability mechanisms cannot compensate for over-scaling and under-funding. Indeed they may contribute to loss of diversity and responsiveness.

The combination of higher education expansion and increasing efficiency is putting at risk the quality of advanced human capital formation. Expansion at lower per student unit costs may result in standards not being met, e.g., student/staff ratios. The tension between funding and standards will become more pressing once the government has set up TEQSA. It would be unreasonable for the government to mandate quality standards without allowing universities access to sufficient funds to meet those standards.

It was a courageous step for the government to agree to an open-ended funding commitment to higher education enlargement. As enrolments expand, particularly over the decade 2015–2025 when school leavers surge, the cost to government will rise and, in the context of increasing costs for health and social security associated with the ageing population, will stretch the limits of fiscal capacity. There will need to be a rebalancing in the sharing of costs between government and students, greater pricing flexibility for institutions, and increased supply by lower cost providers that do not carry the cost overheads of research universities.

Some may argue that supply will sort itself out in a more competitive student-driven environment, but that is to overlook the potency of academic norms (van Vught 2007). Without structural differentiation there will simply be mission drift. The framework of national standards, and the assumption of parity of esteem of qualifications, however and wherever obtained that underpins the national qualifications framework, will give this drift a wide spread.

Registration of universities requires meeting research standards, but if these are set merely at world average, that is a policy for mediocrity. Some might claim that it reflects a *world class system*, but a national higher education system cannot be world class if it cannot sustain real centres of internationally-benchmarked excellence. However, if the research standards are set above world average many universities may not meet them. They could forfeit their university accreditation and would be relegated to another provider category. Governments would come under considerable pressure to prevent relegation and adopt an equity policy for research.

Expansion of university staff under a policy promoting research expansion in all universities would add to the volume of applicants for competitive research grants and put greater pressure on success rates. A notable outcome of the 2011 round of funding compact discussions between government officers and universities was that all universities are seeking to increase their success in national competitive grants for research. Greater demand for research funding, without a commensurate increase in funding for research, threatens to reduce concentration and thereby erode Australia's research competitiveness.

Changing State University Relationships

The uncomfortable trade-off for universities, in return for greater procedural autonomy through admissions flexibility and improved public funding in aggregate, is some erosion of substantive autonomy over academic matters. Policy instruments which were previously descriptive for guidance purposes, such as the national qualifications framework, now have a regulatory application to established universities which in future will have to satisfy national requirements for re-registration.

The Commonwealth's regulations relating to universities have previously been tied to its funding of them. The TEQSA model regulates universities in all their activities, whether or not the Commonwealth is paying. To be licensed to operate, a university must satisfy TEQSA that it meets the standards set by the Australian government minister. If it fails to satisfy, after a period wherein it has had the opportunity to improve, it may no longer be able to enroll and teach students, regardless of its establishment as a university under the law of a state or territory. This is a consequence of the Commonwealth drawing upon the Corporations power under the Constitution, as interpreted broadly by the High Court of Australia.

The Need for a More Nuanced Policy Framework and a More Mutual Process of Policy Development

Universities and other institutions have a responsibility to address the community's need to have confidence in higher education. If the institutions are not responsive, then governments will be obliged to impose their own solutions. The solutions that governments prefer are typically common and crude; they are simple measures regardless of complexity; and they are applied flatly across all providers regardless of institutional differences.

The risk is that this approach will be counterproductive. It will not provide meaningful information to the community. It will stifle diversity, erode quality, and reduce the flexibility necessary for postsecondary institutions to respond to unexpected needs and challenges.

A more nuanced and mutual approach to policy development would achieve a better result, because of the complexity of the matters involved and because of the capacity of experts in the university community and elsewhere to contribute.

A model that recognizes mutual responsibilities and expertise, facilitates different provider models and outcomes, and respects the concerns of the diverse range of stakeholders having a direct interest in higher education outcomes, will go much further in improving performance, promoting diversity, and achieving excellence, than will a centrally-mandated compliance model.

For instance, the imperatives identified earlier could be addressed effectively by greater use of customized, rather than common, measures:

- *The probity threshold:* Institutions satisfying core criteria as bona fide providers.
- *The transparency requirement:* Institutions making clear (i) what they offer—the objectives and learning experiences of programs, (ii) what they expect of students—by way of readiness and during the program, and (iii) and how they assess student learning.
- *The effectiveness imperative:* Institutions delivering what they promise, demonstrating that they have fulfilled their side of the contract with students and the community, and validating their claims about quality.

- *The comparability challenge:* Institutions defining their distinctiveness, how their programs and graduates meet external expectations, and how they differ.

A Focus on Assessment

The primary nexus between improvement and accountability is assessment. There are clear international trends towards accepting that students' academic attainment is the primary reference point for monitoring academic standards, and that attainment in the final year of study is a suitable point for benchmarking:

> If academic standards are primarily defined by academic attainment, the quality and robustness of [the] process for assessing, grading and reporting individual and group attainment are paramount. (Richard James, 2010, presentation to the AUQA Auditors Meeting)

Assessment is the basic means of evaluating the effectiveness of the structured learning experiences of the curriculum in achieving educational objectives. Because different institutions in their various programs have different educational objectives and organize learning experiences variously to meet the needs of their students in achieving those objectives, assessment must be program specific. Common assessment can only apply validly in circumstances of common curriculum.

Comparable assessment may be applied for programs that have similar educational purposes and seek to achieve equivalent learning outcomes standards, such as in the case of universities that self-select in forming national and international networks.

The Go8 Quality Verification System

Concurrently, universities themselves are exploring ways to verify their claims to the general community. Group of Eight (Go8) universities are collaborating in the development of an external peer-based verification of the appropriateness and reliability of assessment and the quality of student work. The Go8 is exploring the viability and benefits of establishing a *Quality Verification System (QVS)* to:

- demonstrate the appropriateness of the standards of learning outcomes and grades awarded in Go8 universities;
- maintain and improve the academic standards of Go8 universities;
- enable comparisons of learning outcomes in similar programs across Go8 universities; and
- promote discussion on good practice in teaching and learning in the Go8 universities.

The Go8 QVS is a process of external, discipline-led, academic peer review of final year undergraduate student outcomes. The QVS will review two core subjects, or the equivalent of a quarter of a year's work, in each undergraduate program across Go8 universities. Based on their academic judgment and the set of documents provided, the *Go8 QVS External Reviewers* will:

- review the appropriateness and comparative quality of the specified learning outcomes, assessment tasks, assessment criteria, and assessment processes set for samples of final year subjects; and
- report on the appropriateness of the grades awarded to stratified random samples of student work in these subjects.

Distinctive features of the proposed Go8 QVS are:

- the timing and scope of the review is designed by individual university's faculties or departments;
- the QVS focuses upon assessment in a sample of final year subjects in undergraduate programs (the review must cover a minimum of 25 percent of final year requirements);
- the QVS concentrates on benchmarking for comparing grades awarded in similar programs across Go8 universities;
- the QVS is conducted by senior discipline-specific academics (level D and above) who will have an understanding of academic standards in leading universities around the world; and
- the QVS is sufficiently flexible to complement other quality assurance mechanisms within Go8 universities to minimize duplication of efforts.

The QVS involves quality verification by external reviewers. It is not moderation of grades by external examiners. The QVS reviewers will retrospectively verify the appropriateness of grades awarded to a sample of student assessment after their results have been published. The QVS review will not influence the grades awarded to students enrolled in the subjects being reviewed. The QVS reviewers are *not* expected to design assessment tasks, re-mark student work, or standardize student grades.

Conclusion: The Debates We Have Yet to Have

Conventionally, the notion of *measuring the value of a postsecondary education* implies an emphasis on the private economic benefits of higher education. Typically, this concern focuses on the relative employment and income gains of graduates. Such a focus may be contrasted with a concern for *appreciating the worth of postsecondary education,* inferring an interest in broader private and social benefits. Regrettably, across many countries, interest in the latter seems to be largely confined to those engaged as education professionals, whereas employers of graduates alongside politicians (and perhaps students and the general community—although that needs to be tested rather than assumed) seem ever narrower in their concerns and seek tangible evidence of direct and immediate utility.

Contemporary public policy may be seen to focus on "cost-effectively enlarging higher education access and success through greater operating flexibility for institutions with stronger accountability for results and without diminution of quality" (Gallagher 2010). This approach has several dimensions: (i) expanding higher education opportunities, and increasing total public and private spending on higher education; (ii) diversifying modes of provision; (iii) framing procedures that enable progressive learner attainment and mobility across different providers, including through recognition of prior learning and credit transfer; (iv) assuring acceptable threshold standards of provision; (v) validating quality beyond the threshold; (vi) improving the productivity of teaching; and (vii) accounting for learning effectiveness.

Taken together, these emphases give rise to an agenda for greater accountability for quality in higher education. This relatively recent approach is ambitious and ambiguous. It involves new forms of financing, often with the assertion on the part of central policy makers of less attention to input controls and more discretion over ways and means of using resources but with tighter associated conditions relating to the outcomes achieved with the available funds. In practice, governments and their officials are reluctant to relinquish their controls over resource inputs, such that institutions find little by way of greater operating discretion but rather an additional overlay of regulatory and reporting burdens.

The accountability for quality agenda involves a dual push: first, to make more transparent to the lay community what may be opaque and self-referenced judgments of academic teachers, such as the assessment of student learning, the grading of student work, and the awarding of credit for prior learning; and second, to validate internal academic assessments against externally set standards.

This agenda may be seen to reflect a new "realism," involving an uncomfortable trade-off of professional autonomy in academic matters for continuing community support. It is based on the view, on the one hand, that there are compelling imperatives for reform in teaching, assessment of learning and reporting of learning outcomes, and, on the other hand, that there are important aspects of university autonomy which need to be safeguarded in the interests of quality, diversity, and the free pursuit of knowledge. The main risks are that governments conflate rather than clarify their objectives, and the means they adopt may be overly simplified to suit their political purposes with adverse consequences for higher education. The challenge is to establish mutually agreed purposes and useful performance reporting frameworks.

Australia is pushing ahead with a suite of far-reaching reforms to higher education. Yet, the policy purposes are not always clear and not all of the available options have been considered. In comparison with Britain, Europe, and North America, Australia has not had conversations on the issues at stake within the academic community and across stakeholder groups, with employers, students, and public policy personnel.

Among the questions we have to debate seriously in Australia are the following:

- Why are conventional indicators of quality and effectiveness not indicating serious problems?
- Whose standards matter most?
- What do we mean by the qualifiers: "consistent," "equivalent," "comparable" in relation to academic standards?
- What is the place of standards in a diversified system?
- Is there an implicit agenda for a common curriculum in higher education, as for schooling?
- To what extent do threshold standards and standardized tests lead to standardization of ends and means?
- Can academic standards be assessed absent peer review?
- Can a customized, rather than a common, approach to standards satisfy community concerns about higher education quality?

NOTES

[1] The views expressed in this paper do not necessarily reflect the views of Go8 vice-chancellors and presidents.

[2] FEE-HELP loans are provided by the Australian government to cover tuition costs where students are enrolled with institutions or in courses that do not attract a government tuition subsidy. The loans which may not exceed AUD$85,000 over a lifetime (except for medicine where the loan limit is AUD$105,000) are repayable after graduation according to the level of graduate income.

[3] Initially, the government set out to achieve integrated reform of the full tertiary (postsecondary) education system. However, without consent of the states and territories, the federal government fell back to the area where it had legal power to act unilaterally, viz. higher education financing. Importantly, in so doing, the federal government extended its regulatory powers over the state-established universities in unprecedented ways.

REFERENCES

ALTC. 2011. *Learning and Teaching Academic Standards Project Final Report.* Sydney: Australian Learning and Teaching Council.

Australian Government. 2009. *Transforming Australia's Higher Education System.* Canberra.

Australian Qualifications Framework. 2011. *Australian Qualifications Framework First Edition.* Adelaide: AQF.

Bleiklie, I. and H. Byrkjeflot. 2002. Changing Knowledge Regimes: Universities in a New Research Environment. *Higher Education* 44 (2-3): 1-14.

Borden, V.M.H. 2010. The Accountability Improvement Paradox. *Inside Higher Ed*, 20 April. At http://www.insidehighered.com/views/2010/04/30/borden.

Bradley, D., P. Noonan, H. Nugent, and B. Scales. 2008. *Review of Australian Higher Education: Final Report.* Canberra: DEEWR.

Craddock, D. and H. Mathias. 2009. Assessment Options in Higher Education. *Assessment & Evaluation in Higher Education* 34 (2): 127-140.

Department of Education, Employment and Workplace Relations. 2011. *Student 2010 Full Year: Selected Higher Education Statistics.* Canberra: DEEWR.

Evans, C. 2011. University Reward Funding to focus on improving participation and social inclusion. At http://ministers.deewr.gov.au/evans/university-reward-funding-focus-improving-participation-and-social-inclusion

Floud, R. 2006. Convergence and Diversity. In *EUA Bologna Handbook: Making Bologna Work.* European University Association. Berlin: Raabe Academic Publishers.

Gallagher, M. 2010. The Accountability for Quality Agenda in Higher Education. Canberra: Group of Eight. At http://www.go8.edu.au/university-staff/go8-policy-_and_-analysis/2010/the-accountability-for-quality-agenda-in-higher-education.

Grm, S. and J. Bjornavold. 2010. Development of National Qualifications Frameworks (NQFs) in Europe. *EQF Newsletter*, April.

Harris, R. 2006. *Private Training Providers in Australia: Their Characteristics and Training Activities.* Melbourne: Australian Council of Private Education and Training.

Heaney, J-G., M. Heaney, and P. Ryan. 2010. Branding Private Higher Education in Australia to International Students. At http://www.consulted.biz/Papers/Heaney,%20Ryan%20&%20Heaney%20-%20Branding%20Private%20Higher%20Education.pdf.

James, R., K. Krause, and C. Jennings. 2010. *The First Year Experience in Australian Universities: Findings from 1994-2009.* University of Melbourne: Centre for the Study of Higher Education.

National Centre for Vocational Education Research. 2011. *Australian Vocational Education and Training Statistics: Students and Courses 2010.* Adelaide: NCVER.

Raggat, P. and C. Williams. 1999. *Government, Markets and Vocational Qualifications: An Anatomy of Policy.* London: Falmer Press.

van Vught, F. 2007. "Diversity and Differentiation in Higher Education Systems." Presentation to the L.H. Martin Institute. University of Melbourne.

Walls, S. and J. Pardy. 2010. *Crediting Vocational Education for Training and Learner Mobility.* Adelaide: National Centre for Vocational Education Research.

Wolf, A. 1995. Competence-Based Assessment. In *Competence in the Learning Society*, ed. J. Raven and J. Stephenson, 453-466. New York: Peter Lang Publishing, Inc.

Young, M. 2007. Qualifications Frameworks: Some Conceptual Issues. *European Journal of Education* 42 (4): 445-457.

APPENDIX 1
AQF Qualification Types in the Levels Structure, 2011

Level	*Level 6*	*Level 7*	*Level 8*	*Level 9*	*Level 10*
Qualification type	Advanced diploma Associate's degree	Bachelor's degree	Bachelor's honours degree Graduate certificate Vocational graduate certificate Graduate diploma Vocational graduate diploma	Master's degree	Doctoral degree
Level summary	Graduates at this level will have broad knowledge and skills for paraprofessional/highly skilled work and/or further learning	Graduates at this level will have broad and coherent knowledge and skills for professional work and/or further learning	Graduates at this level will have advanced knowledge and skills for professional or highly skilled work and/or further learning	Graduates at this level will have specialized knowledge and skills for research, and/or professional practice, and/or further learning	Graduates at this level will have systematic and critical understanding of a complex field of learning and specialized research skills for the advancement of learning and/or for professional practice
Knowledge	Graduates at this level will have broad theoretical and technical knowledge of a specific area or a broad field of work and learning	Graduates at this level will have broad and coherent theoretical and technical knowledge with depth in one or more disciplines or areas of practice	Graduates at this level will have advanced theoretical and technical knowledge in one or more disciplines or areas of practice	Graduates at this level will have advanced and integrated understanding of a complex body of knowledge in one or more disciplines or areas of practice	Graduates at this level will have systemic and critical understanding of a substantial and complex body of knowledge at the frontier of a discipline or area of professional practice

... continued

APPENDIX 1
(Continued)

Level	Level 6	Level 7	Level 8	Level 9	Level 10
Skills	Graduates at this level will have a broad range of cognitive, technical and communication skills to select and apply methods and technologies to:	Graduates at this level will have well developed cognitive, technical and communication skills to select and apply methods and technologies to:	Graduates at this level will have advanced cognitive, technical and communication skills to select and apply methods and technologies to:	Graduates at this level will have expert, specialized cognitive and technical skills in a body of knowledge or practice to independently:	Graduates at this level will have expert, specialized cognitive, technical and research skills in a discipline area to independently and systematically:
	• analyze information to complete a range of activities;	• analyze and evaluate information to complete a range of activities;	• critically analyze, evaluate and transform information to complete a range of activities;	• critically analyze, reflect on and synthesize complex information, problems, concepts and theories;	• engage in critical reflection, synthesis and evaluation;
	• interpret and transmit solutions to unpredictable and sometimes complex problems; and	• analyze, generate and transmit solutions to unpredictable and sometimes complex problems; and	• analyze, generate and transmit solutions to complex problems; and	• research and apply established theories to a body of knowledge or practice; and	• develop, adapt and implement research methodologies to extend and redefine existing knowledge or professional practice;
	• transmit information and skills to others	• transmit knowledge, skills and ideas to others	• transmit knowledge, skills and ideas to others	• interpret and transmit knowledge, skills and ideas to specialist and non-specialist audiences	• disseminate and promote new insights to peers and the community; and
					• generate original knowledge and understanding to make a substantial contribution to a discipline or area of professional practice

... continued

APPENDIX 1
(Continued)

Level	Level 6	Level 7	Level 8	Level 9	Level 10
Application of knowledge and skills	Graduates at this level will apply knowledge and skills to demonstrate autonomy, judgment and defined responsibility: • in contexts that are subject to change and • within broad parameters to provide specialist advice and functions .	Graduates at this level will apply knowledge and skills to demonstrate autonomy, well developed judgment and responsibility: • in contexts that require self-directed work and learning and • within broad parameters to provide specialist advice and functions	Graduates at this level will apply knowledge and skills to demonstrate autonomy, well developed judgment, adaptability and responsibility as a practitioner or learner	Graduates at this level will apply knowledge and skills to demonstrate autonomy, expert judgment, adaptability and responsibility as a practitioner or learner	Graduates at this level will apply knowledge and skills to demonstrate autonomy, authoritative judgment, adaptability and responsibility as an expert and leading practitioner or scholar

Source: Australian Qualifications Framework (2011).

APPENDIX 2
Level Nine Master's Degree Descriptors

Qualification	Purpose	Volume of Learning
Master's degree (research)	The master's degree (research) qualifies individuals who apply an advanced body of knowledge in a range of contexts for research and scholarship and as a pathway for further learning.	The volume of learning of a master's degree (research) is typically one to two years; in the same discipline one and a half years following a level 7 qualification or one year following a level 8 qualification; in a different discipline two years following a level 7 qualification or one and a half years following a level 8 qualification.
Master's degree (coursework)	The master's degree (coursework) qualifies individuals who apply an advanced body of knowledge in a range of contexts for professional practice or scholarship and as a pathway for further learning.	The volume of learning of a master's degree (coursework) is typically one to two years; in the same discipline 1½ years following a level 7 qualification or one year following a level 8 qualification; in a different discipline two years following a level 7 qualification or one and a half years following a level 8 qualification.
Master's degree (extended)	The master's degree (extended) qualifies individuals who apply an advanced body of knowledge in a range of contexts for professional practice and as a pathway for further learning.	The volume of learning of a master's degree (extended) is typically three to four years following completion of a minimum of a three-year level 7 qualification.

Source: Australian Qualifications Framework (2011).

4

THE VALUE OF LEARNING OUTCOMES: A CANADIAN PERSPECTIVE

Virginia Hatchette

My lens for approaching the issue of measuring the value of postsecondary education is quality. Learning outcomes are the most explicit and direct expressions of what we collectively value in postsecondary education. They are also, possibly, the most difficult to measure.

The mandate of my agency, the Postsecondary Education Quality Assessment Board (PEQAB), is to review degree programs against recognized quality standards in Ontario. Learning outcomes are at the centre of our approach. PEQAB has several standards and benchmarks it uses in the course of its reviews. One criterion, in which samples of student work reflect the appropriate learning outcomes, has the potential to trump all the others.

In this chapter, I will share PEQAB's experiences with articulating and measuring learning outcomes, some lessons we learned in the process, and those we think are yet to be learned.

QUALITY ASSURANCE IN ONTARIO

Degree Credentials

Ontario degree education has a long history of quality assurance. Public universities have a 50-year history of ongoing quality assurance of graduate credentials and a 20-year history of cyclical audit of the institutional policies that assure the quality of undergraduate credentials. The Ontario Universities Council on Quality Assurance (OUCQA) is responsible for assuring quality in Ontario public universities that offer degree programs on the basis of statutory authority. It approves new programs and reviews institutional quality assurance procedures on an eight-year cycle.

Measuring the Value of a Postsecondary Education, ed. K. Norrie and M.C. Lennon. Montreal and Kingston: Queen's Policy Studies Series, McGill-Queen's University Press. © 2013 All rights reserved.

PEQAB was created in 2000, in a context of worldwide dynamic changes in degree granting that included the introduction of new kinds of postsecondary education providers offering new postsecondary credentials, an increase in degree mill activity, and the emergence of accreditation mills. The circumstances that led to these changes in degree granting, (e.g., internationalization, globalization, new information, and communication technologies) also inspired concerns about the quality of degree programs. Most jurisdictions, including Ontario, responded with the creation of quality assurance agencies to protect learning outcomes in a period of rapid transformation.

PEQAB is responsible for reviewing degree programs offered on the basis of ministerial consent. PEQAB engages teams of experts in the discipline and in higher education institution management to review both new and existing programs and organizational capacity to offer quality programs. Most degrees offered by consent are offered either by private providers, public colleges of applied arts and technology, and public universities from outside Ontario. Consents are typically time limited and require regular renewal.

PEQAB reviews proposals for new programs against a set of standards and benchmarks that must, by legislative obligation, reflect standards in Ontario and elsewhere. The range of matters considered by PEQAB is comprehensive and includes curriculum; human, financial, and physical resources; and the policy environment of the institution.

The minister's consents for new programs are typically for a period of five to seven years and are tied to the requirement that the institution implement the program as it was proposed, with the full range of resources as committed to in the proposal. At each renewal of consent, PEQAB reviews both the program (including the comprehensive range of matters indicated previously) and the ability of the institution to assure its own quality.

Learning outcomes are important components of the quality assurance processes of both the OUCQA and PEQAB, and each requires institutions to articulate the knowledge and skills expected of graduates.

Diploma and Certificate Credentials

As at the degree level, both private and public providers offer postsecondary diplomas and certificates in Ontario. The Ontario College Quality Assurance Service (OCQAS), created in 2002, is responsible for assuring the quality of programming offered by public colleges of applied arts and technology. OCQAS offers two services to colleges: (i) credential validation and (ii) institutional quality assurance.

The Credentials Validation Service is responsible for ensuring, at a sector level, the consistency of programs and nomenclatures for certificates, diplomas, advanced diplomas, and graduate certificates. The Program

Quality Assurance Process Audit (PQAPA) ensures that colleges have effective processes for internal institutional quality assurance and continuous improvement.

As at the diploma level, learning outcomes are specified for all similar programs offered by colleges and expressed as program standards. Knowledge and skill expectations are identified in three categories: (i) vocational, (ii) essential employability skills, and (iii) general education.

WHAT DO WE VALUE?

Before we can measure what we value about postsecondary education, we have to be clear about what it is that we value. The quality of our measures will be directly affected by how clearly we identify the thing we are measuring. Until about 20 years ago, our assumptions about the outcomes of degree education, i.e., the knowledge and skills degree graduates possessed, were largely implicit. With the introduction of new providers, new types of credentials, new technologies to deliver education, foreign providers, and so on; however, it was no longer possible to take those learning outcomes for granted.

The first jurisdiction to make the knowledge and skill outcomes of its higher education credentials explicit was the United Kingdom, through the UK Quality Assurance Agency (QAA). The QAA introduced a qualifications framework in 1997 that identified the knowledge and skills expected of graduates of all credentials. Many countries have since followed suit and introduced frameworks or are in the process of doing so.

Ontario, through PEQAB, was a reasonably early adopter of qualifications frameworks. We introduced the first qualifications framework (of degree credentials) to Ontario and Canada in 2003. The framework was adopted by British Columbia's Degree Quality Assessment Board; and in 2004, the Council of Ministers of Education Canada (CMEC) struck a Quality Assurance Subcommittee to explore the adoption of a pan-Canadian quality assurance framework for degree education. The PEQAB qualifications framework, program and institutional standards were the reference points for this initiative; and these were revised to accommodate the variability in credentials and practices across the provinces and territories. A pan-Canadian framework for the quality assurance of degree education was adopted by CMEC in 2007.

Also in 2004, PEQAB initiated consultations with the public university sector through the Ontario Council of Academic Vice-Presidents (OCAV) and the Ontario Council on Graduate Studies (OCGS). PEQAB is obligated by legislation to implement standards recognized in Ontario and elsewhere, and was keen to ensure that its degree framework had captured the knowledge and skills expected of degree graduates. In 2005, OCAV released its degree framework, which was the PEQAB framework with two modest revisions.[1] PEQAB then adopted the OCAV degree level expectations, and the province had a common framework of degree expectations for all degree providers in the province.

Following the establishment of a common framework at the degree level, the Ministry of Training, Colleges, and Universities began consultations with stakeholders on a framework for other postsecondary credentials offered in the province. In 2007, the ministry released an expanded framework to encompass the learning outcomes expected of all graduates of all postsecondary credentials from apprenticeship certificates to doctoral degrees.[2]

For each credential in the Ontario Qualifications Framework (OQF) of postsecondary credentials, six categories of outcomes—the knowledge and skills a graduate is intended to achieve—are identified:

- depth and breadth of knowledge (inside and outside the field of study),
- conceptual and methodological awareness / research and scholarship,
- communication skills,
- application of knowledge,
- professional capacity / autonomy, and
- awareness of limits of knowledge.

Like all qualifications frameworks, the aims of the Ontario framework include that it sets a standard for each credential that can be used to assess the quality of particular programs at that credential level, and that it facilitate international recognition of credentials, credit transfer, and graduate mobility.

The outcomes identified in the framework are, of necessity, written at a very general level. Each set of outcomes has to capture the variability among programs offered at any given level. For example, the outcomes identified for the master's qualification have to accurately and comprehensively describe an MBA, an MSc in physics, and every other master's degree program offered in Ontario.

The generic framework is useful for communicating to the public and other jurisdictions about the expectations for graduates of Ontario credentials and may be useful for program design. But, the framework's greatest utility comes when those generic outcomes are operationalized for particular disciplines or institutions.

There are generally two options for operationalizing the credential-wide outcomes in the qualifications framework: (i) discipline-wide and (ii) program-specific. Discipline-wide outcomes are those that could be articulated for a subject area at a particular credential level within a jurisdiction, e.g., all psychology programs at the baccalaureate level in England. The discipline-wide approach is the approach taken by the

European Tuning approach. The Tuning process has articulated outcomes for almost 30 subject areas (e.g., history, engineering, economics, and so forth), at the various credential levels in Europe.

PEQAB, on the other hand, requires all degree learning outcomes to be articulated at the program level, i.e., the outcomes are specified for each particular program offered at each particular credential level at each particular institution (e.g., the learning outcomes in the bachelor of commerce in accounting offered by Humber College Institute of Technology and Advanced Learning).

Table 1 captures some of the differences among the three levels of outcome-specificity (credential-wide, discipline-wide, and program-specific). These are examples of a very small subset of outcomes for an honours bachelor of science degree in psychology. The categories and the generic outcomes are drawn from the Ontario Qualifications Framework (OQF); the discipline-wide and program-specific are hypothetical.

These examples illustrate the usefulness of the exercise of operationalizing the general outcomes identified in the framework for particular programs. It

- identifies the particular knowledge and skills expected from graduates of that program;
- allows for the comparison (within and across jurisdictions) of those program outcomes with outcomes that have been operationalized for other programs;
- informs students, employers, other institutions, and the general public about the knowledge and skills graduates of that program will have; and
- facilitates judgments about credit transfer/advanced standing and the recognition of credentials for employment and further study.

PEQAB uses the framework and its outcomes as a quality assurance tool. Institutions are required to articulate expected program-specific outcomes for graduates of the proposed program, and these must map to the credential-wide outcomes. The ability to accurately assess whether the outcomes have been met is directly related to the clarity with which they have been articulated.

Measuring Value

Statements of outcomes should allow a measure of whether and the extent to which outcomes have been met. All things being equal, the greater the specificity with which outcomes can be articulated, the greater the confidence in their measurement.

TABLE 1
Sample Learning Outcomes at Three Levels of Specificity

Knowledge and Skill Category	Level of Specificity	Outcome
Depth and breadth of knowledge This category addresses the range and mastery of knowledge expected to be achieved within and outside the discipline.	OQF: credential-wide	Graduates will have … a developed understanding of many of the major fields in a discipline …
	Discipline-wide (BSc Honours Psychology in Jurisdiction X)	Graduates will have introductory knowledge in many of the major fields within psychology and have advanced and specialized knowledge in some of them …
	Program-specific (BSc Honours Psychology at a Particular Institution)	Graduates will have knowledge in at least six and no more than nine of the following fields, 60% of which will be at an advanced level, and 15% of which must be at a specialized level: sensation, perception, learning, cognition, history, developmental, abnormal, biological; social, motivation, personality and linguistics; and will have advanced knowledge of statistics, research methods, and psychological measurement.
Conceptual and methodological knowledge/research and scholarship This category is focused on the graduates' grasp of the methods used to create and evaluate knowledge in their discipline.	OQF	Graduates will have … an understanding of the methods of enquiry … in their primary area of study.
	Discipline-wide	Graduates will be able to calculate a range of descriptive statistics and use them correctly in the appropriate circumstances.
	Program-specific	Graduates will be able to select and calculate the appropriate statistics to test hypotheses and interpret data, including: measures of central tendency; Pearson's r; Student's t; Wilcoxon T; Chi-square; Fisher's F; and R^2.
Communication skills This category is concerned with graduates' ability to communicate effectively, using where appropriate, techniques specific to their discipline. It also covers those skills normally referred to as general education skills that cut across this category of credentials (the honours bachelor's degree), namely quantitative reasoning, critical thinking skills, and those knowledge and skills relevant to civic engagement.	OQF	Graduates will have … the ability to communicate information, arguments … informed by … techniques of the discipline.
	Discipline-wide	Graduates' communications will reflect the ability to deploy a range of rhetorical strategies using the appropriate format for the circumstances.
	Program-specific	Graduates will be able to write essays, psychometric reports, and research reports consistent with stylistic and format requirements of the American Psychological Association, and will be expected to select and use, as appropriate, persuasion, logical analysis, exemplification; description; narration; process analysis; comparison and contrast; division and classification; definition; cause and effect analysis; and argumentation.

TABLE 1
(Continued)

Knowledge and Skill Category	Level of Specificity	Outcome
Application of knowledge This category of knowledge and skills pertains to the graduates' abilities to apply knowledge of their own and other disciplines to novel contexts.	OQF	Graduates will have … the ability to use a basic range of established techniques to … solve a problem …
	Discipline-wide	Graduates will be able to conduct experiments under supervision and/or write major research papers.
	Program-specific	Graduates will be able to write major research papers and conduct experiments under supervision.
Professional capacity/ autonomy This category covers the expectations that graduates will have learned how to learn, and their abilities to work in isolation and as members of teams.	OQF	Graduates will have … the ability to manage their own learning in changing circumstances.
	Discipline-wide	Graduates will be able to use a variety of sources to further their learning and to solve problems in novel contexts.
	Program-specific	Graduates will be proficient in identifying credible sources through library searches, databases, and the internet.
Awareness of the limits of knowledge This category is about the graduates' orientation to their own level of knowledge, an openness to ambiguity, and an appreciation that there are ways of knowing outside the methods of their own discipline.	OQF	Graduates will have an understanding of the limits to their own knowledge and ability, and an appreciation of the uncertainty, ambiguity and limits to knowledge …
	Discipline-wide	Graduates will have more than an introductory knowledge in disciplines outside psychology.
	Program-specific	Graduates will have specialized, interdisciplinary knowledge in three of the following disciplines: humanities, natural science, other social sciences, modes of reasoning, and mathematics.

Source: Author's compilation.

At renewal of consent, PEQAB requires institutions to demonstrate (among other things described later) that the learning outcomes it commits to delivering have been achieved. We do so through a review of random samples of student work in the terminal stages of the program that reflects exemplary, average, and minimally acceptable performance. Institutions are required to preserve work that students have created in the terminal portions of the program, and these are reviewed by scholars both in and outside the field to assess whether the expected outcomes are reflected in the work. This ensures that the knowledge and skills that have been committed to have been achieved at an acceptable level of performance.

In the best-case scenario, demonstrating that learning outcomes have been met is that simple. There are, however, some lessons we have learned over the last decade that show that effective measurement of learning outcomes can be a great deal more complicated.

LESSONS LEARNED

PEQAB has learned a number of lessons in its first decade of operations. Chief among these is that demonstrations that learning outcomes have been achieved:

- require clarity in their expression and expertise in their measurement;
- underlie our confidence in other, related measures; and
- are a necessary and (under the right circumstances) sufficient measure of program quality.

Two Requirements for Successful Measurement

Institutions have to articulate their intended outcomes with sufficient clarity, and the appropriate expertise has to be brought to bear on determining whether or not they have been achieved. In the absence of a clear and comprehensive statement of expectations, outcomes have to be inferred, not just by experts charged with advising on whether appropriate outcomes have been achieved, but also by students, employers, and other postsecondary institutions.

Assuming clear statements of outcomes, the right expertise must be engaged to determine whether the outcomes are present in samples of student work. Scholars with expertise in the field have to be engaged to determine whether the appropriate discipline/field-specific outcomes have been realized. Scholars with expertise in assessing generic communication and critical thinking skills are also required.

In PEQAB's experience, learning outcomes expertise at both the institution and on the part of expert assessors is variable. The practice of articulating and measuring the sorts of outcomes set out in a qualifications framework is new and not yet perfected by all providers and assessors. Over time, the utility of the framework as a quality assurance tool will develop, particularly in light of the efficiencies it affords in transparency and quality assurance.

Demonstrated Outcomes are a Necessary Condition for Interpreting Related Metrics

Most institutions collect metrics about their students and graduates, (e.g., graduation rates; retention rates; and participation rates). These metrics, in and of themselves however, tell us little about whether the learning outcomes we expect are being achieved. If we value high numbers on all of these metrics, (and why would we not?), they still need to be grounded in a demonstration that the learning outcomes we associate with graduation have been met. If an incentive were provided, for example, for achieving high targets on each of these metrics, one option for earning the incentives would be to drop admission standards to enroll more students, and then drop the expectations for the program in order to retain and graduate students who were not adequately prepared to enter the program in the first place. Knowing that we have achieved the outcomes we expect at graduation provides critical context for interpreting these kinds of metrics.

Measures of student engagement are also often used as an indicator of the likelihood that certain outcomes will be achieved. Students are surveyed, for example, on whether they were required to submit written assignments during the course of their studies. But this approach too has its shortcomings. Were all students to answer in the affirmative, this would be no guarantee that a single student learned how to write at the level appropriate to the credential awarded. Similarly, were all students to answer in the negative, this still would provide no insight into the actual outcomes achieved. Conceivably all students could be writing at the appropriate level at the time of graduation. Students could have entered with a high level of skills and developed writing skills over the course of a degree program through other means (for example, through reading assignments, note taking, other school assignments requiring communication skills, through civic engagement, and participation).

This is not to dismiss such metrics; rather, it is to underscore that unless we know that the appropriate outcomes are being achieved, such metrics tell only part of the story.

Direct Review of Student Work is a Necessary, and Can Be a Sufficient, Measure of Program Quality

Traditional approaches to quality assurance typically measure those things we assume to be associated with achievement of the appropriate outcomes. Proposals for new programs normally include hundreds of pages of plans outlining the expected outcomes and how the institution intends to achieve them. Since there is no way to assess actual learning outcomes until there has been a graduating cohort, these proposals of necessity have to be assessed in light of those institutional and programmatic factors we assume to be associated with the achievement of outcomes at the degree level.

Table 2 captures the typical range of matters normally assessed by administrators of higher education institutions and scholars in the discipline of study when new programs are proposed, and that are then reviewed by quality assurance bodies (e.g., PEQAB, Maritime Provinces

TABLE 2
Factors Considered in Review of a New Program

Category	Typical Measures
Mission	• Clear, consistent, and well-articulated statement of mission and academic goals • Programs are related to the mission and goals • Resources and policies advance the mission
Administrative capacity	• Legal status of the institution is appropriate for its goals • Organization has an appropriate governance structure • Qualified senior administrative staff • Coordinated business and academic plans • Staff and student involvement in the development of the curriculum, academic policies, and standards
Policy environment	• That recognize and protect the rights of individuals in their pursuit of knowledge • Pertaining to academic honesty, procedures for their enforcement, and ensuring staff and faculty understanding • On the ownership of the intellectual products of employees and students • Concerning ethical research standards • Concerning compliance with copyright law • That protect student and consumer interests • For academic appeals, complaints, grievances, and/or other disputes of students, faculty, staff, and administration consistent with principles of natural justice • For the periodic review of the institution and program that include an external review of a comprehensive self-study • Governing academic remediation, sanctions, and suspension for students who do not meet minimum achievement requirements
Student protection	• Accurate and truthful reports, materials, and advertising • Ethical recruitment procedures • Transparency about key information about the organization
Admissions	• Set at a level such that incoming students will be able to benefit from the course of study appropriate to the learning outcome goals of the program and the degree level standard
Curriculum	• Reflects current knowledge in both the core and non-core fields • Is at the right depth and covers sufficient breadth • Type and frequency of student assessments demonstrate achievement of the learning outcomes • Programs leading to occupations that are subject to government regulations and are designed to prepare students to meet the requirements of the relevant regulatory and/or accrediting body

Category	Typical Measures
Resources	• Budgets are sufficient to provide and maintain the necessary learning, physical, technological, human, and other resources for the program and to supplement them as necessary
	• Reasonable student and faculty access to learning and information resources (e.g., library, databases, computing, classroom equipment, laboratory facilities) sufficient in scope, quality, currency, and kind to support the program
	• Access to an appropriate range of academic support services, (e.g., academic counselling, tutoring, career counselling, and placement services)
	• Faculty qualifications and scholarship
Delivery methods	• Appropriate to course content and design
	• Supported by the appropriate expertise and resources

Source: Author's compilation.

Higher Education Commission, Campus Alberta Quality Council, British Columbia Degree Quality Assessment Board, US regional accrediting bodies, etc.).

Once the initial proposal is reviewed, the typical situation is that credible quality assurance agencies review programs cyclically, every five to ten years. Such cyclical reviews are normally either a series of repetitions of the initial paper-based review (with the addition of a visit to the site to interview faculty and students and to assess facilities and resources), audits of the institution's self-review of these matters, or some combination of the two.

All degrees providers in Ontario are required to have policies and procedures in place that identify the internal institutional activities that will ensure the achievement of outcomes, the quality of programs, and continuous improvement. PEQAB, OUCQA, and PQAPA review these institutional policies and procedures on a cyclical basis. Depending on the quality assurance body responsible for the particular institution, degree programs themselves are subject to further cyclical review (PEQAB) and/or potential cyclical audit (PEQAB, OUCQA).

Few quality assurance agencies review samples of student work during the course of cyclical reviews as PEQAB does. As indicated earlier, every five to seven years (depending on the length of the consent) after a new program has been approved, PEQAB reviews the program again. For existing (as opposed to new) program reviews, PEQAB includes a review of samples of student work in the terminal phase of every program (e.g., theses or capstone projects). Assessors are required to randomly sample student work that has been graded by the institution as exemplary, average, and minimally acceptable performance to ensure that the knowledge and skills expected of graduates are reflected in the work.

No agency that PEQAB is aware of makes decisions about program quality solely on the basis of a demonstration that the learning outcomes had been met. Institutions that have demonstrated that they have the appropriate inputs and the appropriate policies and procedures to ensure ongoing program quality should be able to have only learning outcomes reviewed from that point forward. If the learning outcomes are judged to be appropriate, and it is demonstrated that students are achieving the outcomes, it should not matter whether the traditional factors associated with their achievement are present. It is only in the case when the outcomes have not been achieved that a subsequent review of the curriculum and the resources and policies that support its delivery would need to be revisited for diagnosis and remediation.

Lessons to Be Learned

Much has changed in degree granting and quality assurance over the past 20 years and many features of the landscape are still being shaped. Two of these, discussed below, were addressed as common concerns at the recent conference of International Network of Quality Assurance Agencies in Higher Education, a worldwide network of nearly 300 quality assurance agencies.[3]

Innovation vs. Stagnation

Some have expressed concerns that the articulation of expectations will necessarily have a conservative effect on innovation in educational outcomes. Internationally, there is concern of a hegemonic imposition of standards and expectations associated with the English-speaking world on the expectations for education in countries whose language is not English. Locally, there is concern that traditional approaches and outcomes will unduly limit the ability of non-traditional providers to achieve different, but no less appropriate, outcomes.

Qualifications frameworks, the vehicles used to structure outcomes statements, have been in existence fewer than 20 years. If the fear is that all programs will have to be designed to achieve the generic outcomes articulated in the framework, that is already true in Ontario. Few would argue that this particular brand of sameness is a bad outcome. If the concern is that innovative curricula and outcomes will not be recognized as falling within the framework, it remains to be seen whether this will be borne out. In part it is an empirical question and can be assessed by analyzing the failed proposals in the quality assurance process. What cannot be tracked so readily are the programs that are not proposed because of the concern that they will not be recognized as meeting the standard set in the framework.

The Role of Liberal Education in Civil Society

Discussions concerning the importance of advanced education for economic prosperity often include discussions about the appropriate emphasis of higher education, i.e., whether it should be more vocationally oriented and less oriented to the liberal arts. I am pretty familiar with what quality assurance agencies value and what institutions value, so, as I was preparing to deliver my presentation, I conducted a very unscientific survey to see what the top ten Google hits were using "value of postsecondary education" as my search terms. This is as good an anecdotal approach to measure the social discourse on these matters as any.

There were no surprises in the results. Of the first ten results that were returned by Google, eight sites contained information related exclusively to the economic benefits of postsecondary education. One addressed both the economic benefits and the costs of postsecondary education. References about the relationship of higher education to the economy included discussions of:

- increased labour force participation,
- higher earnings,
- greater productivity and competitiveness,
- greater innovation,
- higher revenue generation for governments (through taxes on income), and
- a higher standard of living.

Two of the sites addressed the social benefits (one of them exclusively). Unlike the sites that addressed the economic benefits of higher education, these two sites were vague about what those social benefits might be, beyond the broad expectation that higher education, specifically, liberal arts education, enhances a civilized society and contributes to personal enhancement and satisfaction. This state of affairs mimics most professional discourses on these two broad categories of outcomes. We have a good handle on what we think the benefits are of higher education for our economy. Our understanding of the social benefits is murky and relatively ignored.

When we measure the social return on investments in education, we usually look at such things as an increased likelihood to volunteer, vote, stay out of jail, donate blood, and so on. These kinds of measures are interesting as far as they go, but that is not very far. They are unsatisfactory not only because they are easy prey for confounds (e.g., socioeconomic status) and are therefore unconvincing measures of the value of a liberal education, but also because they do not adequately capture the importance of the knowledge and skills required to engage in a modern, networked society. Those factors that have created the need for advanced education to participate in the knowledge economy have also altered our social worlds. Our participation in both the economic and social spheres requires increasing skill.

Information and communication technologies allow for instant communication of information through social media, and it increases the burden on citizens to be skilled in critically evaluating that information. Some examples of the power of social media to inform and influence citizens were recently provided by events in Yemen, Tunisia, Syria, Libya, and Egypt where citizens assembled en masse in powerful protest. In this modern, networked context, citizens are required to respond to an intense and relentless stream of information that is impossible to receive passively and that needs to be evaluated critically. The orientation and skills required to consider other perspectives, to expect and welcome disagreement, and to engage in reasoned debate are assumed to be related to a broad education. Yet, our discourse on such matters is sparse relative to our understanding of the connections between education and economic prosperity.

Underlying any discussion of how we expect to benefit economically or socially from higher education are our assumptions about the knowledge and skills that credential holders bring to our economy and broader society.

PEQAB currently clarifies its expectations for knowledge and skills outside the discipline (at the undergraduate level) as follows:

The non-core (liberal arts) curriculum contributes to the achievement of:

- more than introductory knowledge in the humanities, sciences, social sciences, global cultures, and/or mathematics;
- knowledge of society and culture and skills relevant to civic engagement; and
- a more than introductory knowledge of the distinctive assumptions and modes of analysis of a discipline outside the core field(s) of study.

These requirements for an exposure to disciplines outside the core field of study are assumed to be important for achieving key outcomes in the qualifications framework, the realization of the social benefits alluded to earlier, and the ability to bring to bear the critical skills necessary for peaceful civil engagement in modern society. The importance and expectations concerning these and related skills deepens at the graduate levels.

As a body charged with reflecting standards here and elsewhere, PEQAB is keenly aware of discussions about the professional and vocational aspects of higher education versus those concerning aspects broadly categorized as liberal education. Whether these discussions will lead to new standards remains to be seen.

CONCLUSION

Current economic, social, and technological contexts have focused a spotlight on the knowledge and skills required for participation in a modern economy and networked society. Increasing demands for innovation in postsecondary programming; new methods of delivery; laddered, lifelong learning; and internationally recognized, portable credentials can only sharpen our focus on the identification and measurement of learning outcomes. There are likely to be many more lessons to be learned as learning outcomes are increasingly pursued as an efficient measure of an effective, quality education.

NOTES

[1] First, where PEQAB had two categories of expectations of knowledge and skills for Depth and Breadth of Knowledge (Depth and Breadth of Knowledge Inside the Field of Study; and Depth and Breadth of Knowledge Outside the Field of Study), OCAV collapsed these categories into one: Depth and Breadth of Knowledge. The liberal arts, or breadth component, became a benchmark within the new category, rather than a separate expectation at the category level. Second, two other PEQAB categories were collapsed. The expectations in one category (Level of Analytical Skill) were included in another (Application of Knowledge).

[2] See Appendix 1 at http://www.tcu.gov.on.ca/eng/general/postsec/oqf.pdf.

[3] See http://www.inqaahe.org/madrid-2011.

SECTION II

APPROACHES TO MEASUREMENT

5

ASSESSING AND IMPROVING STUDENT LEARNING AND EDUCATIONAL QUALITY

Jillian Kinzie

INTRODUCTION

Improving educational quality through better measurement and accountability could be the contemporary catchphrase in US postsecondary education. The slogan may also reflect recent international efforts in higher education, which have expanded from a primary focus on developing rankings to include direct evaluation of student performance and an emphasis on improving educational quality. The Assessment of Higher Education Learning Outcomes (AHELO) promises a global test of what students know and can do upon graduation and to provide data on the quality of teaching and learning in higher education. The concomitant emphasis on assessing quality, developing better measures, and improving student learning has garnered significant attention in higher education across the globe and shows no signs of abating.

Concern about quality in undergraduate student learning in the United States is, of course, not new. Current concern emanates from the National Institute of Education's 1984 report, *Involvement in Learning*, that proposed research on improving educational quality and on assessing effectiveness to maximize student learning. The report's emphasis on improving educational quality and challenge for institutions to adopt organizational strategies, policies, and processes that would optimize the use of evidence to inform institutional improvement is considered to be one of the founding documents of the assessment movement.

Since the mid-1980s, when assessment was primarily externally driven and accountability focused, the movement has shifted to an internal force

Measuring the Value of a Postsecondary Education, ed. K. Norrie and M.C. Lennon. Montreal and Kingston: Queen's Policy Studies Series, McGill-Queen's University Press. © 2013 All rights reserved.

emphasizing improvement as accountability. The roots of assessment are political and public policy oriented. However, it is also grounded in measurement practice and had been given impetus by the growing interests of state governments in using newly available tests and surveys to demonstrate return on investment. Over the last decade, the focus on assessment measurement in US higher education has only become sharper.

In this chapter I present a broad overview of current assessment issues relevant to the discussion about approaches to measurement. I draw from literature on assessment and my direct experience working with two national assessment projects, the National Survey of Student Engagement (NSSE) and the National Institute for Learning Outcomes Assessment (NILOA). I begin by highlighting the current context in US higher education related to student learning and educational quality and then specify issues in assessment and accountability. Next, I introduce a framework for examining perspectives on student learning, assessment, and accountability; and then explore what is happening on the ground at campuses across the country, revealing insights about theory in action. I close with a discussion about current issues in measurement and assessment of student learning outcomes.

CURRENT CONTEXT FOR US HIGHER EDUCATION

The current context in US higher education is characterized by a pressure to document and improve student learning and success in college. Legislative bodies, the system of regional accreditation, and the broader public are pressing to make higher education more accessible and affordable to a wider range of students, improve graduation rates, and assume more accountability for what students are supposed to learn and how well they are, in fact, learning it (Ewell 2002; Suskie 2004). In particular, the need to increase graduation rates has been mandated by several sources, including President Obama and the Lumina Foundation for Education.[1] President Obama's goal is for the United States to retake the world lead in college graduation rates by 2020, while Lumina is challenging states to increase the percentage of adults with high-quality degrees and credentials to 60 percent by the year 2025.

Although the scrutiny applied to higher education during the Secretary of Education's Commission on the Future of Higher Education (2006) (commonly known as the Spellings Commission) seems to have subsided, public doubt about the value of college lingers. New York Times reporter David Leonhardt's (2009) query emphasizes the connection between measurement and public suspicion: "Colleges do so little to measure what students learn between freshman and senior years. So doubt lurks: how much does a college education—the actual teaching and learning that happens on campus—really matter?" The Spellings

Commission's emphasis on the need for more effective data gathering and transparency of results, particularly the need for comparable data about the benchmarks of institutional success—student access, retention, learning and success, educational costs, and productivity—to stimulate innovation and demonstrate accountability, remains a strong influence in higher education.

These broad issues in higher education influence assessment and accountability in specific ways. First, pressure to demonstrate the value of higher education has placed greater emphasis on assessing student learning outcomes and providing evidence that student performance measures up. Second, the need for comparable data leads naturally to standardized tests. Third, doubt and public scrutiny promptly call for greater transparency of evidence of effectiveness. Fourth, the combined mandates for increased graduation rates and improved student learning translate into a need for more and better approaches to measurement and greater use of results to improve the conditions for learning and success.

Although the current issues in higher education and assessment provide an important context, the perspective from institutions of higher education reveals more about current circumstances and challenges. In other words, what is happening on the ground at colleges and universities? Over the last decade, nearly all postsecondary institutions report that their assessment activity markedly increased (Banta, Jones and Black 2009; Kinzie 2010; Kuh and Ikenberry 2009). While much of this additional activity is about data collection to satisfy reporting requirements of federal and state agencies, governing boards, and to be in compliance for accreditation, a fair amount of this activity has worked its way into continuous improvement and regular institutional assessment processes, such as annual program reviews. In fact, while in the early 1990s only about half of college and university administrators surveyed believed that assessment can lead to improvement in undergraduate education (El Khawas 1995), more recent reports suggest that the perception of assessment to improve is more favourable (Banta, Jones and Black 2009; Kuh and Ikenberry 2009).

The topic of student learning outcomes is also getting greater attention on campuses, both in the form of ensuring that outcomes are specified and explicit and that educators are attending to outcomes assessment. For example, according to an Association of American Colleges and Universities (AAC&U) report, *Learning and Assessment: Trends in Undergraduate Education* (2008), the majority of campuses reported that they have a common set of intended learning outcomes for all their undergraduate students and are focused on assessing students' achievement of these outcomes across the curriculum. Greater interest in what improves student learning has also captured campus attention. For example, interest in adopting engaging, high-impact practices, such as service-learning, first-year seminars, and capstone projects, have increased along with encouragement for faculty to experiment with new pedagogical approaches. However, there is a disconnect between evidence and improved student learning. Although institutions have increased their assessment activities, there is less evidence that results are leading to improvements in student learning and success (Banta, Jones and Black 2009; Suskie 2004).

A significant challenge for colleges and universities is to promote the use of evidence for systematic improvement. Few institutions have well-developed assessment plans to sustain a culture of assessment. In fact, as the international discourse about educational quality, improvement, and accountability for results in higher education has ratcheted up, the calls for the establishment of a culture of evidence or of assessment have increased (Dwyer, Millett and Payne 2006; Millett et al. 2007; Millett et al. 2008). The first volume in the series on this topic produced by the Educational Testing Service (ETS) makes strong claims about the seriousness of the need to measure student learning in postsecondary settings and the need for a national initiative to create a system for collecting data (Dwyer, Millett and Payne 2006). Although the ETS recommendation focuses, perhaps predictably, on the development of a national system to assess learning in college, efforts to develop a culture of evidence commonly focus on actions to be taken by colleges and universities themselves (for example, Jenkins et al. 2009; Kinzie, Buckley and Kuh 2008).

In an effort to learn more about assessment practices and the establishment of a culture of evidence on campuses, the National Institute for Learning Outcomes Assessment (NILOA)[2] set out to document student learning outcomes assessment work and support institutions in their assessment efforts. Since its establishment in 2008, NILOA has conducted two national surveys of all accredited colleges and universities in the United States and has gathered information about assessment practices, completed an inventory of commonly used measures, conducted scans of institutional websites and those of organizations engaged in assessment-related efforts, produced a series of commissioned papers addressing pressing topics in assessment, and developed case studies of promising practices in collegiate learning assessment—particularly the use of assessment data to improve student learning and approaches to public reporting of assessment data.

NILOA is just one of a number of national initiatives to advance assessment in the United States. Examples of other efforts include the Lumina Foundation's Achieving the Dream project, which facilitates data collection and use to promote student success at community colleges, and the Teagle Foundation, which has supported institutional collaboration for the systematic improvement of student learning and the examination of the use of evidence to improve learning. Another initiative involving more than 300 public universities is the Voluntary System of Accountability (VSA). In response to escalating calls for accountability by higher education, the Association of Public and Land-grant Universities (APLU) and the American Association of State College and Universities (AASCU) jointly launched the VSA in 2006. It was created to provide basic, comparable information on the undergraduate student experience (McPherson and Shulenberger 2006). To participate, institutions must assemble specific forms of evidence and display this information using a common template.[3] The VSA proposes to help institutions demonstrate accountability and stewardship to the public; measure educational outcomes to identify effective educational practice; and assemble information that is accessible, understandable, and comparable.

The VSA is primarily a tool to promote transparency. There is little question that the project has affected data collection and display by participating institutions, and it has likely contributed to data consumption by its broader public audience. However, it is too soon to determine if, by making institutional performance data transparent and readily accessible, all stakeholders will be better equipped to make data-informed decisions about the performance of participating colleges and universities.

FRAMEWORKS FOR UNDERSTANDING ACCOUNTABILITY, ASSESSMENT, AND IMPROVEMENT

Central to any conversation about current issues in higher education and the press for greater accountability and assessment is the consideration of the tension between the concepts. The two purposes of assessment—accountability and improvement—have not rested comfortably together in higher education. The tension is rooted in concern about the impact of increasing expectations for accountability and whether these demands will alter the educational process and how assessment data are used. Moreover, differing perspectives on assessment influence the context on quality and approaches to measurement. The review of two frameworks—the first, distinguishing accountability vs. improvement, and the second, outlining a marketplace vs. an academic perspective—provide analogous models for thinking about quality and approaches to measurement.

Peter Ewell (2008) distinguishes the purpose of assessment in two paradigms. The first is the accountability paradigm, characterized by external influence, summative judgment, and a compliance and reporting ethos. The second is the improvement paradigm, distinguished by an internal, institution influence and formative feedback loops. The two frames suggest very different approaches to measurement. The accountability paradigm advocates for standardized, quantitative, and comparative or fixed measures that are publicly reported. In contrast, the improvement frame promotes multiple instruments, triangulation among quantitative and qualitative measures, longitudinal and comparative designs, and communication via multiple feedback loops. How assessment is framed influences approaches to measurement.

The second framework for understanding the tension that exists around accountability distinguishes a marketplace perspective from an academic view of accountability (Kean and Thompson 2007). The marketplace perspective emphasizes an external definition of standards for academic quality, focuses on an end product and individual student achievement, puts institutions in competition, and uses results to rank and evaluate institutions. In contrast, the academic view of accountability emphasizes the evaluation of educational processes, with a focus on evidence of learning gains, and an approach that is improvement-oriented, promotes collaboration among institutions, and results that are used to demonstrate institutional distinctiveness.

These two models provide useful frameworks for thinking about how the purpose and role of assessment influences approaches to measurement. The adoption of the accountability and marketplace perspectives, for example, advocate the use of standardized, comparable measures of student achievement within institutions that are then put into a formula to rank institutions. In this view, the purpose of measurement is to assess institutional quality and to provide information to consumers—students and families—so that they have information about which institution provides the best education. The marketplace perspective drives the development of rankings and focuses attention on reporting comparable institutional summaries like that provided in the VSA. While the marketplace perspective seems to positively advocate for greater consumer information, it actually disregards the fact that the student experience, outcomes, and the quality of learning vary more within than between institutions (Borden and Young 2008). The finding that there is greater variation in outcomes among students within institutions than between students at institutions has been documented in college impact research (Pascarella and Terenzini 1991; 2005) and has been further illustrated in analyses of NSSE results that show the lion's share of the variation in benchmark scores is among students within institutions (National Survey of Student Engagement 2008). What this means is that restricting attention to institutional comparison overlooks most of the variation in educational quality.

In contrast, the improvement paradigm and academic perspective emphasizes diversity of measures, quantitative and qualitative; educational processes; and learning outcomes that the institution can influence and change. This perspective emphasizes the personal and societal benefits of educational quality, promotes a view that institutions will hold themselves accountable by continuously engaging in systematic, iterative processes to improve the quality of teaching and learning, and that information should help students and families identify institutional programs that match a particular student's interests and talents. This view of systematic improvement through self-correcting processes with regard to teaching and learning characterize universities' approach to academic scholarship and inquiry. Furthermore, it acknowledges the importance of assessment results that provide information to guide the development and implementation of curricular and pedagogical approaches that improve student learning. In terms of measurement, this perspective suggests that it is not a matter of developing a better test or assuring adequate student motivation to perform optimally on tests, but rather a matter of interpretative and consequential validity relating to the use of a test or measure (Borden and Young 2008).

These two frameworks outline important distinctions in purpose, approach, and use of evidence about educational quality. Even more, they can help shed light on the source of opposition to, or strong advocacy for, particular approaches to measurement. Explicating assumptions that underlie particular stances in assessment and accountability is a vital component to discussions about measuring the value of postsecondary education.

PERSPECTIVES ON LEARNING OUTCOMES

Any consideration of measurement in postsecondary education must emphasize outcomes. What is it that colleges and universities are supposed to measure and then use to demonstrate educational effectiveness? Whereas, most institutional assessment activities still involve a variety of measures, including satisfaction, degree progression, and graduation rates, grades, performance activities, etc., the need to measure student learning outcomes has taken on a sharper focus.

As colleges and universities face pressure to attend to student learning outcomes, more have established explicit institution-wide learning goals to define and set expectations for the skills and abilities their undergraduates are expected to master and to provide an intellectual framework for building a common curricular and co-curricular learning experience. The increased prominence of student learning outcomes is demonstrated in several national reports.

According to the 2009 NILOA report, *More Than You Think, Less Than We Need: Learning Outcomes Assessment in American Higher Education* (Kuh and Ikenberry 2009), based on survey responses from provosts from a national sample of colleges and universities, about three-quarters of all institutions have adopted common learning outcomes for all undergraduate students, an essential first step in guiding efforts to measure learning outcomes campus-wide. This relatively high percentage of schools with common learning outcomes is consistent with data assembled by the Association of American Colleges and Universities (AAC&U) in a late 2008 survey of its member institutions.

To explore students' awareness of common learning outcomes, NSSE appended a set of items to the 2010 survey regarding students' understanding of institutional learning goals and how they are reinforced through the academic program and course assignments. The majority of first-year students (75 percent) and seniors (70 percent) responding to these questions believed their institution had a common set of learning goals, and of these, the vast majority (95 percent) had at least "some" understanding of these goals.

Student learning outcomes are also getting greater attention at the program or department level. Results from the NILOA 2011 National Survey report, *Down and In: Assessment Practices at the Program Level,* revealed that 80 percent of programs had established intended student learning outcomes. Correspondingly, senior students responding to NSSE's additional questions about learning outcomes in their major revealed that four out of five seniors were aware of a common set of learning goals for their primary academic major, and of these, 85 percent substantially understood them. The creation of clear goals for learning is an important step toward measuring outcomes. Of course, the important step is ensuring that institutions have established processes and identified appropriate measures to capture information about student performance on the stated learning goals.

MEASURES USED BY COLLEGES AND UNIVERSITIES

Assessment measurement tools and technologies have evolved alongside increased concerns about quality in undergraduate education. Many standardized, commercially available, and "homegrown" instruments and surveys are available to institutions to assess dimensions of educational quality, such as incoming student values, attitudes, and expectations; student satisfaction with and use of educational services; participation in and perception of educational processes and experiences; and alumni and employer surveys, among others. These measures are generally categorized as "indirect" or "process" measures because they provide information about salient aspects of the educational program and student behaviours and institutional practices but are based on self-report. In contrast, "direct" or "outcome" measures are standardized tests and authentic measures, typically defined as performance assessments that require students to generate rather than choose a response to demonstrate what they can do, to demonstrate what students have learned and can do.

One example of a popular indirect or process measure is the National Survey of Student Engagement (NSSE). Since 2000, nearly 1,500 institutions in the United States and Canada have participated in NSSE to obtain information about their student and institutional investment in educational practices associated with student learning and success. Reports include comparative data for customized groups and cohort norms as well as longitudinal comparison for benchmarking. NSSE results have been determined to be good proxies for desirable learning outcomes (Pascarella, Siefert and Blaich 2010). Other commonly used indirect measures include several at the Higher Education Research Institutes (HERI), including the Cooperative Institutional Research Project (CIRP) Freshman Survey or the College Senior Survey, as well as commercial instruments, including an array of instruments from Noel-Levitz, such as the Student Satisfaction Inventory. Several commercially available tests have been widely adopted to measure learning outcomes, including ACT's Collegiate Assessment of Academic Proficiency (CAAP), the ETS® Proficiency Profile, and the Collegiate Learning Assessment (CLA), which is being promoted in AHELO, the international project to assess learning outcomes.

Collecting both process and outcome measures is valuable for institutional assessment. Process measures help identify what contributes to outcomes and where attention may be warranted. Outcome measures provide evidence of achievement or learning goals, but alone do not indicate how this occurred or suggest what requires attention or where to improve. By collecting process and outcome data, and reflecting on it in combination with, and in consideration of, institutional mission and goals, it is possible to develop a more complete story about the quality of student learning, overall educational effectiveness, and where improvement may be warranted. The combined use of indirect and direct measures is generally advocated in good assessment work (Maki 2004; Suskie 2004), particularly to address the mutual goals of assessment for accountability and improvement.

Information about the types of instruments and assessment methods utilized by institutions provides useful information about the variety in approaches to measurement. As reported in *More Than You Think, Less Than We Need* (Kuh and Ikenberry 2009), a wide range of approaches were being used to gather evidence on campus, such as nationally normed measures of general knowledge and skills (e.g., the Collegiate Learning Assessment, or CLA, the American College Testing program's Collegiate Assessment of Academic Proficiency, or CAAP), portfolios, national or locally developed surveys, and alumni and employer surveys and interviews. However, in terms of institution-wide assessments of student learning outcomes, most campuses (76 percent) tended to rely on national surveys (representing indirect measures of learning), such as NSSE. Two-fifths (39 percent) of all colleges and universities reported using a standardized measure of general knowledge and skills (e.g., CLA, CAAP, WorkKeys). Far less common uses with institutionally valid samples were external expert judgments of student work (9 percent) tests of specialized knowledge (8 percent), student portfolios (8 percent), and employer interviews (8 percent).

In contrast, NILOA 2009 results regarding program-level activities as reported by provosts within institutions show that the most common approaches to assessing learning outcomes were student portfolios, measures of specialized knowledge and other performance assessments, and rubrics. More than 80 percent of institutions indicated at least one of their academic programs was using one of these approaches. Essentially, while campus-wide assessments tended to rely on surveys, such approaches were infrequently used for program assessment. Assessment tools and approaches understandably vary depending on what the data are intended to represent.

In addition, approaches to institution-level and program-level assessment seem to be consistent with the varied missions of institutions of higher education in the United States. For example, more private colleges used alumni surveys with institutionally valid samples, and more public colleges and universities collected data about their students from employers using program-level surveys and interviews. This variation in approach and use suggests that if the results of outcomes assessment are to be useful to campuses and policy makers, they need to reflect the differences in institutional mission, type, organization, governance, and constituency.

An alternative perspective on measures used by colleges and universities is captured in a survey of employers regarding the most effective sources of evidence of college graduates' skills and knowledge (Hart Research Associates 2009). Employers were satisfied that the majority of college graduates possess a range of skills that prepare them for success in entry-level positions, including solid skills in the areas of teamwork and intercultural skills, but they were less confidant about graduates' skills in global knowledge and writing that typically prepare them for promotion and advancement.

The survey showed that, in terms of assessment practices, what employers trust to indicate a graduate's level of knowledge and potential to succeed in the job are assessments of real-world and applied-learning approaches, including evaluations of supervised internships, community-based projects, and comprehensive senior projects. Employers also endorsed individual student essay tests, electronic portfolios of student work, and comprehensive senior projects as valuable tools both for students to enhance their knowledge and develop important real-world skills, as well as for employers to evaluate graduates' readiness for the workplace. On the other hand, employers dismissed tests of general content knowledge and found multiple-choice tests particularly ineffective. Employers also indicated that the academic transcript does not provide much in terms of assessing college graduates' potential for success. Interestingly, employers were not interested in institutional scores of student competencies that show how a university compares to other institutions.

As the NILOA 2009 and 2011 institution and program level surveys indicate, although only a small minority of institutions rely on portfolios and rubrics for institution-wide assessment, many more programs have adopted these approaches or a combination of national and local approaches in their efforts. Assessment experts Trudy Banta, Merilee

Griffin, Theresa Flateby, and Susan Kahn (2009) define measures such as portfolios, rubrics, performance assessments, and examinations of student work, as authentic assessment measures that require students to generate rather than choose a response to demonstrate what they can do and provide a more holistic picture of learning gains over time. These approaches tend to bring the assessment process and the teaching and learning process closer. These measures are considered to be preferred by faculty and represent a more meaningful educational experience for students.

Banta et al. document the development of several promising, authentic measures and processes to assess student learning outcomes and include specific instances in which portfolios, common analytic rubrics, and online assessment communities are being effectively used to create a shared set of standards and expectations for student learning and for demonstrating accountability. The authors make a strong case for authentic assessment as both an approach to yield deeper understanding of individual student learning and an efficient and effective method to assess learning outcomes and demonstrate institutional accountability.

Another development associated with increased assessment activity and greater attention to measurement in colleges and universities has emerged from educational organizations and foundations. Organizations, including the Association of American Colleges and Universities (AAC&U), the Council for Independent Colleges, and the Teagle Foundation, have brought together educators and other university administrators to share assessment strategies, discuss results, and engage in collective experimentation, evidence, and process to promote the development of systematic assessment of undergraduate learning. AAC&U has led the way, calling for colleges and universities to take responsibility for assessing the quality of student learning, formulating a number of key higher-order learning outcomes, and by engaging faculty nationally in creating rubrics that can be used to define and assess essential learning outcomes at diverse institutions.

AAC&U supported the creation of 15 rubrics aligned with their essential learning outcomes, such as critical and creative thinking, intercultural knowledge and competence, written and oral communication, quantitative literacy, information literacy, and teamwork.[4] Each rubric contains the most common and broadly shared criteria or core characteristics considered critical for judging the quality of student work in that outcome area. AAC&U encourages institutions to test and use the existing rubrics, and to share their experience with the organization and with colleagues. Hundreds of campuses participated in the initial testing, and even more have taken up the invitation to adopt the rubrics in their assessment efforts. The broad interest in AAC&U's rubrics reflects both greater interest in the use of authentic measures for assessment and also the potential learning that can occur when educators and teams are sharing information to further the development of assessment processes and approaches to improve student learning.

Comparing information about widespread and emerging institutional practices to employers' views regarding the preferred evidence of graduates' skills suggests some interesting points of convergence and disconnects for assessment. Although a range of assessments are being used at institutions, it seems that employers' perspectives are more aligned with the kinds of assessment being undertaken at the program level in colleges and universities and the variety of authentic measures demonstrated by Banta et al. (2009) and in the approaches to assessment being employed by groups of institutions in organization-sponsored consortia.

LESSONS ABOUT STUDENT LEARNING OUTCOMES ASSESSMENT

Reviews of current assessment literature and work by NILOA to examine the higher education landscape lead to several general conclusions about student learning outcomes assessment. By all accounts, institutions are using a variety of tools and multiple, meaningful measures in their assessment work. These measures are being used for diagnostic, milestone, and culminating assessments. A wider range of approaches to assessment are getting attention on campus, including authentic assessment, portfolios, capstones, more direct learning outcomes, and value-added approaches. Institutions also seem to be shifting from a pure emphasis on collecting data to developing systems for integrating and using data in decision-making and actually acting on data. While there is less evidence that institutions are "closing the assessment loop"—in other words, acting on data and then following up to measure the impact of change—it is clear that more campuses are setting up feedback systems. If assessment is to make a difference for student success, it is necessary to dedicate more attention to converting data about student and institutional performance into action that makes a demonstrable difference for student learning.

What is stalling institutions' progress to act on data and then assess if change leads to improvements in student learning? Blaich and Wise (2011), who have been collaborating with hundreds of institution to gather and use evidence to strengthen liberal arts education at the Center of Inquiry at Wabash College, identified several practices that inhibit efforts to use assessment evidence to advance educational improvement. They observed that gathering data is much easier than using the information to improve student learning. As they monitored institutions that had significant amounts of quality data and their use of these results, it became clear that evidence was having limited impact, with only about one in four institutions having engaged in any active response to the data. While institutional personnel had more than enough actionable assessment evidence, they lacked experience reviewing and making sense of the data. Blaich and Wise (2010; 2011) concluded that using evidence to promote improvement is as much a political and socio-cultural process as it is an analytical process, and that scaffolded processes for making meaning of results and bringing representatives from different campuses together to interpret assessment evidence and discuss possible responses are important to move institutions from simply collecting evidence to using it to effect improvement.

Most institutions of higher education seem to share a struggle for using evidence to promote improvement. It is clear that institutions have more than enough actionable assessment evidence, including national surveys, standardized measures, dynamic student-information systems, interviews with students, reports conducted by external evaluators, and more than a third report having evidence of a holistic picture of student learning gains over time. The challenge is not about collecting data or having the right measures. The challenge begins once faculty, staff, administrators, and students try to use the evidence to improve student learning.

Conclusions drawn by Blaich and Wise (2010; 2011) about using evidence and Kinzie and Pennipedes (2009) regarding converting NSSE data into action indicate that the challenge is data utilization. Several assumptions seem to block the use of evidence. One of the most dominant mistaken beliefs is that there is insufficient, high-quality data available to analyze and make decisions. This belief simply promotes more data collection in the hopes that additional data will result in better, more accurate decision-making. It is also evidenced in the practice of regularly administering surveys and tests or massing data in pockets of the institution, but failing to bring it all together to put it to use. Although more data may be needed to inform decisions or to advance action, perpetual data pursuit can overshadow the important aspect of using good, available data to guide institutional improvement efforts. A related stumbling block is about design, that a lack of control group or small sample sizes, makes data use impossible or worse, dangerous. Although standardized research design and data quality considerations are important in assessment, the application of rigorous approaches to research design is simply beyond the purpose of assessment for institutional improvement. Another obstacle is the belief that simply providing a detailed report to the campus should be enough to stimulate action. Reports are more likely to be used if they are connected to institutional interests, provided to individuals and committees who have relevant influence accompanied by a structure for responding to results, and if concerns are tailored to offer insights into institutional problems. Finally, action on data is frequently paralyzed by requests for more analysis and additional data collection.

Several of these obstacles could be addressed by developing more practical understandings and expectations for assessment and measurement.

Reviews of the learning outcome assessment work reported by institutions that have made strides in utilizing evidence to improve demonstrate the following practices were critical to their utilization efforts:

- investment of faculty in the development of approaches and identification of measures;
- use of multiple measures;
- sharing results and communicating how results were used;
- greater awareness among faculty of student learning and success markers (graduation rates, progression to degree, troublesome courses);
- tangible examples of having "closed the loop"—illustrations of how data influenced action, and how data show improvement; and
- evidence of meaningful changes in student learning.

These indicators suggest some activities that could be encouraged and reinforced to support advancements in outcomes assessment.

CONCLUSION

So what approaches to measurement are needed to respond to the public scrutiny and national concern about quality and student learning outcomes in higher education? To move the educational quality and assessment agenda forward, colleges and universities must have evidence of student performance, use these results to make improvements, and demonstrate how changes have improved student learning and success. Institutions must measure things that matter in the context of mission, values, and desired outcomes and focus on educationally meaningful indicators that the institution can do something about.

Measuring the value of postsecondary education and advancing assessment to improve student learning and educational quality requires thoughtful consideration of the current context in higher education, assumptions about accountability and assessment, greater attention to the assessment of student learning outcomes, and evidence that assessment results help in the improvement of educational quality. The following prompts might also be useful for further discussion:

- How are student learning outcomes made explicit to students and the public?
- How are institutions collecting student performance results and utilizing this information in institutional decision-making?
- Are we measuring what really matters to student learning?
- What kinds of information about institutional performance and educational quality should be comparable and for whom? Are there

some measures that can be made comparable, while still honoring evidence about distinctive aspects of institutional mission and signature learning experiences?

- How might evidence of institutional response to assessment results and documentation of improvement be included in expectations for accountability?
- What do effective models for the systematic management of assessment and improvement include?
- What can be done to help more institutions measure the relationship between evidence-based improvement activities and actual enhancements in student learning?
- What might stimulate more opportunities for institutions to share lessons learned from their assessment processes and enter into collective initiatives with other institutions around shared questions of inquiry?

Given global concern about quality in undergraduate learning, now is the time to improve our capacity to measure what matters to educational quality and student learning and demonstrate the value of postsecondary education.

NOTES

[1] See www.luminafoundation.org/goal_2025.html.

[2] NILOA is a national project to study learning outcomes assessment in postsecondary education and to advance assessment practice. It is supported by funding from the Lumina Foundation for Education, the Carnegie Corporation of New York, and the Teagle Foundation. More information about NILOA is available on the Website: www.learningoutcomesassessment.org.

[3] See the College Portrait, www.collegeportraits.org.

[4] See http://www.aacu.org/value/rubrics/index_p.cfm.

REFERENCES

Association of American Colleges and Universities (AAC&U) and Council for Higher Education Accreditation (CHEA). 2008. *New Leadership for Student Learning and Accountability: A Statement of Principles, Commitment to Action.* Washington, DC: Authors.

Banta, T.W., M. Griffin, T.L. Flateby, and S. Kahn. 2009. Three Promising Alternatives for Assessing College Students' Knowledge and Skills. NILOA Occasional Paper No. 2. Urbana: University of Illinois and Indiana University, National Institute of Learning Outcomes Assessment.

Banta, T.W., E.A. Jones, and K.E. Black. 2009. *Designing Effective Assessment: Principles and Profiles of Good Practice.* San Francisco: Jossey-Bass.

Blaich, C. and K. Wise. 2010. Moving from Assessment to Institutional Improvement. In *Longitudinal Assessment for Institutional Improvement: New Directions for Institutional, Research Assessment Supplement*, ed. T. Seifert, 67-78. San Francisco: Wiley Periods, Inc., A Wiley Company.

———. 2011. From Gathering to Using Assessment Results: Lessons from the Wabash National Study. NILOA Occasional Paper No. 8. Urbana: University of Illinois and Indiana University, National Institute for Learning Outcomes Assessment.

Borden, V.M.H. and J.W. Young. 2008. Measurement Validity and Accountability for Student Learning. In *New Directions for Institutional Research*, 19-37. Wiley Periodicals, Inc., A Wiley Company.

Dwyer, C.A., C.M. Millett, and D.A. Payne. 2006. *A Culture of Evidence: Postsecondary Assessment and Learning Outcomes*. Princeton, NJ: Educational Testing Service.

El-Khawas, E. 1995. Campus Trends 1995: New Directions for Academic Programs Higher Education Panel Report No. 85. Washington, DC: American Council on Education.

Ewell, P.T. 2002. An Emerging Scholarship: A Brief History of Assessment. In *Building a Scholarship of Assessment*, ed. T.W. Banta, 3-25. San Francisco: Jossey-Bass.

———. 2008. Assessment and Accountability in America Today: Background and Context. In *Assessing and Accounting for Student Learning: Beyond the Spellings Commission* (New Directions for Institutional Research, Assessment Supplement 2007), ed. V.M.H. Borden and G. Pike, 7-18. San Francisco: Jossey-Bass.

Hart Research Associates. 2009. Learning and Assessment: Trends in Undergraduate Education. Washington, DC: Author. At http://www.aacu.org/membership/documents/2009MemberSurvey_Part1.pdf.

Jenkins, D., T. Ellwein, J. Wachen, M.R. Kerrigan, and S. Cho. 2009. Achieving the Dream Colleges in Pennsylvania and Washington State: Early Progress toward Building a Culture of Evidence. At http://www.achievingthedream.org/d8190309-5307-48b4-ba53-dce97c2dbf5d.asset.

Kean, R.C. and R.J. Thompson. 2007. Student Learning Outcomes: From Assessment to Accountability. Presentation at the Reinvention Center, Vice President Network Meeting, University of Miami, Miami, Florida.

Kinzie, J. 2010. Perspectives from Campus Leaders on the Current State of Student Learning Outcomes Assessment. *Assessment Update* 22 (5): 1-2, 14-15.

Kinzie, J., J. Buckley, and G. Kuh. 2008. Using Assessment to Cultivate a Culture of Evidence on Campus: An Evaluation of Six Teagle Foundation-Funded Collaboratives. Teagle Foundation.

Kinzie, J. and B. Pennipedes. 2009. Converting Engagement Results into Action. In Using NSSE in Institutional Research, ed. R. Gonyea and G. Kuh. *New Directions for Institutional Research, 141*, San Francisco: Jossey-Bass.

Kuh, G.D. and S. Ikenberry. 2009. *More Than You Think, Less than We Need: Learning Outcomes Assessment in American Higher Education*. National Institute for Learning Outcomes Assessment. University of Illinois and Indiana University Bloomington.

Leonhardt, D. 2009. The College Calculation. *The New York Times Magazine*, 24 September.

Maki, P. 2004. *Assessing for Learning: Building a Sustainable Commitment Across the Institution*. Sterling: Stylus Publishing.

McPerson, P. and D. Shulenberger. 2006. Toward a Voluntary System of Accountability Program (VSA) for Public Universities and Colleges. Washington DC: American Association of State Colleges and Universities and Association of Public and Land-grant Universities. At http://voluntarysystem.org/docs/background/DiscussionPaper1_April06.pdf.

Millett, C.M., D.A. Payne, C.A. Dwyer, L.M. Stickler, and J.J. Alexiou. 2008. *A Culture of Evidence: An Evidence-Centered Approach to Accountability for Student Learning Outcomes.* Princeton: Educational Testing Service.

Millett, C.M., L.M. Stickler, D.A. Payne, and C.A. Dwyer. 2007. *A Culture of Evidence: Critical Features of Assessments for Postsecondary Student Learning.* Princeton: Educational Testing Service.

National Institute of Education. 1984. *Involvement in Learning: Realizing the Potential of American Higher Education.* Washington, DC: U.S. Department of Education.

National Survey of Student Engagement (NSSE). 2008. *Promoting Engagement for All Students: The Imperative to Look Within.* Bloomington: Indiana University Center for Postsecondary Research.

Pascarella, E.T., T. Seifert, and C. Blaich. 2010. How Effective are the NSSE Benchmarks in Predicting Important Educational Outcomes? *Change* 42 (1): 16-22.

Pascarella, E.T. and P.T. Terenzini. 1991. *How College Affects Students: Findings and Insights from Twenty Years of Research.* San Francisco: Jossey-Bass.

———. 2005. *How College Affects Students: A Third Decade of Research.* San Francisco: Jossey-Bass.

Suskie, L. 2004. *Assessing Student Learning: A Common Sense Guide.* Bolton: Anker Publishing Co., Inc.

6

TEACH, LEARN, ASSESS[1]

Roger Benjamin

INTRODUCTION

Achieving a close alignment of teaching, learning, and assessment[2] is the ultimate goal we must pursue if we are to fully realize the promise of the new assessments and new pedagogies emerging in postsecondary education. If we think of postsecondary education as producing two principal goods, research and undergraduate education, it is instructive to review the progress made with respect to research. We have developed a continuous system of improvement for research. No one can simply assert that they have produced the greatest advance in stem cell research. They need to have their work scrutinized through the peer review process of major journals that publish work or grant agencies or foundations that fund the research.

The reward system associated with research is well understood so that all parties, the federal and state governments in the case of the United States, the president and her/his administrators at a university, the dean, the chairperson, and the principal investigator, understand the stakes involved in pursuing research, i.e., the rewards for the principal investigator, if he or she produces research that is well received, garner substantial research contracts, etc. The game is thus viewed as worth the arduous process of peer review which involves subjecting oneself to rigorous criticism by anonymous reviewers. It is not perfect, but over time the peer review process has led to improvement in field after field of research.

We do not have anything like a continuous system of improvement for undergraduate education, the other principal public good. The question is whether we can begin to develop one. This is the theme I pursue in this chapter.

Measuring the Value of a Postsecondary Education, ed. K. Norrie and M.C. Lennon. Montreal and Kingston: Queen's Policy Studies Series, McGill-Queen's University Press. © 2013 All rights reserved.

The discussion moves through three steps. First, I discuss the rationale for assessment, which is perhaps much stronger than previously realized. Second, I outline a strategy for assessment. Third, I make a brief case for performance assessment, focusing on a novel testing paradigm I am involved with. There is nothing wrong with the multiple-choice testing paradigm, but many have made the case for it over the past century. Performance assessment seems to be appropriate for today's knowledge economy. My examples are taken from the American experience. However, I extrapolate from my examples to other countries where appropriate.

THE RATIONALE FOR ASSESSMENT

The assumption that human capital is the only real national or individual resource is becoming ascendant in the United States. That means that education or training is the formal and really the only practical way for individuals to improve their human capital. But, the reality is that we have a very large group of unskilled citizens and high school dropouts for whom we do not offer postsecondary training or education opportunities. The society as a whole cannot be successful in today's knowledge economy with such a large proportion of our population without the skills to contribute to the economy. It should therefore be the right of all citizens to purse some form of postsecondary education or training.

Despite this clear need, there appears to be significant under-spending on postsecondary education in the US. The consequence of inadequate revenue is a hollowing out of the sector's infrastructure, particularly that devoted to instruction. Institutions are forced to reduce the number of instructors in the classroom and to eat their capital stock through deferring maintenance and not renewing technology. The inevitable results are a reduced ability of colleges and universities to admit students and a decline in the quality of education they are able to provide. If this situation continues, we risk tipping over into a permanent social and economic crisis.

That is why I argue we need a fundamental debate about higher education in the United States.[3] Why are we under-investing in higher education when its role in securing our economic and social well-being is so evident?

This debate must start by thinking carefully about the balance between the public and private responsibilities for postsecondary education. One may think of goods as a continuum from pure public to pure private goods.[4] In reality, there few, if any pure public goods that warrant that description. Nor are there many pure private goods. Most goods produce some distortion effects or exhibit free rider problems. That has led to the introduction of terms, such as quasi-public, quasi-private, or collective goods as descriptors of goods.

Unlike elementary education, which most countries would accept has large positive social benefits and therefore merits extensive public support, the situation in postsecondary education is less clear. There are significant financial and non-financial returns to the individual, which is the usual justification for students paying at least part of the cost of their higher education through tuition and other fees. But, it would not be accurate to label postsecondary education a pure private good. There are clear public good dimensions to research and in teaching in postsecondary education, justifying the infusion of public funds into the sector. This social dimension to higher education was recognized in the United States when the land grant university was created to permit universal access of all citizens who meet admissions requirements through the *Morrill Act* by Congress in 1866.

I suggest viewing postsecondary education's problems through the common pool problem (CPP) because the reality is that there is not sufficient public *or* private spending on the postsecondary education good. CPPs develop whenever a group depends on a public good that everyone uses but no one owns, and where one person's use affects another person's ability to use the good. The result is that either the population fails to provide the resources, over consumes, and/or fails to replenish it. Another important characteristic includes confusion about property rights.[5] In this case, the question is who is responsible for seeing to the under-investment in higher education.

There also is widespread confusion about what we should do about it. In the United States there is a historic legacy that treated postsecondary education through the Land Grant model in recognition of its large social benefits. In recent decades, accelerated by the knock on effects of the recent recession, net tuition revenues outstrip local and state subsidies in over one half of the states.

We need a public debate about the issues the postsecondary sector confronts, including how we treat the sector conceptually.

THE NEW LIMITS OF EDUCATION POLICY

One can see the portents of change regarding the place and role of education policy in the debates over K-12 education in the United States. The need for significant education reform in K-12 education appears to be one area upon which Republicans and Democrats agree. The recognition that the K-16 education system is the formal venue for preserving and enhancing human capital will continue to grow; education policy should be regarded as the central obligation of the state to focus on. This is so because the quality of a nation's human capital determines the success in all other policy domains. In other words, there is a compelling argument that education policy is central to the success of health, economic, and even national defence policy.

However, currently education policy in the United States (and in most countries) is of marginal rather than central importance. For example, of the US$150 billion federal government non-defence budget, the share for postsecondary education is approximately US$132 million.[6] Education policy is taught in public policy schools but the subject is not central to the curriculum. The major social science departments, such as economics and political science, attract the best and brightest faculty to focus on national security policy, economic, and health policy, but not on education policy. The subject is taught in colleges of education but again is rarely central to the curriculum or research program of the faculty. Finally, the entering GRE scores of graduate students are lower in education than 29 other fields of study (Benjamin 2012). Education policy has a long way to go to achieve the higher status it should have.

Whether education policy will be accorded greater status remains to be seen. It is likely that there will be a significant national debate about the importance of increasing the nation's focus on the subject as more leaders confront the question as to whether the social and perhaps even the private returns to postsecondary education are under appreciated. Rising costs and declining revenues are becoming a serious challenge to public and private colleges and universities. For-profit, online colleges now account for approximately 12 percent of the undergraduate market in postsecondary education. The for-profit sector has been growing at over 10 percent per year while the non-profit higher education sector has remained flat.

A safe projection is that the next decade will be turbulent for the post-secondary sector overall (Christensen et al. 2011). Under these conditions we can expect substantial restructuring of many colleges and universities as they respond to fiscal and market pressures. There will be many more experiments with online teaching and learning solutions as administrators attempt to substitute technology for personal interaction. Under such conditions that require decisions of consequence to be made, there will be a greater need for evidence-based decision-making to improve the quality of student learning and reduce costs. In this context benchmarking student learning outcomes becomes the critical metric against which to evaluate changes in curriculum or the reallocation of funding to departments directed at improving learning or reducing costs. This is so because such decisions will be of the high stakes nature and greater systematic evidence will be required by all involved parties.

What is reasonable to expect, then, are increasing demands for transparency, restructuring, and accountability from local, state, and national leaders, private sector leaders, potential students and their parents, and boards of trustees and central administrators. This new emphasis will include demands for institutions to benchmark the growth and level of student learning achieved of graduating seniors.

Fortunately, we can also expect increased attention to using assessment for improvement of teaching and learning. This is fortunate because it will be important to connect the role of assessment for improvement, something the faculty buy into, with the increased demands for accountability. This is critical because higher education institutions possess a high level of legitimacy and relative autonomy, featuring a decentralized system of accountability anchored by department-based governance. In this system the faculty decide what subjects are taught within disciplines, how they are taught, and whether or how students are assessed. Therefore, assessment instruments must be developed that are viewed as authentic by faculty and of direct use to them in their classroom activities.[7]

In sum, the challenges to traditional postsecondary education will come from external sources. However, the methods of adaptation of assessment into the classroom and into internal-based incentive systems will be developed by faculty and administrators themselves. The reasons for expecting the role of assessment to increase significantly are compelling. Discussions today are no longer about whether postsecondary institutions should focus on measuring the quality of student learning but how. Next, I outline the strategy for assessment over the next decade.

THE STRATEGY FOR ASSESSMENT

The fundamental issue to address is the misaligned incentives that do not encourage faculty to focus on improving both teaching and learning. Department-based governance reflects the dominance of research metrics for the evaluation of faculty (Tierney 1998). There are few if any incentives for focusing on improvement of teaching and learning. One of the challenges is to encourage experiments or pilots designed by faculty that give them incentives that encourage improvement of student learning. Right now there are no models of incentive systems that go beyond the research metrics in place to evaluate faculty productivity. We need examples of incentive systems directly linked with student learning goals that can be scrutinized, improved, and hopefully eventually adopted more widely.

The incentive system is so important because the faculty role must be recognized as central for any progress to be made. Because the faculty decide whether and how to assess, the most important question to ask is whether they want assessment instruments being considered for use. In other words, the assessment must be known to be reliable and valid, but that is only a necessary, not sufficient, condition for adoption of an assessment. The assessment must also be seen as authentic by faculty and of direct use in the classroom.

Elimination of Seven Red Herrings about Assessment in Postsecondary Education

A number of shibboleths have grown up over the years that make it easier for stakeholders within postsecondary education to avoid systematic, standardized assessments. By standardized assessment I mean that the questions, conditions of administering, scoring procedures, and interpretations are consistent and are administered and scored in a predetermined, standardized manner. The list of skeptical stakeholders includes faculty, administrators, boards of trustees, accrediting groups, and membership associations. I will state the most familiar arguments used against arguments for and against standardized assessments in higher education that have confused participants on each side of the debate about the need for and the possibility of new benchmarks of student learning outcomes.

We need appropriate standardized assessments to permit faculty and administrators to signal faculty and administrators how well they are doing in comparison with other higher education institutions. Most importantly, we need good standardized assessment instruments to encourage the development of assessment strategies that directly assist faculty to improve teaching and learning in a systemic, continuous improvement way. In fact, appropriate standardized instruments that permit comparison are a necessary condition for progress in developing a more systematic approach to assessment in higher education. However, nuance is important here. While standardized tests are necessary, they are *not sufficient* for assessment to be integrated with teaching and learning within institutions. Formative assessments developed by faculty at institutions are also critically important.

Why has the view that both formative and standardized assessments are needed not prevailed? Here are the seven red herrings that tell us why.

1. Since it is impossible to measure all of what is important in education, it is impossible to measure anything that is important.
Response: Just because we cannot measure every aspect of education does not mean we cannot measure important components of it perfectly well. For example, it is possible to benchmark critical thinking, analytical reasoning, problem solving, and written communication, often called higher order skills. These skills are considered crucial in the knowledge economy by most colleges and universities (see mission and general education statements), faculty, many employers, and observers (Stevens 2010; Bok 2006; Wagner 2010).

2. Comparison of higher education institutions is not possible or, in any case, not needed. Missions and visions of colleges and universities are so different that it makes no sense to compare them.

Response: Inter-institution comparison is essential for formative assessment. It is true that the postsecondary education sector presents a diverse set of institutions pursuing distinctive goals. However, most higher education institutions commit to improving higher order skills as a fundamental part of their compact with students. The fact that there can be at least two standard deviation differences between similarly situated colleges and universities means there is a substantial canvas of similar institutions where researchers may study best practices producing substantial improvements in teaching and learning as measured by the Collegiate Learning Assessment (CLA),[8] Academic Proficiency Profile, or CAPP in institutions doing better than expected which can be adapted for institutions not doing as well.[9]

Second, what conclusion or implication can adherents of formative assessment draw from the fact that the standard deviation for any variable (and thereby its confidence interval) is larger when the student is the unit of analysis rather than when a group (such as a college) is the unit of analysis? For example, suppose one finds that 30 percent of an institution's students report reading a book during the past two weeks that was not assigned by their professors. Is that percentage good, bad, or indifferent? Interpretation of this finding would be much more meaningful if one also could inform the faculty and administrators at the institution that this percentage was one of the highest (or lowest) rates reported by students at colleges and universities that were similar to this one. Similarly, suppose colleagues at a college are told that the percentage of students making some choice or other increased by 20 percentage points over the previous year. Again, is that bad, good, or indifferent? One needs a comparative-based benchmark to frame this finding in order to give the specific finding meaning.

To argue that between institution comparisons and standardized tests, in particular, have an important role in assessment does not mean formative assessments at an institution that are focused on assisting faculty to improve teaching and learning are not needed or inappropriate. Quite the reverse is the case; appropriate standardized tests[10] should be combined with formative, within-institution assessments. Both are necessary if we are to achieve something like a continuous system of improvement of teaching and learning many in the academy desire.

3. What is really important is what goes on in the classroom between the teacher and the student.

Response: Yes, this remains true. However, there is growing consensus about the need for reform of undergraduate education that can be characterized along three dimensions noted above, comprising a shift to: (i) a student-centred approach, (ii) a case or problem approach in courses and curriculum, and (iii) more open-ended assessment instruments. To achieve such changes, faculty need assistance; tools that help them make the shifts in their pedagogy, such as course design, text selection, and assessments that tell them whether and how much they are improving. Of course, we have always needed stronger theories of teaching and learning but we have yet to achieve them. In these circumstances the ability to compare the outcomes of one's courses, programs and overall institutional contribution to student learning outcomes is essential.

4. All standardized tests are bad.

Response: Faculty are skeptical of standardized tests. However, most faculty equate standardized tests with the multiple-choice tests that characterize the implementation of the *No Child Left Behind Act* for K-12 education in the United States. Faculty and administrators rightly celebrate the diversity of American higher education and therefore cannot see how one standardized test could be used across this range of institutions. However, it is incorrect to hold that colleges are so diverse that they do not share some important common goals. For instance, most faculty and virtually all college mission or general education statements agree that critical thinking and writing skills are essential for all college graduates to possess.

5. One-size-fits-all measures to compare institutions are inappropriate.

Response: This is correct. No one measure can capture the complexity of a college or university. Consider the CAAP, Academic Proficiency Profile, and CLA tests. The mean scores on these tests at the institutional level should be set in the context of multiple indicators collected and analyzed by faculty at the institution itself. We need to establish what will become a reinforcing system of continuous improvement of teaching and learning.[11] The institution's global score provides a critical signal that should trigger an internal focus on what correlates with the score. It does not really matter where the institution is on the initial test administrations. The important questions become related to: (i) understanding what led to those results, and (ii) deciding what improvement goals might make sense for the future.

6. Content is what is important in undergraduate education.

Response: Of course content is important. But, in today's knowledge economy equally, if not more, important is the application of what one knows to new situations. Before the onset of the knowledge economy, there was a sense that there was a knowable stock of knowledge. It was the job of lecturers to pour content into students who were passive receptacles to be filled to the brim. We now live in an age where one can "Google" to access "facts." It is more important to be able to access, structure, and use information than merely accrue facts.[12] None of this means that academic majors, for example, are unimportant; they are the fundamental building blocks for both the transmission of knowledge across generations and the creation of new knowledge. But, employers want employees who can navigate the increasing flood of information and come to reasoned judgments about the course of action to take.

7. If colleges and universities engage in standardized assessment, the results will be used by state and federal authorities to control and punish institutions that are ranked by arbitrary and capricious indicators.

Response: Base assessment in higher education on the peer review analogy. Consider the response of public authorities to the production of the other main public good universities produce, i.e., research. The initial comparisons of student learning outcomes at the institutional level, noted above, are important signals to faculty and administrators about how well they are doing. What is much more important is what institutions do to improve. Higher education institutions are much more complex and relatively autonomous than K-12 education. Because of this, higher education leaders can lead the way in deciding what is appropriate to report about student learning publically. That is what two national associations of higher education, the American Public Land Grant Universities (APLU) and the Association of American State Colleges and Universities (AASCU) are attempting to do now (see their Voluntary System of Accountability website). More important than outside forces demanding accountability is the need to develop assessments that are embraced by the faculty as concrete aids to their efforts to improve teaching and learning. This is so because only when faculty accept assessment instruments as an important aid to their classroom success, will the higher education community and the groups that hold it accountable remove the blinders and move past these seven false arguments.

THE PEER REVIEW ANALOGY

As in the case of peer review of research, comparative-based assessments should be designed to be objective characterizations of institution-level performance on student learning outcomes, offering evidence that is judged to be reliable and valid, and in particular, to be thought authentic by the faculty. Such assessments that meet the measurement science requirement of minimum standards of reliability and validity offer a powerful reality check for institution-based formative assessment. The fundamental point, by analogy, is that the organization that does the testing should not make the results public. The testing organization should report assessment results for the institutions it tests back to them only. Otherwise, why would an institution, department, or program want to permit comparative-based testing across institutions? Of course, the question of what to report and who gets to report it under what review conditions are central issues being debated today. The peer-review analogy suggests the position to take.

Since it is possible to learn from other institutions that are producing advances in teaching and learning, there is no intellectual argument for not doing so. The stakes, i.e., for improving the quality of undergraduate education, are too high. Peer review anchors the continuous improvement system that continues to provide advances in scholarship and scientific research. We may never achieve such clearly positive results in teaching and learning as have been achieved in research. Surely, however, we can build on the basic strategy presented here to move the subject of teaching and learning forward to a much more evidence-based systematic subject in which verifiable best practices are continually adjusted or changed and improvement of student learning demonstrably occurs in higher education to all standardized assessment and accountability initiatives.

If the principle of peer review is adhered to, colleges and universities should be able to define the terms under which accountability systems are developed although there is little doubt that increased transparency of student learning results will bring less institutional autonomy to administrators and faculty. If progress is made in integrating assessment and accountability systems through the peer review concept and demonstrable improvements in student learning are made, colleges and universities are likely to maintain control over most of the accountability discussion. And because student learning will have been made more systematic, that would be a good result for those interested in the human capital argument.[13]

Why are the seven red herrings not more widely debunked? One answer is that there may be deeper underlying assumptions that account for resistance in postsecondary education to all assessment and accountability initiatives. A basic reason for the relatively small progress in assessment in higher education involves the power of institutional inertia. All institutions, including universities and colleges, are stable, enduring patterns of behaviours formed to undertake certain services deemed important by private or public reasons. Institutions, like the individuals that inhabit them, tend to continue the patterns of behaviours they are familiar with and not carve out new ones because that would require a decision. And, decisions are by definition risk taking. Unless or until an attractive or even acceptable institutional design alternative that truly integrates assessment into teaching and learning and produces positive results as seen and defined by the faculty as having relevance for their classroom activities, the status quo will remain.[14] We are not there yet, but the pieces are there to be put into a design such that exogenous and endogenous forces come together to warrant executing it.

The Response to the Need for Assessment in Postsecondary
Education: All Hands on Deck

To meet the challenge of improving the quality of undergraduate education, we need to change attitudes toward assessment, to experiment with several types of assessment approaches available, and reinvent the concept of the college of education. Here is a list of major approaches.

Formative assessment, meaning assessments developed by and for faculty in departments and programs for their use on a campus, remains critical to success. The formative assessments developed are viewed as authentic by the faculty and stand a good chance of being aligned with curriculum and pedagogy. If incentive systems that guide faculty are adapted to encourage focus on teaching and learning, much more attention to formative assessment will be stimulated. One form of formative assessment that deserves special mention is portfolios championed by many groups.[15]

Standardized Surveys and Tests

The National Survey of Student Engagement (NSSE) pioneered interest in studies of best practices that encourage improvement in student learning. Widely used, the leaders of NSSE have produced an important set of recommendations about improvement of undergraduate education.[16]

Because of the salience of the issues associated with the common pool problem in postsecondary education, there are increasing calls for direct measures of student learning results. There are now three principal standardized tests that benchmark critical thinking, problem solving, analytic reasoning, and written communication: Academic Profiles developed by the Educational Testing Service, the Collegiate Assessment of Academic Progress (CAAP) developed by ACT, and the Collegiate Learning Assessment (CLA) developed by CAE. A recent joint study conducted by researchers from all three of these groups concluded all three measures were reliable and valid (Klein et al. 2009). The CLA is an example of performance assessment, rather than multiple choice assessment, and represents a novel testing paradigm. Performance assessments, case studies, or realistic problems complete with written documents, graphs, and tables are also now being used to benchmark new common core standards, the new college readiness standards in mathematics and English. I will discuss performance assessment further below.

Finally, the Wabash Survey integrates standardized tests, NSSE results, and their own surveys to provide in-depth studies of best practices associated with student learning growth (Wabash National Study of Liberal Arts Education 2001).

Over the past decade, then, the landscape of assessment instruments has changed significantly. There are a number of credible choices to make by faculty and administrators.

However, there are also promising innovations that attempt to directly meet the challenge of linking teaching, learning, and assessment. One very interesting design is the Open Education Initiative (OEI) at Carnegie Mellon University that brings together content specialists in science and technology fields, cognitive scientists, education technologists, and assessment specialists to create improved courses, for example, in introductory statistics, a gateway course that many students do not pass. Their results are extraordinary.[17] There are also a number of developments associated with the Open Education Resource (OER) movement that give promise of permitting the development of a virtual academic community. The concept is to place intellectual property, texts in PDFs, courses, curriculum, and assessments in Internet platforms to be accessed without charge by faculty and administrators. The goal is to create a user friendly infrastructure for teaching, learning and assessment at no cost for both faculty and students. This is an attractive new development that consortia of colleges and universities should evaluate carefully for possible use.[18]

In addition to the rich knowledge base of pedagogy, a new college of education could be based on four additional cornerstones. First, cognitive science (now a source of science-based findings relevant to learning) should be a prominent new component of the new education school.[19] Second, measurement science, a small but well-defined school of measurement experts that work in the fields noted above, should be a building block.[20] Third, educational technology offers innovative new ways to reach students.[21] Finally, education policy should be a final building block that generates a greater understanding of and practical recommendations for addressing the common pool problem (Benjamin 2012).

The Case for Performance Assessment[22]

Here I will note the principal rationale for performance assessments which appear to be better aligned with the needs of the Knowledge Economy and recent theories of learning that emphasize the importance of applying what one knows to new situations (Simon 1996; Pellegrino, Chudowsky and Glaser (eds.) 2001).

What Are Performance Assessments?

Performance assessments are distinctive in that they can be used as standardized tests, but faculty also find them of direct use in the classroom. More broadly, there is a connection between performance assessment and an emerging education reform movement in postsecondary education in the United States comprising a shift from the lecture to a student-centred approach to teaching, a change in emphasis from a focus on content in curriculum and textbooks to case-based materials, and a change in assessment from multiple choice to open-ended essays now possible because of the Internet and computer-assisted scoring (Klein 2005; Elliot 2011).

One example of performance assessment is the Collegiate Learning Assessment (CLA) which measures critical thinking, analytic reasoning, problem solving, quantitative reasoning, and written communication skills. It asks two questions: (i) how much value added growth in these skills occurs from the point students enter the institution to when they graduate, controlling for student SAT or ACT scores, and (ii) what absolute results do students achieve on the CLA when they graduate?[23] Because performance assessment is a novel paradigm, here is a brief description of the CLA testing protocol, including an example of a performance task.[24]

CLA performance tasks require constructed essay responses. Students are allowed up to 90 minutes for completion. They present realistic problems drawn from all across the arts and sciences and feature a document library that the student may use in answering the questions. The tasks require students to apply what they have learned to solve problems and make recommendations. Each performance task is designed to be judged authentic by faculty in the fields from which the task is constructed, i.e., faculty agree that graduating college students should be able to perform these tasks. Finally, the tasks are designed to be engaging to the students. For an illustration see Table 1.

TABLE 1
Example of CLA Tasks

Swiftaire 235

- You advise the president of DynaTech
- DynaTech makes airplane navigation and communication equipment
- DynaTech's sales manager suggests buying a Swiftaire 235 to visit customers and demo its products
- Recent accident—wing came off in flight
- Student's tasks
  - Review document library
  - Write memo discussing pros and cons of DynaTech getting a Swiftaire 235
  - Justify your recommendations

Document Library

- Newspaper article about recent accident
- Transcript of interview about accidents
- DynaTech email exchanges regarding reasons to buy a Swiftaire 235
- Trade magazine article that compares Swiftaire 235's performance and safety characteristics to similar planes
- Manufacturer specifications and required pilot training for Swiftaire 180 and 235
- Charts about airplane accidents and sales

Source: CAE (2008).

Performance assessments cannot stand alone. Faculty need to be taught how to develop their own tasks and how to teach the types of problem-solving skills employed in CLA's performance tasks. To date the CLA Education program has completed over 100 faculty academies in the United States and several countries reaching over 2,000 instructors. The new goal is to link performance assessment to curriculum reform working with college-based, faculty-developed performance tasks on internet sites and place CLA-developed performance tasks on Internet Open Education Resource sites for faculty use. Sample courses that seek to teach the skills associated with the CLA performance tasks include the following:

- performance is reality—developing a performance task (PT) in legal studies,
- using CLA in the classroom—PTs for assessment in a quantitative reasoning course,
- a cognitive psychology PT: a referendum on cell phone use while driving, and
- a CLA-based biology course: development of a protocol for breast cancer treatment.

CONCLUSION

The size of the student learning problem is much larger than many have realized. Most advanced countries may not face the size of the challenges noted here for the United States which should qualify for designation as a common pool problem in postsecondary education. However, most advanced countries do face similar challenging deficits in access and quality of student learning results due to immigration and other social-economic inequality related issues. Moreover, all countries face the stark challenge brought by the new consensus that human capital is any nation's principal resource. The challenge is to preserve and enhance the nation's human capital through education development. Just now a huge part of that challenge is to figure out how to benchmark the quality of student learning results, something in which postsecondary education has traditionally not engaged.

A useful start has been made in developing new approaches to assessment over the past decade. However, much more work remains to be done. Significant investments in the assessment enterprise will be needed. As I think about the investments needs, perhaps a new blueprint for colleges of education may well make a great deal of sense as a framework for the investments. My idea for a blueprint comes from the Flexner Report issued in 1910. Commissioned by the Carnegie Corporation, Abraham Flexner surveyed the quality of the 155 medical colleges in the United States and

Canada. As a result he proposed a new medical and science curriculum to these colleges and universities (Flexner 1910). Since that watershed moment medical schools have embarked on the journey to make medicine a science-based enterprise. In a similar sense, then, we have an opportunity to integrate cognitive science, state of the art pedagagy, measurement science, the core arts and science disciplines, and educational technology into a new college of education.

Finally, it may be useful to end with the following six steps, the recommendations for thinking about assessment and accountability that flow from eliminating the seven red herrings:

- Focus on improvement.
- Align teaching, learning, and assessment.
- Do not rank colleges or universities.
- Do standardized assessment comparisons between colleges, but for framing the meaning of information from formative (single-institution) assessments.
- Use the principle of peer review as basis for reporting results.
- Insist that accountability systems respect the peer review principle in their reporting systems.

NOTES

[1] This chapter builds on the arguments presented in Benjamin (2012).

[2] This is the goal of CLA Education. See a description of its goals at cae.org.

[3] I thank Dr. Ken Norrie for his suggestions on the points addressed in this section.

[4] For the need to differentiate among public goods and private goods see Buchanan (1965), Downs (1967), and Ostrom (1990).

[5] Examples include water, fishing or grazing rights, and climate change. If no solution to the CPP is reached, they can tip into a permanent crisis by which is meant the problem can no longer realistically be solved. This is what Hardin (1968) calls a tragedy of the commons.

[6] The Federal 2009 research budgets for the National Institute of Health, the National Science Foundations are from the American Association for the Advancement of Science (2009), "September R&D Funding Update," Washington, DC: American Association for the Advancement of Science. The research budget for the U.S. Department of Defense for the fiscal year 2009 is from the Office of Management and Budget Historical Tables (2010), Table 3.2, Outlays By function and Sub Function, 1962-2014. Office of Management and Budget, Washington, DC. The figures for the research budget of the U.S. Department of Education's Fund for Post Secondary Improvement is from the U.S. Department of Education 2009.

[7] For accountability systems to be sustainable they need to take these points into account. In other words the accountability systems need to be aligned with the assessment needs of the faculty.

[8] Similarly situated colleges are defined here as colleges with student populations that are similarly based on the entering competencies of the students as measured by the ACT or SAT. See Benjamin (2008).

[9] The measures are the Collegiate Academic Proficiency Progress (CAAP) of ACT, the Academic Proficiency Profile (formerly MAPP) of ETS and the Collegiate Learning Assessment (CLA) of CAE. All three measures were selected as appropriate assessment instruments for the student learning outcomes section of the Voluntary System of Accountability (VSA). ETS, ACT, and CAE co-operated in a study to see whether and the extent to which the three assessment instruments are correlated (see Klein et al. 2009; also Steedle, Kugelmass and Nemeth 2010). I will occasionally refer to the CLA because it is the assessment instrument I am involved with and know best. However, to restate, as corroborated in the Klein et al. *Test Validity Study Report*, all three measures are reliable and valid indicators of higher order skills. The criteria for choosing one or another of these assessment instruments rests on other grounds not discussed here.

[10] In the internet age possibilities to move beyond the multiple choice testing paradigm are emerging. We need to continue to experiment with a variety of versions of performance assessment and any other new standardized tests.

[11] This is precisely what higher education has in the research realm. Through peer review, research has a public face that encourages and requires researchers to respond to criticism and evaluate the claims of other researchers; in short, engage in a never ending process of continuous improvement. If we followed the above steps for undergraduate assessment, we could hope to eventually also create a continuous system of improvement of teaching and learning.

[12] See recent adjustments to the meaning of knowledge: Simon (1996) and Pellegrino, Chudowsky and Glaser (2001).

[13] It will also be good for the reduction of inequality which is the other important imperative to solve for in all societies through educational reform. See Task Force on Inequality and American Democracy (2004).

[14] This will also include incentive systems for faculty that encourage a focus on aligning teaching, learning and assessment.

[15] The Association of American Colleges and Universities is taking a lead role in promoting portfolios. See their website www.AAC&U.org.

[16] See Annual results at NSSE.org.

[17] See the Carnegie Mellon University website cmu.edu/openlearning for more details.

[18] See hewlett.org/programs/education-program/ open-educational-resources.

[19] A good review of this field is Miller (2003).

[20] I am thinking of individuals such as Edward Haertel, Stanford University; Paul Holland, chief research scientist, emeritus, ETS; Robert Linn, professor of psychology, University of Colorado; Henry Braun, Boise Chair in Education and Public Policy, Lynch School of Education, Boston College; Larry Hedges, professor of statistics and social policy, Institute of Policy Research, Northwestern University; William Mehrens, professor of education psychology, emeritus, Michigan State University; George Englehard, professor of education measurement, Emory University; Paul Sackett, professor of psychology, University of Minnesota; Lauri Wise, Human Resources Organization among others. To ignore the measurement science community is unacceptable if we are to succeed in developing testing paradigms that solve for both formative and summative assessment requirements.

[21] There is a vast literature on this subject. To start, see Monahan (2005).

[22] I note my involvement with the CAE-based Collegiate Learning Performance Assessment.

[23] For example, Klein et al. (2008) found that students did just as well on CLA tasks that were aligned with their academic major (such as science or business) as they did on tasks in other content areas. Factor analyses done by Robert Linn and others have found that on both the multiple choice and essay portions of the bar exam, examinees do just as well on two questions in the same content area (such as torts) as they do on questions in different areas (such as contracts and criminal law). Differential subject matter expertise is not evident when the test and job emphasize higher order skills, such as analysis. For an example of a CLA performance task see StartTest.com. A third example further illustrates the importance of generic skills. For over 70 years, the SATs (along with high school grades) have provided reasonably accurate predictions of a student's success in college. And, recent longitudinal studies have shown that the combination of high school grades and CLA scores do just as well (Klein et al. 2009). Adding subject matter tests to the battery provides little incremental accuracy. The dominant predictors (i.e., the ones that contribute the most to predictive accuracy) are the ones that measure generic skills.

[24] Performance assessment development is currently being encouraged by the U.S. Department of Education for use in K-12 and postsecondary education which means there will soon be other examples of this testing paradigm to review.

References

Benjamin, R.W. 2012. *The New Limits for Education Policy: Avoiding A Tragedy of the Commons*. London: Edward Elgar.

——. 2008. The Case for Comparative Institutional Assessment of Higher Order Skills. *Change* 40 (6): 15-21.

Bok, D. 2006. *Our Underachieving Colleges: A Candid Look at How Much Students Learn and Why They Should Be Learning More*. Princeton: Princeton University Press.

Buchanan, J. 1965. An Economic Theory of Clubs. *Economica* 32 (125): 1-15.

CAE. 2008. Swiftaire 355: A Sample Performance Task. New York: CAE.

Christensen, C., M.B. Horn, L. Caldera, and L. Soars. 2011. *Disrupting College: How Disruptive Innovation Can Deliver Quality and Affordability to Postsecondary Education*. Center for American Progress and Innosight Institute. Accessed 3 July 2012. http://www.americanprogress.org/issues/2011/02/pdf/disrupting_collegepdf.

Downs, A. 1967. *Inside Bureaucracy*. Boston: Little, Brown & Co.

Elliot, S. 2011. Computer-Assisted Scoring of Performance Tasks for the CLA and CWRA. The Council for Aid to Education. Accessed 3 July 2012. http://www.collegiatelearningassessment.org/files/ComputerAssistedScoringofCLA.pdf.

Flexner, A. 1910. Medical Education in the United States and Canada: A Report to the Carnegie Foundation for the Advancement of Teaching. The Carnegie Foundation for the Advancement of Teaching (4): 346. Accessed 3 July 2012. http://www.carnegiefoundation.org/sites/default/files/elibrary/Carnegie_Flexner_Report.pdf.

Hardin, G. 1968. The Tragedy of the Commons. *Science* 162 (3859): 1243-1248.

Klein, S. 2005. Characteristics of Hand and Machine-Assigned Scores to College Students' Answers to Open-Ended Tasks. In *Probability and Statistics: Essays in Honor of David A. Freedman*, ed. D. Nolan and T. Speed, 76-89. Beachwood: Institute of Mathematical Statistics.

Klein, S., R. Bolus, B. Bridgeman, H. Kugelmass, O.L. Liu, J. Scorning, et al. 2009. *Test Validity Study Report*. Washington, DC: Fund for the Improvement of Post-secondary Education. At http://www.voluntarysystem.org/docs/reports/TVSReport_Final.pdf.

Klein, S., D. Freedman, R. Shavelson, and R. Bolus. 2008. Assessing School Effectiveness. *Evaluation Review: A Journal of Applied Social Research* 32 (6): 511-525.

Miller, G. 2003. The Cognitive Revolution: A Historical Perspective. *Trends in Cognitive Sciences*, 7 (3): 141-144.

Monahan, T. 2005. *Globalization, Technological Change and Public Education*. New York: Routledge.

Ostrom, E. 1990. *Governing the Commons: The Evolution of Institutions for Collective Action*. Cambridge: Cambridge University Press.

Pellegrino, J., N. Chudowsky, and R. Glaser, eds. 2001. *Knowing What Students Know: The Science and Design of Educational Assessment*. Washington, DC: The National Academy Press.

Simon, H. 1996. *The Sciences of the Artificial*, 43. Boston: M.I.T. Press.

Steedle, J., H. Kugelmass, and A. Nemeth. 2010. What Do They Measure? Comparing Three Learning Outcomes Assessments. *Change: The Magazine of Higher Learning*. 42 (4): 33-37.

Stevens, A. 2010. *Summary of Mission Statement Research*. Unpublished. New York, New York: CAE.

Task Force on Inequality and American Democracy. 2004. American Democracy in an Age of Rising Inequality. *Perspectives on Politics* 2 (4): 651-666.

Tierney, W.G., ed. 1998. *The Responsive University: Restructuring for High Performance*. Baltimore: The Johns Hopkins University Press.

Wabash National Study of Liberal Arts Education. 2001. Center of Inquiry in the Liberal Arts at Wabash College. At www.liberalarts.wabash.edu.

Wagner, T. 2010. *The Global Achievement Gap: Why Even Our Best Schools Don't Teach the New Survival Skills Our Children Need—and What We Can Do About It*. New York: Basic Books.

7

OECD Assessment of Higher Education Learning Outcomes (AHELO): Rationale, Challenges and Initial Insights from the Feasibility Study

Diane Lalancette

Introduction[1]

Today, given the central role it plays in the success and sustainability of the knowledge economy, higher education represents a critical factor in innovation and human capital development. Countries and individuals around the world recognize the strategic value in investing in higher education. For the last decades, higher education has been expanding fast globally with some 135 million students now studying worldwide in more than 17,000 higher education institutions.

With this substantial rapid expansion in student numbers and the growing internationalization comes an increasing recognition that greater attention should now be paid to the quality and relevance of postsecondary education. Policymakers, as well as the public, devote considerable attention to the outcomes of higher education given its importance for human capital development, its cost to public finances as well as to students and their families, and the needs of business and industry.

At the same time, efforts to improve the quality of teaching and enhance the learning outcomes of students enrolled in higher education suffer from a considerable information gap. There is no reliable information which enables comparative judgments to be made about the capabilities of students in different countries and different institutions or about the quality of teaching. The reputations of higher education institutions are based largely on research performance and international rankings derived from inputs or research-driven outputs are distorting decision-making by individuals, institutions and governments. Developing measures that give due weight to teaching practices and learning outcomes has thus become essential.

There is currently considerable interest within institutional, political, and scientific circles for measures of higher education learning outcomes, but uncertainties and doubts of some actors as to whether it is scientifically and operationally feasible to measure learning outcomes across higher education institutions of very different types and in countries with different cultures and languages nevertheless exist. In order to answer this question, the Organisation for Economic and Co-operation and Development (OECD) has consulted a number of international experts over the past four years. Three meetings were held in 2007, bringing together international specialists in the field.[2] The main conclusion of the experts was that while it might be both desirable in terms of public policy and theoretically possible to assess and compare central components of education outcomes, it would be necessary to conduct a feasibility study to test this proposition before undertaking any more systematic assessment. The feasibility study would have to test both the science of the assessment and the practicality of implementation.

In response, the OECD has embarked on a feasibility study to explore the viability of developing an international Assessment of Higher Education Learning Outcomes (AHELO) that would measure learning outcomes in ways that are valid across cultures and languages, but also across the diversity of institutional settings and missions.

DESIGNING THE AHELO FEASIBILITY STUDY

Purpose

The purpose of the AHELO feasibility study is to assess whether it is possible to measure at the international level what undergraduate degree students know and can do. Ultimately, by developing different performance measures (summative performance measures as well as measures that capture the learning gain at an institution) and by identifying contextual factors that influence learning outcomes in different areas, AHELO will provide better information on teaching and learning quality than is currently available to higher education institutions, governments, and other stakeholders including students and employers.

The intent of the AHELO feasibility study is not to develop predetermined quality standards to be applied to all higher education institutions irrespective of their individual mission, nor to develop a single performance measure that would then be used for a uni-dimensional ranking of higher education institutions or countries. On the contrary, the feasibility study endorses the concept of a "multi-dimensional quality space," in which a set of quantifiable criteria for higher education quality establish the dimensions of the space. Within this concept of "quality space" higher education institutions, departments, and faculties can then be situated depending on the prevalence of different quality attributes. Students would then be able to choose programs and higher education institutions depending on the configuration of the quality attributes that are most relevant to them, rather than depend on ratings that combine quality attributes in predefined ways, which may not necessarily be the most relevant ones for either students or providers. It would also become possible to portray policy trajectories of higher education institutions and systems over time, as they change their position on the different dimensions of this "quality space," which in turn could become a powerful tool for public policy.

AHELO also recognizes the diverging views on how knowledge about learning outcomes in higher education institutions can and should be used. Some see such information primarily as a tool to reveal best practices, to identify shared problems among higher education institutions, and to encourage collaboration and lateral capacity building among research and teaching personnel. With this approach, emphasis would be placed on the relevance of performance information for the institutions themselves and on contextualizing performance data with other information on the learning environment in higher education institutions. Other views extend the purpose of learning outcome measures to support contestability of public services or market-mechanisms in the allocation of resources, e.g., by making comparative results of higher education institutions publicly available to facilitate choice.

The underlying motivation for AHELO is that this information could contribute to higher education institutions' knowledge of their teaching performance, and thereby provide a tool for development and improvement. As such, the AHELO central emphasis is on the improvement of teaching and learning and in providing higher education leaders with tools to empower them and foster positive change and enhanced learning.

Two Key Aims

Based on the recommendations that have resulted from the expert groups' meetings conducted in 2007 and given its purpose and underlying motivation, the AHELO feasibility study has been designed with two key aims:

- test the science of the assessment—whether it is possible to devise an assessment of higher education outcomes and collect contextual data that facilitates valid and reliable statements about the performance/effectiveness of learning in higher education institutions of very different types and in countries with different cultures and languages; and

- test the practicality of implementation—whether it is possible to motivate institutions and students to take part in such an assessment and develop appropriate institutional guidelines. In addition, the feasibility study will involve related work exploring other options for capturing indicators of higher education quality indirectly.

Four Strands of Work

Given the two key aims of the feasibility study, the focus of AHELO is on providing proof of concept by exploring different approaches, methodologies, and instruments that might eventually be envisaged as parts of a fully-fledged assessment. As a result, the feasibility study has been designed to cover four different strands of work. The approach chosen is not to develop comprehensive assessment instruments, but rather to explore how best to assess student performance in higher education institutions around the world.

FIGURE 1
AHELO Four Strands of Work

Source: Author's compilation.

A Cross-Discipline Strand: The Generic Skills Strand

The generic skills strand is an essential component of the feasibility study. Indeed, competencies in critical thinking, analytic reasoning, problem solving, or the generation of knowledge and the interaction between substantive and methodological expertise are widely viewed as critical for the success of individuals and of rising relevance in the information age.

It is therefore important for AHELO to measure these transversal higher-order competencies that are necessary for success in both academic and business contexts, not only cognitive knowledge. A key advantage is that such competencies are largely invariant across occupational and cultural contexts and could be applied across higher education institutions, departments, and faculties. Moreover, a focus on higher-order skills allows the coverage of a more diverse population representing the whole undergraduate student body, whereas the discipline strands will only cover a subset of students enrolled in given disciplines.

Two Discipline Strands: Economics and Engineering

Despite the fact that generic competencies underlie most facets of under-graduate education, institutions and learners invest most of their effort on discipline-specific knowledge and skills. The limitation of an approach entirely restricted to generic competencies is that it would not assess the kind of subject-matter competencies that most higher education departments or faculties would consider their primary work. There would thus be a risk that what is measured becomes too far removed from what goes on in faculties and departments and does not capture the competencies that are uniquely the province of higher education institutions.

For the purposes of the feasibility study, AHELO focuses on assessing learning in the fields of economics and civil engineering. This approach covers disciplines that are common among higher education institutions in OECD countries, are relatively divergent in terms of substance and context, are less likely to be influenced by unique cultural features, and reflect the dynamics of disciplinary change.

The economics and engineering assessments will help gauge the vi-ability of measuring discipline-specific skills, representing both scientific and social sciences domains, with the understanding that a fully-fledged AHELO main study could aim at expanding the number of disciplines covered over time.

The interest in assessing student performance in economics and en-gineering is to assess competencies that are not only fundamental, but also "above content," i.e., competencies indicating students' capacity to extrapolate from what they have learned and apply them in novel contexts unfamiliar to them. In this regard the AHELO approach follows the PISA dynamic model of lifelong learning in which new knowledge and skills necessary for successful adaptation to a changing world are continuously acquired throughout life. AHELO focuses on aspects that higher educa-tion students will need in the future and seeks to assess what they can do with what they have learned. The development of the assessment instru-ments is not to be constrained by the common denominator of program curricula which are very diverse in higher education, but instead examine students' ability to reflect and to apply their knowledge and experience to novel and real world tasks and challenges.

A Research-Based Strand: The Value-Added Measurement Strand

Should the performance assessment instruments demonstrate the feas-ibility of assessing student learning outcomes across different countries and institutions, AHELO will implement a value-added measurement strand to explore methodologies and approaches to capture value-added or the contribution of higher education institutions to students' outcomes, irrespective of students' incoming abilities.

Measuring the value-added in higher education, i.e., the learning gain that takes place during the higher education experience, imposes layers of complexity that, though theoretically well-understood, are still challenging in the context of large-scale assessments. Given the complexity of measuring marginal gain, the feasibility study will first scrutinize possible methods for capturing marginal learning outcomes that can be attributed to attendance at different higher education institutions, both from a conceptual/theoretical perspective and in terms of psychometric approaches. It will build upon similar work carried out at the school level by the OECD (2008) and review options for value-added measurement in higher education. Researchers will be invited to study potential data sources, methodologies, and psychometric evidence on the basis of datasets existing at the national level, with a view to providing guidance towards the development of a value-added measurement approach for a fully-fledged AHELO main study.

FIGURE 2
Substantive Focus of the Four AHELO Strands of Work

Generic Skills	Economics	Engineering	Value-Added Measurement Strand

• Using an adapted version of the Collegiate Learning Assessment to measure students' generic skills:
  • critical thinking,
  • analytical reasoning,
  • problem solving,
  • written communication.
	• The economics assessment measures economics learning outcomes.
	• The test assesses whether students close to graduating have the competencies required to apply their economics knowledge in effective professional practice.
		• The engineering assessment measures civil engineering learning outcomes.
		• The test assesses whether students close to graduating have the competencies required for effective professional practice as global engineers.
			• Developing a value-added measurement approach in the context of higher education by researching and exploring
			  • potential data sources,
			  • methodologies, and
			  • psychometric evidence.

Source: Author's compilation.

Adding a Contextual Dimension

While the main focus of the AHELO feasibility study is to gauge the feasibility of assessing learning outcomes, it is also necessary to assess the feasibility of gathering contextual variables that will be needed to interpret performance measures and help institutions understand the performance of their students and improve their teaching accordingly. The contextual variables will allow for disaggregation of assessment results by different kinds of institutional/program characteristics and student populations and provide information to help construct appropriate comparisons across institutions. Further, the contextual data collected through student, faculty, and institution instruments will be used to rehearse some psycho-metric analyses to identify relevant contextual variables for longer-term development and demonstrate the analytical potential of AHELO for institutional improvement.

This aspect of the feasibility study also requires ensuring that the contextual surveys developed are internationally valid and reflect the cultural context of the countries in which the AHELO feasibility study is implemented. The contextual information will be collected from existing documentation at the country level and through three surveys: (i) a student survey, (ii) a faculty survey, and (iii) an institution survey.

Institutional, Cultural and Linguistic Diversity

To test the scientific and practical feasibility of an assessment of higher education learning outcomes, the selection of participants requires a sufficiently broad coverage of institutional, cultural, and linguistic diversity. Therefore, the AHELO feasibility study has been designed to ensure the participation for each strand of work of a minimum of four or five countries that represent a diverse set of cultures and languages. Similarly, in each participating country, the selected higher education institutions should reflect the diversity of higher education at the national level. The required number of participants is large enough to assess the measurement properties of the various instruments and small enough to keep the process manageable.

As of 1 August 2011, 15 countries were involved in the AHELO feasibility study, representing a range of geographic, linguistic, and cultural backgrounds. Figure 3 indicates the countries involved and the strand(s) of work in which they participate.

IMPLEMENTING THE AHELO FEASIBILITY STUDY

Following the definition of the scope of the AHELO feasibility study which involves assessing, in countries with different cultures and languages, higher education student performance in different areas along with related contextual information, the feasibility study has been designed to unroll in several phases.

The first phase, conducted between January and June 2010, provided an initial proof of concept. In this phase, the goal was to develop provisional assessment frameworks and testing instruments suitable for an international context for each of the three strands of work (generic skills, economics and engineering) and to validate those tools through small-scale testing (cognitive labs and think aloud interviews) in participating countries in order to get a sense of cross-linguistic and cross-cultural validity.

FIGURE 3. AHELO Country-Specific Strands of Work

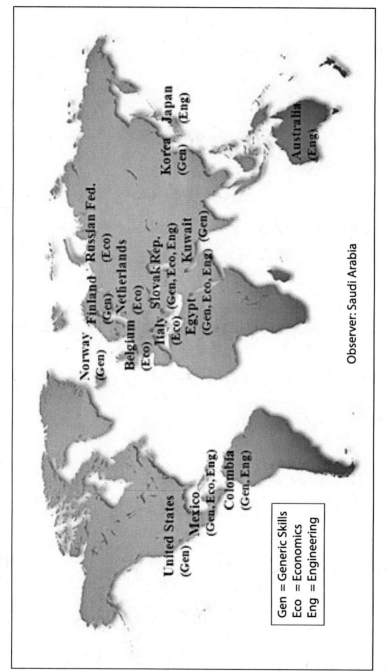

Gen = Generic Skills
Eco = Economics
Eng = Engineering

Observer: Saudi Arabia

Source: Author's compilation.

The second phase, scheduled from March 2011 to December 2012, consists of establishing the scientific and practical feasibility by focusing on the practical aspects of assessing students' learning outcomes. During this phase, the implementation of assessment instruments and contextual surveys in small groups of diverse higher education institutions will not only allow for the exploration of the best ways to implicate, involve, and motivate leaders, faculty, and students to take part in the testing, but also allow for the exploration of the relationships between context and learning outcomes and the factors leading to enhanced outcomes.

Should those two phases demonstrate the feasibility of assessing student learning outcomes in countries with different cultures and languages, the subsequent phase consists of developing a value-added measurement strand to explore methodologies and approaches to capture value-added or the contribution of higher education institutions to students' outcomes, irrespective of students' incoming abilities.

With the completion of the feasibility study, the information collected on student performance and the analysis of the results will help to assess whether a fully-fledged AHELO study could feasibly be taken forward from both scientific and practical standpoints. The outcomes of the AHELO feasibility study will guide the decision to be made by the OECD member countries of whether to launch a fully-fledged study in the longer term.

Selecting/Developing Assessment Instruments and Contextual Surveys

The Generic Skills Strand

When the international experts gathered in 2007 and reviewed the various initiatives taken in countries to assess higher education learning outcomes (Nusche 2007), they were impressed with the Collegiate Learning Assessment (CLA)[3] approach taken by the Council for Aid to Education in the United States. The CLA is an initiative designed to assess the quality of undergraduate education by directly measuring student learning outcomes. The CLA measures focus on skill sets that students will need as they graduate and enter the workforce, namely critical thinking, analytical reasoning, problem solving, and written communication. These skills are intertwined. Thus, the CLA measures are holistic: they require students to use these skills together to respond to tasks. All CLA measures are administered online, using open-ended prompts that require constructed responses. Each task also has an accompanying library of information which students are instructed to use in preparing their answers. Tasks often require students to marshal evidence from these diverse quantitative and qualitative sources and exercise judgment on their relevance. Tasks are appropriate for students across a wide range of undergraduate academic majors and general education programs.

After considerations by the AHELO Group of National Experts,[4] the development work for the generic skills strand has been contracted to the Council for Aid to Education. The development work consisted then in selecting and adapting two performance tasks for the assessment of generic skills, using the existing US Collegiate Learning Assessment performance-based assessment.

This portion of the study is well on its way to proving that an international tool to measure generic skills can indeed be developed. Two performance tasks, chosen by participating countries and their supporting materials, have been translated and culturally-adapted in different languages for a first set of participating countries. The same will be done for a group of latecomer countries. The tasks have also been put to the test with students from countries as different as Finland, Korea, Kuwait, Mexico, and Norway who have taken the CLA test in their own language and provided qualitative validation that this test of generic skills is relevant to them. This qualitative testing has also identified cultural issues that will have to be addressed in an AHELO main study (perceived reliability of information sources, students' familiarity with performance tasks). All in all, emerging insight suggests that measuring generic skills across languages, cultures, and types of institutions is feasible.

The Economics and Engineering Strands

The development work for the economics and engineering frameworks has been contracted to a consortium led by the Australian Council for Education Research (ACER). As with the generic skills strand, the discipline strands explore the feasibility of directly measuring learning outcomes in the selected disciplines and across different cultural and linguistic contexts. A prerequisite for this is to reach international agreement on expected learning outcomes in these contrasting disciplines to provide proof of concept that it is possible to develop domain assessment frameworks in the disciplines within the context of great curriculum diversity in higher education programs. Early progress on this front has been made using the Tuning approach, which has been successfully applied in Europe in many disciplinary fields and is now being piloted in other parts of the world (as discussed in Chapter 1).

On this basis, the consortium developed economics and engineering assessment frameworks intended to demonstrate that agreements on domain definition can be reached in two disciplinary fields as distinct as economics and engineering. Two international expert groups in engineering and economics were convened at the end of October 2010 in order to develop provisional frameworks and discuss actual test items. The resulting instruments have then been translated and adapted by participating countries in preparation for qualitative validation which started in late spring 2011 with focus groups of students at a range of institutions across each country. Both students and faculty were invited to provide feedback on the instruments.

In economics, the Educational Testing Service (ETS) has developed an economics instrument that tests the skills and knowledge of final-year bachelor's degree students. The AHELO Economics Expert Group reached agreement on a draft economics framework, based on the Tuning-AHELO document and the United Kingdom "QAA subject Benchmark Statement for Economics 2007." The Economics Expert Group reviewed draft test items, which were then mapped against the framework. The instrument comprises 45 multiple-choice questions and one constructed-response question to provide additional coverage.

In engineering, ACER has been working since mid-2010 with experts from Japan's National Institute for Educational Policy Research (NIER) and the EUropean and Global ENgineering Education (EUGENE) network to develop a framework and test for the field of engineering. The AHELO Engineering Expert Group approved the draft engineering framework based on the Tuning AHELO document. Experts also reviewed draft test units developed around a key civil engineering problem and included a range of multiple-choice and constructed-response questions.

In both discipline strands, the instruments have been translated and adapted by participating countries, and their qualitative validation has been conducted[5] with focus groups involving small numbers of students at a range of institutions within each country. Both students and faculty were invited to provide feedback on the instruments. Initial feedback from the focus groups suggests that the authentic scenario tasks that have been developed stimulate students' interest in the tasks and are engaging.

The Contextual Dimension

The ACER-led consortium also worked on the development of a framework and survey instruments for the contextual dimension in collaboration with the Centre for Higher Education Policy Studies (CHEPS) at the University of Twente (the Netherlands) and the Center for Postsecondary Research (CPR) at Indiana University (United States).

The design of the contextual framework and instruments commenced in 2011, building on 2008/2009 foundation work by the OECD, the AHELO GNE, and commissioned experts. Feedback from consultations in March/April 2011 with the AHELO Group of National Experts, National Project Managers and members of the Stakeholders Consultative Group provided a basis for item and instrument development, validation, small-scale testing, and delivery. Three context survey instruments have been developed: (i) a student context instrument, (ii) a faculty context instrument, and (iii) an institution context instrument. They will be used to identify factors that may help to explain differences in observed learning outcomes of the target population.

The student survey will be administered with the AHELO assessment instruments themselves. The intent is to collect information on student characteristics, such as demographics, experiences, and behaviours, such as exposure to specific teaching and learning practices, and self-reported outcomes, such as attainment of particular learning outcomes.

The faculty survey will be administered to all faculty members in the chosen department or to a random sample where departments are very large. Faculty preferably will be from department/schools of economics and engineering to provide comparability within institutions participating in these two discipline strands. The intent is to collect information on faculty characteristics, such as status of teaching, teaching modes, and unit/program characteristics, such as faculty perception of the status of undergraduate teaching.

The institution survey will be administered to institutional leaders in each participating institution. The intent is to collect information on institutional characteristics, such as retention, graduation outcomes, degree structure, and curriculum.

Initial Insights: What Have We Learned So Far?

As of 1 August 2011, the assessment frameworks and instruments for the three strands of work have been validated through small-scale testing and are currently being reviewed by expert groups and participating countries. The contextual dimension framework and the three survey instruments have been developed and are also being currently reviewed by participating countries. The implementation of the assessment instruments and contextual surveys is scheduled to start at the beginning of 2012. The field testing of those instruments and surveys will involve about one to two hundred students per institution and about ten higher education institutions per country. By the end of 2012, the information collected on student performance and the analysis of the results will help assess whether a fully-fledged AHELO study could be taken forward from both scientific and practical standpoints.

Although results from field testing are yet to come, the AHELO feasibility study has already proven that international agreement on learning outcomes to be measured can be reached in contrasted disciplines. The outcomes of the Tuning-AHELO project have already demonstrated that reaching agreements on expected learning outcomes can be achieved across diverse national and cultural settings, and in contrasted disciplines.

With respect to instrument development, the international co-operation on the cultural adaptation and translation of the CLA performance tasks has already provided valuable lessons on the instrument development and translation/adaptation processes. The initial adaptation of the performance tasks by participating countries was minimal (names, city/

government structures, date format), and the translation process went smoothly but brought some adaptation issues to light. Reports from cognitive labs in participating countries indicated that the performance tasks functioned as anticipated and can be considered valid, with slight modifications to help with understanding. As the performance tasks concept was not as familiar in some countries, there may be a need—in the event of an AHELO main study—to provide students with an example (mini-performance task and answer) prior to the actual test administration. Finally, the perceived confidence and trust in the sources of information provided to students as accompanying test materials also differed according to different national contexts, especially information from government sources depending on the extent of corruption. Further insights will be documented as the work deploys with the additional countries participating in this strand.

Likewise, the development of the economics and engineering instruments and their testing with focus groups of students for which results are currently being reviewed will provide further insights on the feasibility of developing internationally valid assessment instruments in the disciplines, as well as some initial data on the reliability of the measures.

There was a lot of uncertainty on the feasibility of getting academics from different countries to agree on what to measure in the disciplines and to agree on an assessment instrument. These doubts were part of the rationale for including an economics strand in the feasibility study, to gauge whether agreement was possible in a social science. One of the remarkable findings of the feasibility study to date is that it has, in fact, been easier than anyone thought to get economics experts to agree on what an AHELO should cover and measure. The reason for this is that AHELO goes above content knowledge and rather focuses on the "language" of economics.

In the long term, the outcomes of the AHELO feasibility study will inform the decision by OECD countries on whether to proceed and launch a fully-fledged AHELO main study. But, there are many more outcomes for the higher education sector in the short and longer term.

First and foremost, the launch of the AHELO feasibility study has raised awareness of quality data and advocated for its use in higher education. By implication, it also contributes to shifting emphasis from the research performance of institutions towards greater weight on their teaching mission. A longer term outcome in this respect will be to spur reflection—once learning outcomes are defined and measured—on their relevance to the needs of the workforce.

For participating institutions, a short term outcome will be to obtain objective information and benchmarks on their teaching and learning practices and on their outcomes. In the longer term, the conduct of the feasibility study will allow them to build capacity with assessing learning outcomes and using quality data for improving student performance.

They will also grasp the benefits of international exchange and discussions in this area.

CONCLUSIONS

Despite the fact that higher education has been expanding fast globally and the fact that it represents the key to success in the knowledge economy, there is still a significant gap of information about its quality. There are no tools available to compare the quality of teaching and learning in higher education institutions on an international scale. The few studies that do exist are nationally focused, while international university rankings are based on reputation and research performance and do not reflect the quality of teaching and learning, nor the diversity of institutions' missions and contexts.

The AHELO project is a unique and innovative attempt to fill this gap. It aims to develop criteria that will make it possible to evaluate the quality and relevance of what students learn in institutions around the world. For frontline higher education practitioners—from academics to institutional leaders—AHELO will provide valuable information on effective teaching strategies to enhance learning outcomes. Students, governments, and employers also stand to benefit. AHELO will shed light on whether the considerable resources invested in higher education are being used effectively and on the capacities of graduates to enter and succeed in the labour market.

The OECD has launched the AHELO feasibility study to determine by the end of 2012 whether an international assessment of higher education learning outcomes is scientifically and practically possible. The outcomes of the feasibility study will guide the decision to be made by the OECD member countries of whether to launch a fully-fledged study in the longer term.[6]

NOTES

[1] This paper summarizes a presentation of the OECD AHELO initiative delivered at the HEQCO conference *Measuring the Value of a Postsecondary Education*, organized in Toronto on 19-20 May 2011. The information presented in this chapter reflects the status of the AHELO project as of 1 August 2011.

[2] The expert meetings took place in Washington (28 April), Paris (5–6 July) and Seoul (26–27 October). The Washington meeting was primarily about the usefulness and desirability of an OECD international assessment of higher education learning outcomes, the Paris meeting focused on the conceptual possibility, and the Seoul meeting concerned how to move from possibility to feasibility. See www.oecd.org/edu/ahelo for the summary records and lists of participants from these meetings.

[3] For a sample Collegiate Learning Assessment performance task, please visit: http://starttest.com/CLA sample.

[4] The governance and the management of the AHELO feasibility study involve a wide range of experts from all over the world. This mix provides access to a network of world-class expertise through the various technical and advisory board members. For a description of the governance and the different groups involved in the AEHLO feasibility study, please visit: http://www.oecd.org/document/who's who.

[5] The qualitative validation is still underway for some countries who joined the AHELO feasibility study at a later stage.

[6] For more information about AHELO, visit the AHELO website at www.oecd.org/edu/ahelo.

References

Council for Aid to Education. n.d. CLA: Returning to Earning. Collegiate Learning Assessment. Accessed 4 July 2012. http://www.collegiatelearningassessment.org/.

Nusche, D. 2007. Assessment of Learning Outcomes in Higher Education: A Comparative Review of Selected Practices. Working Paper No. 15. Organisation for Economic Co-operation and Development. Accessed 3 June 2008. www.oecd.org/dataoecd/14/8/40257354.pdf.

Organisation for Economic Co-operation and Development. 2008. *Measuring Improvements in Learning Outcomes: Best Practices to Assess the Value-Added of Schools*. OECD Publishing.

SECTION III

BRINGING ABOUT CHANGE

8

AN INFLUENCE PATHWAY: LEADERSHIP TO CULTURE TO PRACTICE TO OUTCOMES

Lorne Whitehead

As with many fields, educational concepts are hierarchical, ranging from lower-level ideas that are simple to describe to higher-level ones that are progressively more important but difficult to study. At the most basic level, we study the learning of facts, concepts, attitudes, and skills. Although this level is basic in some ways, high quality assessment of it is difficult, problematic, expensive, and slow. The next level up is the study of educational experiences themselves—the situations, activities, and influences that are intended to improve student learning. An impressive and rapidly growing body of academic literature reports very promising research results at this level. Unfortunately, however, this new knowledge is not being adopted nearly as widely as experts feel is warranted.

In order to study the reasons behind this lack of adoption, we may consider yet a higher level, which some call *culture*—the confluence of behaviours, expectations, beliefs, and attitudes that influence the decision-making of teachers. Many feel that although academic culture is beneficial in general, it currently does not sufficiently encourage the adoption of improved educational methods. In considering how to overcome this problem, we can look to the highest level of the hierarchy—the actions of the university leaders and leadership groups that influence academic culture. We all know that universities face many constraints, but a growing number of experts believe university leaders can develop programs and policies that will help catalyze culture enhancements that, in turn, support both better education and academic excellence.

These ideas are discussed here in reference to initiatives at the University of British Columbia and the Carnegie Foundation for the Advancement of Teaching.

Measuring the Value of a Postsecondary Education, ed. K. Norrie and M.C. Lennon. Montreal and Kingston: Queen's Policy Studies Series, McGill-Queen's University Press. © 2013 All rights reserved.

INTRODUCTION

Discussions about improvement of education inevitably lead to concerns about the definition and measurement of education quality. For this reason, it may be helpful to ask ourselves a basic question—why should we measure quality? Two quite different answers come to mind. On one hand, quality measures can provide a way of ensuring that "customers" receive "fair value." On the other hand, they can be used to guide the improvement of quality. These two views are not contradictory, and both have value. But, they affect people quite differently. The latter view, emphasizing improvement, is generally more respectful and motivational; and it is this view that drives most of the ideas presented here.

Part of the widespread appeal of this view may come from the simple fact that we have all had poor educational experiences at some time. Furthermore, based on a great deal of recent research, there is solid evidence that improvements are possible within existing resource constraints. The question, of course, is how we can take advantage of such sentiments to make significant progress. It is in this area that we still face significant challenges.

Returning to the measurement of quality, it may be helpful to look at certain commonplace opinions. For example, business managers often say, "If we do not measure quality, it will not improve." This opinion is supported by strong correlational evidence; there are numerous examples of situations where introduction of the measurement of quality was followed by significant quality improvement.

However, there is a danger here. Some have stretched this idea by saying, "If we *do* measure quality, it *will* improve." Of course that is a logical error. It would be more correct to conclude, "In order to improve quality, one of the things we should do is measure it."

So, it is reasonable and understandable to conclude that measuring the quality of education will be an important contributor to the process of improving it. It may not be guaranteed to work, but at least it cannot hurt. Or can it? This is actually a critical question that raises a significant concern. Unfortunately, harm can arise if quality is measured poorly. For example, if we measure and then optimize the wrong thing, the overall quality could quite possibly decrease. And unfortunately, in education, the easiest things to measure are seldom the most important. The reality is that measurement of education quality, while critically important, is also problematic and controversial.

This should not be surprising, considering the great complexity of the task. After all, education concerns human behaviour, which is exceedingly complex. Furthermore, human organizations such as universities are very complex entities. Worse yet, consider that human understanding itself is, almost by definition, near the limit of human understanding. Finally, consider that we seek to go even further by considering the process of *development* of human understanding! From this perspective, it is difficult to imagine a more daunting task than that of improving higher education. There is no wonder that disagreement exists about how to do so.

The aim of this chapter is to explore some of this complexity and to try to make it more amenable to clear discussion. It is hoped that this will help us to understand and appreciate the diversity of views about improving education and to develop a conciliatory approach for streamlining the process. The discussion will be illustrated by examples of initiatives and experiments underway at the University of British Columbia and Carnegie Foundation for the Advancement of Teaching.

DIFFICULTIES WITH MEASUREMENT

Measurement can be problematic in any field. Common concerns include:

- various forms of measurement error;
- perturbation of the system being measured, by the act of measurement;
- the natural tendency to emphasize the easily measured rather than the most important;
- inadvertently underemphasizing the importance of diversity and complexity;
- time delays inherent in the measurement process;
- the cost and effort required in measurement; and
- sometimes, measurement just *feels* wrong.

The last item in this list may seem out of place. But, it matters a great deal, since the way people feel about any project has a profound impact on its success. The following analogy may help to reinforce this point: Imagine you live in a country in which a benevolent government strives to improve parenting by introducing a program of parental assessment. The plan is that once a year every home will be visited by a government official who interviews the parents, their children, and their neighbours, and based on these interviews provides each home with a "parenting score" that appears in the newspapers. How does that idea sound to you? I have yet to meet anyone who does not instantly dislike this idea, even before they think about it. Then, after thinking it over, most still feel it is a very bad idea and can justify their view with sound arguments. This demonstrates an important point—often the first gut reaction that people have is correct. So it is important to listen to and respect these initial feelings. When possible, our plans for progress should resonate well with people from all perspectives, including generating a positive initial emotional reaction.

HIERARCHY OF FACTORS RELATED TO LEARNING

To further explore the connection between learning and measurement, it will be helpful here to classify systems of higher education into four basic levels as depicted by Figure 1 below:

FIGURE 1
Diagram Depicting Four Levels of Influence in Higher Education

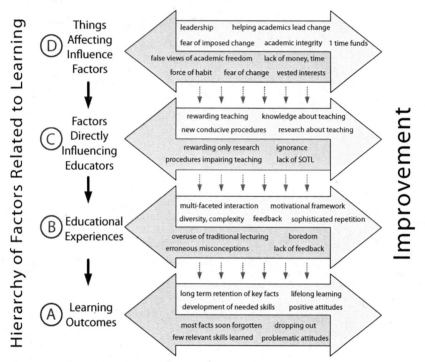

Source: Author's compilation.

At the base of this hierarchy, Level A is the realm of learning outcomes. It includes the benefits we hope our students will obtain from education. In the figure items in the upper areas are examples of positive, desirable things; and those in the lower areas shaded darker gray are examples of things that are generally known to be undesirable. Overall, Level A could be called "Learning."

The next level up is Level B, which contains the educational experience we help our students to have, which in turn helps them to achieve desired educational outcomes. This level could be labelled "Teaching," but only if we use it in the broadest sense of the word to include guidance and encouragement in a wide range of educational experiences.

Next is Level C, which includes the factors that influence the behaviours of teachers. These are all kinds of factors that teachers encounter in their environment, such as policies to which they must adhere, attitudes of their colleagues, time constraints, factors for consideration in promotion and tenure, training experience, etc. In other words, this level consists of all of the things that teachers experience that in turn influence their teaching behaviour. This level could be labelled "Culture." Although people are often largely unaware of the culture in which they find themselves, they are nevertheless strongly influenced by it. Some would prefer not to think much about culture because it can be difficult to describe and define, but it would be wrong to ignore it because it has an immense impact on the success of our educational institutions.

Expanding on that point, most experts agree there are better ways to provide improved educational experiences for our students, which are both practical and affordable. Unfortunately, implementation of these ideas is not happening at nearly the rate that is felt to be both needed and readily achievable. When experts consider the reason for such difficulties, they inevitably loop back to the issue of culture. There are concrete, readily apparent, cultural factors that impede the adoption of improved educational practice.

This raises an interesting question: Is it possible to enhance the culture found within an existing organization? Many believe this is not possible, citing examples in which efforts to change culture have at best succeeded only temporarily. However, despite such counter-examples, sociologists tell us that it *is* possible to enhance cultures in ways that overcome known problems—numerous examples have been documented.[1] Perhaps now is a good time for higher education to follow suit.

Returning to the above figure, the highest realm is Level D, which includes all of the factors that can influence the culture of educational enterprises. This could be labelled "Leadership." While it may be possible for the leaders of an organization to enhance its culture, it is rarely easy. For example, some might hope that a carefully worded message from a university president could have a big impact on a university's culture—but generally it will not. The fact is that few faculty members would read such a message and of those that did, most would ignore it and even if not, they would rapidly forget it. This is human nature, but this does not mean that culture cannot be enhanced—it just suggests that it will require a more significant, sustained, and optimized effort. Universities are especially interesting places because they experience several different forms of leadership, ranging from faculty members on influential committees to external groups, such as funding agencies and accreditation bodies. And of course the president, vice presidents, deans, and department heads can have a huge influence. So, there is a complex sea of influences that have the potential to enhance academic culture.

It is important to emphasize that in this diagram there is an upward flow of information as well as a downward pathway of influence. That is, the activities at Level D influence the factors in Level C. These in turn have the ability to influence the provision of educational experiences at Level B. And those experiences profoundly influence the outcomes at Level A. In other words, there is a long and complex pathway leading from the actions at Level D to the outcomes that matter in Level A. Although this is an indirect influence pathway, it can offer leaders tremendous leverage. At Level D we have the potential to cause profound improvement if this influence pathway can be optimized.

From this perspective, it is now helpful to consider, at all four levels, the need for measurement in education.

Beginning at the base Level A, clearly we carry out measurement all the time. Student grades are the obvious example, but possibly also the least useful from the perspective of guiding improvement. That is because grades tell us little about what ultimately matters most, which is the long term retention of knowledge, skills, and attitudes. Additional assessment efforts may include surveys of alumni and their employers, although typically these are quite general. Recently, more sophisticated tools have been developed for gauging student understanding both in real time and over extended periods. This is critically important—after all, this is where "the rubber meets that road." But, unfortunately, measurement at Level A has a major challenge from the perspective of guiding improvement of teaching—if it is done well, it is quite slow and expensive.

Consider now measurement at Level B, the realm of educational experiences. Here we study what our students are experiencing. Student surveys can study this, and we can directly ask our teachers what they are doing in the classroom. Peer review of teaching, when done well, can also be very helpful. Overall, it is fairly practical to establish the experiences that are actually happening. When done well, this can provide a feedback loop with a shorter response than is possible at Level A. Of course it is Level A that really matters, but we have the encouraging results of considerable research about improved teaching techniques that may enable us to make informed predictions about Level A results on the basis of Level B observations.

Measurement at Level C, the realm of culture, is no less important; but at first glance it appears to be difficult because the concept of culture seems vague. But, it can be made reasonably concrete by considering specific elements of culture that are known to drive changes in educational behaviour. These could include:

- attitudes about educational professionalism and the responsibilities of teachers,
- confidence in fair rewards for excellence in teaching, and
- the perception of policies and procedures about teaching and learning.

It is true that such factors are challenging to define and measure well, but sociologists and psychologists do routinely carry out excellent work in these areas. Even though individual attitudes may be highly subjective, they have linked such views with likely behaviour; and thus, it is possible to link measurements at Level C to likely future outcomes at level B. This provides an even faster effective feedback loop.

While it is even more indirect, measurement at Level C has the advantage of being immediately responsive to leadership action. Examples of things that can be fairly efficiently studied are:

- review of terms of engagement of key academic committees,
- surveying of the beliefs and attitudes of members of such committees, and
- interviews with key university leaders.

Overall, it is important to realize that measurement, for the purpose of guiding improvement, will probably be quite ineffective if constrained to only one or two levels. But, by engaging in prudent measurement at all four levels, it should be possible to obtain valuable information that can guide significant evidence-informed improvement.

Harmful Misunderstandings and Possible Ways to Overcome Them

It is unfortunate that the complexity of teaching and learning can exacerbate misunderstandings that may imperil measurement-informed improvement. In this regard two extreme viewpoints seem to have emerged concerning measurement in education. One sees measurement-based approaches as being overly simplistic and therefore potentially harmful (Regehr 2010, 31-39). The other dismisses such concerns as the avoidance of accountability (Slavin 2008, 5-14). Needless to say, these incompatible views can slow progress because progress in a human endeavour, such as this, is highly dependent on co-operation and mutual respect. Furthermore, emotional rhetoric promoting such views can attract "converts" away from the more reasonable middle ground. Surely, we need more people to believe that although measurement, like any valuable tool, can cause harm if used improperly, this does not imply that we should avoid it. We should pursue, with care, the benefits that are achievable through its proper use.

This raises the questions of whether certain approaches to measurement-informed improvement of teaching and learning could be helpful in strengthening this middle ground. To make this more specific, it may be helpful to consider two quite different initiatives aimed at building consensus while also significantly improving teaching and learning.

The first is the Carl Wieman Science Education Initiative that is underway both at the University of British Columbia and the University of Colorado Boulder (Deslauriers, Schelew and Wieman 2011, 862-864; Wieman 2007; Wieman, Perkins and Gilbert 2010). Although rarely described as such, it is an experimental attempt to enhance the culture of a few selected academic departments in order to promote improved teaching and learning. The initiative encourages simple but important changes in the ways that certain things are done within academic departments, in part by providing additional resources (over a five to seven year period) to departments that apply and are selected to participate. An example of the intended changes include shifting the "ownership" of key academic courses from a series of individuals to the department as a whole and ensuring that investments made in course improvement can provide benefits even after change of responsibilities of the individual professors involved. In any selected department, the initiative proceeds in the following steps:

- Identify the people in the department who are most responsible for educational quality.
- Offer them temporary new resources that will be awarded on a competitive basis.
- These champions consider carefully educational outcomes and their measurement.
- Under their direction and with the help of the new resources, work on improvement begins.
- Inevitably the work identifies problems within courses, which motivates improvement.
- Those responsible are credited with these successes, encouraging the work to expand.
- The culture enhancements within the department are solidified through this process.

It is hoped that even after the temporary new sources end, these new habits will persist. This initiative has been underway for about four years, and all of these points have been observed but we have not yet been underway long enough to verify that the observed culture change will persist after the period of enhanced resources. However, based on early indications, we are cautiously optimistic.

A second example is a network program organized by the Carnegie Foundation for the Advancement of Teaching. It employs a process of building quality through Networked Improvement Communities (Bryk, Gomez and Grunow 2011; Mehta, Gomez and Bryk 2010, 27-36). In this case the steps are:

- A specific well-defined educational problem is selected for collaborative work.

- A group of institutions agree to collaborate on it.
- Each sends a diverse team of members to regular meetings to discuss the problem.
- Various member organizations try various improvement initiatives and share results.
- They share experiences that are not identical, which are viewed as natural experiments.
- By allowing significant independence in research, enthusiasm and creativity will grow.

In this limited space, it is not possible to fully describe these initiatives. They are mentioned here as two very different examples that share the common advantage of minimizing the conflict between views about measurement. In both cases a key characteristic is that the intended enhancements of culture are achieved not through external pressure, but through respectful, open, and internal conversations. Yes, people are changing their attitudes and behaviours, but they are doing so because they want to, and they want to because they have discovered for themselves a more effective framework within which to pursue their own goals. Recently, a number of universities, including UBC, have become involved in discussions centred at the Carnegie Foundation for the Advancement of Teaching in Palo Alto, and plans are under consideration for an initiative that would combine some aspects of these methods. The intent is to apply the concept and methodology of the Networked Improvement Community and select as a goal the appropriate enhancement of academic culture in order to accelerate the rate of adoption of improved methods of teaching in higher education.

Conclusion

The improvement of education can be characterized as a multi-level hierarchy of related factors, and the concept of quality measurement applies at all levels. Appropriate measurement, at the levels of culture, educational methods, and educational outcomes can, in combination, provide considerable guidance to educational improvement initiatives. However, this will only be possible if the measurement processes are appropriately respectful and inclusive of the people involved at all levels of the education process. Preliminary attempts to make progress in this manner are encouraging, and we hope they will form the foundation for considerable future improvement.

Note

[1] An excellent account of the impact of this approach in health care improvement can be found in Berwick (2008).

REFERENCES

Berwick, B. 2008. The Science of Improvement. *The Journal of the American Medical Association* 299 (10): 1182-1184.

Bryk, A., L. Gomez, and A. Grunow. 2011. Getting Ideas into Action: Building Networked Improvement Communities in Education. Stanford: Carnegie Foundation for the Advancement of Teaching.

Deslauriers, L., E. Schelew, and C. Wieman. 2011. Improved Learning in a Large-Enrollment Physics Class. *Science* 332 (6031): 862-864.

Mehta, J., L. Gomez, and A. Bryk. 2010. Schooling as a Knowledge Profession. *Education Week* 30 (26): 27-36.

Regehr, G. 2010. It's NOT Rocket Science: Rethinking Our Metaphors for Research in Health Professions Education. *Medical Education* 44 (1): 31-39.

Slavin, R. 2008. Perspectives on Evidence-Based Research in Education—What Works? Issues in Synthesizing Educational Program Evaluations. *Education Research* 37 (1): 5-14.

Wieman, C. 2007. Why Not Try a Scientific Approach to Science Education? *Change: The Magazine of Higher Learning* 39 (5): 9-15.

Wieman, C., K. Perkins, and S. Gilbert. 2010. Transforming Science Education at Large Research Universities: A Case Study in Progress. *Change: The Magazine of Higher Learning* 42 (2): 7-14.

9

GAUGING IMPACT: CONNECTING STUDENT ASSESSMENT-AS-LEARNING WITH PROGRAMS AND INSTITUTIONAL ASSESSMENT

Jeana M. Abromeit

I was honored to speak at a recent HEQCO conference and to have Alverno College identified in the program as one of the innovators in articulating student learning outcomes and measuring student accomplishment of those outcomes. Being with many leaders from the Ontario postsecondary sector provided me and other attendees with insights about the high quality work already being done in the province of Ontario.

Alverno College is a four-year, independent, Catholic liberal arts college for women, founded by the School Sisters of St. Francis in 1887 ("Time line of Alverno" 2009). In 1973, Alverno implemented an outcomes-based curriculum as a requirement for all students. Graduation requirements were (and are) based on the demonstration of outcomes rather than distribution requirements. Alverno now has several masters' programs, all of which are co-ed. Enrolment is about 2,100 undergraduates and more than 500 graduate students.

What distinguishes Alverno College from other academic institutions is its ground-breaking innovations for educating students—its creation of the first outcomes-based curriculum in higher education, its performance-based assessments, its very early recognition of the power of experiential learning as a way of fostering deep learning, its formation of a coherent developmental curriculum, and its student-centred culture where student learning is at the heart of the college's mission. Beginning in the 1970s, faculty at Alverno College created an outcomes-based approach to learning that transformed our institution and resulted in national and international recognition for our contributions to higher education, especially

Measuring the Value of a Postsecondary Education, ed. K. Norrie and M.C. Lennon. Montreal and Kingston: Queen's Policy Studies Series, McGill-Queen's University Press. © 2013 All rights reserved.

our work on student learning outcomes, student assessment as learning, and accountability of higher education. For example, Alverno College was a 1996 recipient of the John D. and Catherine T. MacArthur Foundation's one-time award to six innovative liberal arts colleges (Arenson 1996). In 1994, Alverno earned TIAA-CREF's prestigious Hesburgh Award, which recognizes exceptional faculty development programs designed to enhance undergraduate teaching, learning, and student achievement.

Alverno College's approaches have been validated in several external studies. For recent examples, Alverno was included in an examination of highly successful institutions for its high graduation rates and student demographics (Kuh et al. 2010) and for its effectiveness in developing students' abilities in moral and civic responsibility (Colby et al. 2010). In addition, many experts in the field have espoused Alverno's principles and practices for advancing student learning, with more recent ones including Maki (2010) and Banta, Black and Jones (2009). Since 1975, through our Institute for Educational Outreach, several thousand educators representing more than 140 institutions in the United States and abroad have come to our campus to attend workshops and institutes to learn about our ability-based curriculum and performance assessment methods, as well as to gain insight from our research on a variety of issues pertaining to women and education. In addition, our faculty have provided consultation services to hundreds of institutions in the United States and around the world.

For nearly 40 years, the Alverno College faculty have been developing and implementing a curriculum centred on student learning outcomes (i.e., ability-based education). In this chapter, I discuss Alverno College's historical context leading to the development of outcomes and how we addressed challenging questions pertaining to student learning and continuous improvement. I offer our experience not as a model for other institutions, but rather as a jumping-off place for meaningful conversation and learning. To all of these challenging questions and others we have not yet imagined, there will be more than one kind of answer.

History of Outcomes and Assessment at Alverno College

Alverno's outcomes-based approach to education was the result of an exploration by the college's faculty that began in the late 1960s when serious questions were emerging nationwide about the meaning and value of college and liberal education.[1] Simultaneously, faculty at Alverno were re-examining the institution's mission as a small, urban, liberal arts college for women.

Joel Read, a School Sister of St. Francis and president of the College, was instrumental in providing the leadership that instigated the work that led to so many innovations, such as instituting the ability-based, assessment-as-learning approach to learning; initiating one of the first internship programs in the country (which was identified by the college in 1971 as the *Off-Campus Experiential Learning program)*; and in 1977 launching its Weekend College (the first of its kind in Wisconsin), now known as Alverno on the Weekend, to reach out to working women so they could earn their degrees.[2]

Early in the 1970–1971 academic year, President Read asked the academic departments a set of questions (Alverno College Faculty 1975; 1989; 1994, 8):

- What kinds of questions are being asked by professionals in your field that relate to the validity of your discipline in a total college program?
- What is your department's position on these?
- How are you dealing with these problems in your general education courses, and in the work for a major in your field?
- What are you teaching that is so important that students cannot afford to pass up courses in your department?

For the rest of that year, the faculty met regularly to hear each department's responses to the questions. Through these sessions, faculty began to notice some commonalities in the departments' responses, which prompted the emergence of a critically important question: "What are the outcomes for the student, rather than the input by the faculty?"(Alverno College Faculty 1975; 2005, *vi*). In retrospect, it is very interesting that the question our faculty posed in early 1971 reflects much of the recent emphasis in higher education and accrediting bodies on how students learn and what we expect students to know and be able to do by virtue of their learning experiences, rather than just the means of instruction.

More specific questions followed:

- How do you want your students to be able to think as a result of studying your discipline?
- What do you want your students to be able to do as a result of studying your discipline?

As faculty addressed these questions and began to see some overarching patterns in departmental responses, a task force volunteered to synthesize and summarize emerging commonalities. In May 1971, this process resulted in the identification of four institution-wide learning outcomes:

- communication,
- problem solving,
- valuing, and
- involvement.

In 1971–1972, under the leadership of the Curriculum Committee (which included administration, faculty, and students) and with input from the faculty's own pedagogical practice and professional expertise, as well as from an extensive review of the literature, the four outcomes were expanded to eight institution-wide student learning outcomes or *abilities* that, taken together, would result from a successful liberal education. Today's eight abilities have very similar (but not identical) names to those that were articulated in 1971–1972. Our current abilities are:

1.   communication,
2.   analysis,
3.   problem solving,
4.   valuing in decision-making,
5.   social interaction,
6.   developing a global perspective,
7.   effective citizenship, and
8.   aesthetic engagement.

We have continually revised and refined a curriculum that requires all students to demonstrate these core abilities in the context of their study across various disciplines. Early on, we recognized that abilities must be carefully identified and compared to what contemporary life requires. Therefore, it should not be surprising that the meanings of the abilities would be re-examined by faculty as needed. To underscore this point, since 1973, re-conceptualizations of one or more of the abilities have occurred 13 times, as revealed in the copyright dates of one of our publications that summarizes each ability ("Ability-Based Learning Program" 1973; 1980; 1983; 1985; 1988; 1991; 1992; 1993; 1994; 1996; 2000; 2002; 2005; 2010).

In our continual efforts to examine and strengthen student learning, we recognized that articulating learning outcomes was only the beginning and that our new curricular approach had implications at every level of practice. This realization led us to:

•   identify key underlying principles,
•   define relationships among outcomes—creating a coherent curriculum, and
•   develop institutional and program assessment measures.

KEY UNDERLYING PRINCIPLES

As we continued to develop our new approach to learning, assessment, and teaching, we recognized the importance of critically evaluating the effectiveness of our approach and the accuracy of our assumptions about student learning. How will we know how students are doing in demonstrating the abilities? How will we judge our performance at the course level, program level, and institution level? In answering these questions, we identified a type of assessment—student assessment-as-learning—with several key principles.

PRINCIPLE: EDUCATION GOES BEYOND KNOWING TO BEING ABLE TO DO WHAT ONE KNOWS

This principle grew organically out of the faculty's commitment to an ability-based curriculum. We recognized that we needed to design forms of evaluation/assessment that correspond to the kinds of abilities we wanted students to develop. Knowledge and its application are inseparable; students should be able to do something with what they know. This meant that the education of an individual, understood in terms of developing ability involving the use of one's knowledge, cannot be adequately plumbed by traditional testing. One-dimensional probes into a student's mine of stored information do not begin to get at how she learns or what she can do (Alverno College Faculty 1979; 1994, 4).

Our concept of assessment-as-learning, which incorporated performance-based assessment, evolved from a central tenet that is now held by accrediting bodies and many educators: what *learners achieve*—not what *teachers provide*—is at the centre of the educational enterprise. In the last few decades, legislators, parents, and educators at every level are asking: What can graduates do as a result of their education?

PRINCIPLE: ABILITIES NEED TO BE DEFINED IN A WAY THAT OUR TEACHING OF THEM CAN BE DEVELOPMENTAL

By 1973, each of the eight outcomes/abilities was defined in six sequenced levels of development. This is another example of some very early and innovative thinking. This principle is now common-place in learning frameworks world-wide.

If students are to develop the abilities, the abilities need to be defined in a way that our teaching of them can be pedagogically developmental. Levels 1–4 correspond to general education and to beginning and intermediate levels in the major and minor areas of study; levels 5–6 correspond to advanced-level, specialized work in the major and minor areas. Following is an example of a brief description of the developmental levels that members of the analysis ability department have articulated for that ability (Ability-Based Learning Program 1973; 2010, 2).

ANALYSIS ABILITY

Beginning Levels

Observes individual parts of phenomena and their relationships to one another:

- Level 1—observes accurately, and
- Level 2—draws reasonable inferences from observations.

Intermediate Levels

Uses disciplinary concepts and frameworks with growing understanding:

- Level 3—perceives and makes relationships, and
- Level 4—analyzes structure and organization.

Advanced Levels

Consciously and purposefully applies disciplinary frameworks to analyze complex phenomena:

- Level 5—refines understanding of frameworks and identifies criteria for determining what frameworks are suitable for explaining a phenomenon, and
- Level 6—applies frameworks from major and minor discipline independently to analyze complex issues.

PRINCIPLE: EDUCATORS ARE RESPONSIBLE FOR MAKING LEARNING MORE AVAILABLE BY ARTICULATING OUTCOMES AND MAKING THEM PUBLIC

Outcomes are made accessible in several ways. They are defined in multiple Alverno publications. In addition, each course syllabus includes the student learning outcomes at the course level as well as the developmental level(s) of the abilities that are relevant to the course. Syllabi for advanced level courses include the relevant student learning outcomes at the program/major level. Further, when students receive an assessment prompt, it includes the student learning outcomes and developmental level(s) of the abilities that are relevant to the particular assessment, as well as the criteria for a satisfactory performance. Making the outcomes and criteria public and explicit help students understand the basis of our actions and expectations.

Students learn and demonstrate abilities over time (developmentally) in the contexts of courses across general education, disciplines, and professions, rather than in separate courses. Because they demonstrate each ability in multiple settings and across disciplines through performance assessments (assessment-as-learning), they learn to use their developing abilities as *metacognitive strategies* across settings, rather than in *just a few situations*. We have found that the process of making student learning outcomes explicit and public to students fosters metacognitive awareness.

By articulating student learning outcomes for ourselves as educators, we create curricular coherence within the diversity of our disciplines and professions, rather than fragmentation or uniformity. In addition, specifying the student learning outcomes is a critical step in holding ourselves accountable to each other, students, and numerous other stakeholders.

Relationships Among Outcomes—Creating a Coherent Curriculum

We specify learning outcomes at three levels: institution wide, program, and course. The institution-wide outcomes are integrated into the program outcomes, one or more program outcomes are directly linked to the course (and course outcomes), and each assessment of the individual student's learning is tied to one or more course outcomes. Thus, assessment at Alverno moves out in concentric circles from the individual student's learning environment to courses, to academic programs, to an institution-wide context. Refer to Appendix 1, Relationships among Outcomes, for a chart that depicts an example of how the levels of the curriculum are related.

The example in Appendix 1 illustrates relationships between a single course (Introduction to Social Science) and the whole sociology program curriculum by presenting a cross-sectional view of our system. We show links between the Alverno College mission, the eight abilities, sociology's program outcomes, outcomes for the specific course, and an example of an assessment and criteria for a student's performance. The arrows in the example trace the connections across the curriculum.

At each of these levels, assessment provides student performance data to be used for the improvement and evaluation of learning. Performance data are used by the student for ongoing learning; by the instructor for reflection on his/her teaching and improvement of the course or assessments; by members of the academic department for program assessment; by staff and administrators for deliberation on the curriculum and co-curriculum; and eventually, by wider publics to critically examine student learning outcomes (Loacker and Rogers 2005).

How did we go about creating this coherent curriculum? There are many ways to create a coherent curriculum (e.g., start with program outcomes and then inductively create institutional outcomes). In Alverno's case, faculty created the institution-wide abilities first. Then each discipline department was required to create the student learning outcomes for each of its programs—that is, to create a *set of statements that describe what a student in a particular major can do with what she knows by the time she graduates, as a result of a set of learning experiences.*

In my consultation work, I have discovered that some faculty find it helpful to begin the process by imagining what the "ideal" majors (students) should know and be able to do by the end of the program. Regardless of the strategy that is used to start the department conversation about program outcomes, the faculty need to consider essential disciplinary knowledge, tools of inquiry, skills, dispositions, and values that they would expect their majors to have by the time they graduate. In addition to the nature of the discipline, other considerations include the institution's mission, professional requirements, needs of society, aspirations of learners, and accreditation standards.

In the social science department, we used the abilities as a backbone for defining our program and articulating sociological themes and content that we would expect sociology graduates to know and be able to do. After the program outcomes were developed, members of the department mapped out the relationships between the program outcomes and the abilities. This process made it possible for department members to see the extent to which the abilities were reflected in the program outcomes and to make adjustments where we deemed necessary.

The abilities are not add-ons. The faculty take collective responsibility for the curriculum by designing their courses in ways that integrate their disciplines with the abilities most germane to their disciplines. In other words, not all abilities are in each program. For example, programs in the social science department (i.e., sociology, political science, global studies, and community leadership) do not teach for the ability of aesthetic engagement; students who are majoring in our programs learn this ability in their arts and humanities general education courses (and possibly in their minor field of study). In contrast, all of our programs in social science teach for the ability of developing a global perspective because we have agreed that learning our disciplines necessarily involves learning the aspects of this ability.

The next step the social science faculty took in creating a coherent curriculum was formulating the outcomes for each course. The instructor created the course outcomes and presented them to the rest of the department members for further dialogue and refinement. Individual faculty designed some of the performance assessments, with the criteria directly related to particular course outcomes. There were other assessments that were developed collaboratively by a few faculty.

A crucially important activity in creating a coherent curriculum is developing an assessment plan for the program, using a collaborative process involving meaningful conversations among department members about the curriculum. There are various formats for assessment plans. Alverno's approach consists of one or two documents (often in chart form) that show: (i) how each program outcome integrates some/all of the institutional outcomes; (ii) how each required course in the program integrates some/all of the program outcomes and, if applicable and necessary, how each course integrates specified external bodies' standards; and (iii) how the course outcomes for each required course are assessed in the course (i.e., a brief description of the key assessments for each course).

There are several benefits of creating an assessment plan, particularly if faculty use a collaborative approach in which they share their descriptions of course outcomes and assessments. The process is likely to elicit many important discoveries about teaching, student learning, assessment, and how the whole curriculum fits together. If the faculty members know their program's entire curriculum, they can require that students apply what they have learned previously and faculty can assist them to do so. This is a huge pay off for having discussions about the program. The assessment plan itself should permit department members to see the extent to which the program outcomes are integrated in courses. The plan might also provide insight into additional courses, program outcomes, course outcomes, or assessments that are needed (or current aspects of the curriculum that are not needed). Faculty could also analyze the extent to which the curriculum is developmental, which might prompt a review of the prerequisite courses. In a nutshell, a good assessment plan provides a foundation for productive program evaluation—it allows faculty to analyze the program from several vantage points and to ask the questions that are most important to them about their programs and student learning.

Today, most universities and colleges have student learning outcomes at the institutional level and/or the program level, although some might not adequately depict expectations regarding what a student can do with what she or he knows as a result of a set of learning experiences. Student learning outcomes at the course level are far less common and, when they exist, might not be systematically aligned with the program and/or institutional outcomes. It is even rarer to find systematic, intentional linkages between the program/institutional outcomes and the assessments in the courses.

INSTITUTIONAL AND PROGRAM ASSESSMENT

If students are to develop their abilities, teaching and assessment processes need to be designed in ways that foster learning and most effectively evaluate whether students are learning what is expected in the outcomes.

One of the key approaches we use is to integrate the abilities into the heart of our teaching within and across disciplines. Our design of courses requires that students develop and demonstrate abilities in the context of academic and professional disciplines.

As Loacker and Rogers (2005, 2) show, some of the implications of the new approach pertained to student learning and program/institutional assessment:

- How will we know how well we are doing as students, as instructors, as departments, as programs, as an institution?
- Can we design our program so that student, program, and institutional assessment ... can be connected together by the same collection of evidence?
- In our efforts to determine our effectiveness as an institution, can we assure a process that would still foreground each student's learning?

One of the solutions turned out to be a kind of assessment with several key principles. *Assessment would be based on explicit public outcomes with generic criteria contextualized into content specific criteria.* For each developmental level of each ability, we developed generic criteria for the ability being performed. These criteria are not tied to specific courses. Rather, they provide the faculty with a standard for (i) judging and certifying that the student has demonstrated the ability, and (ii) creating more explicit performance criteria in language appropriate to the context of specific courses. This assessment practice keeps us, as a college, accountable to students, each other, the academic community, and to other stakeholders. The second principle—*assessment designed and implemented for the sake of learning*—keeps our assessment focused. The third principle—*assessment sustained by dynamic interaction among those responsible for and participating in its processes*—keeps us mutually interdependent with shared responsibility for using results for improvement and evaluation of effectiveness.

As a context for evaluating student demonstration of abilities, we developed the concept of student assessment-as-learning (student assessment) as "a multidimensional process, integral to learning, that involves observing performances of an individual learner in action and judging [her] on the basis of public developmental criteria, with [self assessment and] resulting feedback to the learner" (Alverno College Faculty 1979; 1994, 6). Student assessments are embedded in every course.

When creating plans to conduct program or institutional assessment—which we define as processes that yield patterns of student and alumna learning, development, and performance on a range of educational outcomes—we begin by identifying the specific questions we want to explore and tailor a plan to address them. Yet, we find it useful to consider examples of questions that might frame institutional and program assessment (Hutchings and Marehese 1990):

- Do our graduates know and can they do what our degrees imply? How do we assure that?
- What do we intend that our students learn? At what level are they learning what we are teaching? Is that the level we intend?
- What is our college's contribution to student learning? How do we know it?
- What combination of institutional and student effort would it take to get to a next level of student learning?

It is not unusual for us to use student assessments integral to ongoing instruction that are part of the student's everyday coursework for the additional purposes of program and institutional assessment. In such circumstances, we refer to these assessments as *curriculum-embedded assessments*. There are many good reasons for using curriculum-embedded assessments. They fit with existing roles, responsibilities, and expertise of faculty in carrying out curriculum evaluation and development. By collectively reviewing patterns of student performance as they occur in the curriculum, this approach allows us to use what we have. Further, they are not an add-on for students. In addition, one assessment can serve multiple purposes. It gives students information about how well they are meeting course and program outcomes and how they can improve. It gives faculty information about the effectiveness of the current course; previous courses where the outcomes were taught and assessed; and depending on the level of the course, the overall program.

The following are examples of sources of evidence of student learning that we use for program assessment:

- capstone experiences (research projects, presentations, juried recitals),
- portfolios,
- scores and pass rates of licensure/certificate exams,
- substantial course assignments, and
- group projects that require demonstration of learning.

To further explain how we use some of the sources of evidence in program evaluation and academic planning, an example using student performance data from a capstone course in the social science department is given. At the time of the evaluation, the social science department had four programs: social science, political science, global studies, and community leadership. The five full-time faculty came from three disciplines: sociology, urban planning, and political science.

The problem with our curriculum became evident when the professor of the senior capstone course for social science majors observed that many of the students were unsuccessful in using theory in their final project. After the instructor discussed the problem with department colleagues, department members agreed to examine students' performances in the capstone course using criteria related to three program outcomes for the social science major. Although the initial problem appeared to involve only one of the program outcomes, they decided to do a more comprehensive analysis of student learning and the extent to which students were demonstrating several program outcomes.

We used an approach that was similar to methods used by other social science/sociology departments (Jennings, Lyda and Rienzi 2006). We analyzed a sample of nine students' senior projects from two semesters. Two faculty examined each student's senior project and compared their judgments with regard to the three outcomes, using criteria from the assignment that we had levelled into four categories (strongly met, met, weakly met, not met). We found strong inter-rater reliability. Then we compared these judgments to the instructor's judgments. Again, we found strong inter-rater reliability. From this analysis, we determined that the instructor's judgments were valid and reliable. Next, we examined the instructor's feedback on all of the students' performances from the two semesters and used the same criteria and categories to create a more comprehensive picture of student performance on the three outcomes.

Our analysis showed that a high percentage of the students successfully demonstrated two of the three outcomes. We also confirmed that there was a pattern of student performance showing weakness in the demonstration of one aspect of one of the outcomes pertaining to the application of theory.

Consequently, members of the department reviewed our assessment plan and identified the courses where theory was taught. Our initial discussion revealed that the faculty were teaching theory in the courses that were identified in the assessment plan. However, we discovered that our assessment plan did not contain a sufficient level of specificity regarding theory. This prompted us to describe for each other exactly which theories we taught, how students learned them, and how students were assessed. Our analysis revealed substantial developmental gaps in the curriculum regarding social theory; often, a student would use the same theory only once or twice throughout her program, which is not enough if we expect her to transfer and integrate her learning of theory. The problem was exacerbated by the interdisciplinary nature of the social science department—members of the department used a wide range of theories *from their own discipline.*

What did we do to strengthen students' skills in using theory? What curricular changes did we make? First, we reached consensus on which theories we would include in designated beginning, intermediate, and advanced-level courses. In addition, we made a commitment to offer our social theory course on an annual basis and to require all of our majors to take this specific course. (Prior to our analysis of student learning, we offered the course every other year and gave our students the option of taking our theory course or a theory-based philosophy course.) Further, we made major revisions in the advanced research methods course in order to strengthen opportunities for students to use social theory in their conceptualization of research projects and design. Lastly, we monitored student performances related to their application of theory to determine if our changes were having the intended positive impact, which they did.

In an example involving student portfolios, sample assessment, and interviews with students, the education department at Alverno conducted a program evaluation of teacher education at the mid-program level: (i) Are teacher candidates developing as effective teachers, as described by the program outcomes? And (ii) are they able to reflect on their teaching in a way that will guide their ongoing growth as teachers? The students' portfolio and work sample assessment during student teaching were assessed by faculty and a practitioner (e.g., principal of a school); faculty also conducted a one-on-one interview with the student. The faculty independently judged assessments already validated by the course instructor, using one common "referent" assessment. Then they discussed judgments in small groups, followed by a whole department discussion.

Their review indicated several strengths in students' performances and demonstrations of outcomes. Faculty also identified a few areas for improvement, which they addressed in action plans and continued to monitor.

Although these examples used student performance data from a capstone course and a variety of data from the mid-point of the student's program, similar approaches have been used with some of the other sources of evidence (e.g., substantial course assignments, group projects).

We also use a variety of data sources that provide indirect evidence of student learning, especially with regard to questions dealing with students' attitudes, perceptions, satisfaction, and experiences of the learning environment.

- Student and alumni surveys—On a regular basis we conduct alumni surveys to find out what students are doing after graduation, the extent to which they are working in a field related to their major, and their satisfaction with their learning experiences. Such information has helped us make improvements in career development services and in the curriculum of their major.
- Exit interviews/surveys/focus groups—Many departments at Alverno use one of these methods in their capstone course. Students often provide important information about factors related to student retention, which we share with Alverno's retention committee. In addition, students give us feedback about our curriculum, making specific suggestions for changes (e.g., adding a course that they think would be very helpful, discussing an instructor or course that they thought was particularly effective or ineffective, brainstorming name changes for a program). Generally speaking, faculty seriously

consider students' input and take action when they think it is called for. In the social science department, for example, we added a course based on students' recommendations and our analysis of the situation.

- Course evaluations—All of the course evaluations are read by one of the associate vice presidents of academic affairs, by the dean of the school, and by the associate dean or chair of the department (depending on the school's organizational structure). We are very mindful of our faculty's expertise and skill in teaching. We use the teaching evaluations as one source of information to make decisions about faculty development, tenure/continuous appointment, promotion, re-employment, and our curriculum.

In terms of college-wide sources of evidence of student learning, we use curriculum-embedded assessments as well as several other measures of student learning (e.g., alumni surveys, Noel-Levitz Satisfaction Survey). Our most comprehensive longitudinal institutional assessment is documented in *Learning That Lasts* (Mentkowski et al. 2000).

The following are brief descriptions of other approaches we use for program and institutional assessment.

Mid-Program General Education Assessment

In the paragraphs below, I go into some detail regarding this assessment and how we will use student performance data to analyze the effectiveness of our general education curriculum (and the curriculum in some fields of study). Through the leadership of the Council for Student Assessment, we have developed a new assessment to give students an opportunity to transfer and integrate their learning from specific courses in general education (with implications for some fields of study) that focus on the scientific method and the abilities of quantitative literacy, analysis, or problem solving. It also includes a substantive self-assessment component. Success in this assessment is a requirement for graduation.

The goals of the assessment are to: (i) foster student learning; (ii) provide students with opportunities for self assessment, which includes creating learning goals and plans that can help them strengthen their knowledge and abilities in the future; (iii) assess students' capacity to integrate and transfer their learning across courses and over time; and (iv) use performance data from the assessment to collectively evaluate, as a corporate faculty, student development of abilities and content knowledge and to make needed curricular improvements (or any other improvements deemed necessary).

We designed this mid-program assessment so that it focuses on a narrow cluster of abilities and discipline-based knowledge. The plan is to change the content/focus of the assessment when we are reasonably satisfied with students' demonstrations of integration and transfer of learning of the specified abilities and content areas. Drawing on academic literature on action research, we expect this to take 3–4 action research cycles. We plan to change the assessment every 5–6 years. Over 15 years or so, all eight of Alverno's institutional abilities and a variety of discipline-based content should have been assessed.

Throughout the process, we collaborated with many faculty, academic and ability departments, and administrative departments across the college. We have been keeping detailed documentation of our processes and decisions, partly for validity purposes and partly for creating a more efficient process for the next iteration of the assessment. We piloted the assessment in the fall of 2009 with a small group of students, and we fully implemented it in the 2010–2011 academic year. This summer, I will work with the educational research and evaluation department to analyze the student performance data and disaggregate results by subpopulations. I will also work with members of the Council for Student Assessment to plan all the faculty and academic staff in-service meeting to be held this August; we will present the findings and facilitate discussions about their interpretations and implications for improvement.

Wabash National Study of Liberal Arts Education

Alverno College joined the fall 2008 cohort of the Wabash National Study of the Liberal Arts (2011) to investigate longitudinal change on a range of externally designed measures of student outcomes. The study focuses on key liberal arts outcomes (e.g., critical thinking, moral reasoning) and the educational conditions and experiences that foster these outcomes (e.g., well-being, interest in and attitudes about diversity). Initial findings for Alverno student change during their first year have been presented on campus in the context of all faculty and academic staff in-service meetings and at a board of trustees meeting. In addition smaller deliberative settings, hosted by academic affairs and student services departments, have been used to engage faculty and staff more deeply in the findings, their interpretations, and how they inform our educational practices. Wabash findings are also contributing to the collective discourse on student retention and why some students may be more at risk. Faculty, staff, and trustees examined gains at Alverno in comparison with (i) norms for the other liberal arts colleges in the study, (ii) past research at Alverno, and (iii) statistical standards for estimating the size of the observed effects. In addition, the educational research and evaluation department at Alverno has presented on the statistical relationship between observed gains during the first year at Alverno and progress in the curriculum, as well as disaggregating results by subpopulations.

Consortium for Innovative Environments for Learning

The five institutions in the Consortium for Innovative Environments (2011) that are participating in the Wabash National Study of the Liberal Arts have initiated a data sharing process. The purpose of this project is to use observed differences in outcomes as a stimulus to better appreciation of the diverse practices at our institutions, how these are distinctly aligned with differences in mission and populations, and how and what we may learn from each other that can be adapted to our institutions.

National Survey of Student Engagement (NSSE)

On a regular schedule, we administer this survey to first-year and senior undergraduates to get a reading on the ways that our students are engaging learning in the curriculum. Researchers housed within NSSE at Indiana University oversee the standardized administration of the survey; development of benchmark summary indicators of effective educational practices; and distribution of reports to participating institutions, which include normative comparisons at the level of benchmarks and individual items. Campuses also receive their data at the level of the student, which enables institutions to do their own analyses. The processes we use for using NSSE data are very similar to my earlier description of the Wabash National Study of the Liberal Arts.

WHAT WE HAVE LEARNED

In our years of focusing on student learning and our sustained efforts dedicated to improvement, we have discovered some key ingredients for creating a community of inquiry about student learning.

- *Focus on our most meaningful questions.* Most faculty care about their discipline/profession and student learning. Faculty will be more engaged in conversations about student learning if they are allowed the flexibility to ask questions that matter to them—questions that emerge from their collective analysis of issues that are important to them (Manning 2005).
- *Use what we have.* Take stock of student performance data that we already have; take advantage of curriculum-embedded assessments for program evaluation. Also, be strategic in determining the data that we need. Engage faculty in such decisions to ensure that their questions are of great importance when deciding which data should be collected.
- *Build on the department's assessment plan.* As discussed earlier, a good assessment plan created through collaborative processes can strengthen

student learning and serve as one of the tools for effective program evaluation and improvement.

- *Collectively review patterns* of student performance as they occur in the curriculum.
- *Avoid the lone ranger syndrome.* By collaboratively examining student performance data, making meaning of them, and creating appropriate action plans, we are able to develop shared responsibility for the curriculum.
- *Build program and institutional assessment on our educational principles and mission. Connect it to student assessment.* Based on our experience at Alverno, creating a coherent curriculum fosters deep learning and increases students' capacities to transfer and integrate their learning (Mentkowski and Associates 2000);
- *Develop commitment to focus on student learning.* One of the most important responsibilities of institutional leaders is to structurally create time, space, and processes for sustained conversations about student learning. In the 1970s Alverno College did not have the funds to pay faculty extra money to transform the curriculum. However, President Read showed great resourcefulness and wisdom when she determined that she could give faculty the time to do this important work. She instituted the policy of having no classes on Friday afternoons from 1:00–4:00 pm; instead, this time was set aside for work in the discipline departments, ability departments, and all-college sessions. To this day, we have preserved the Friday afternoon time block, as well as three all-faculty institutes a year, for curricular work.

This article has given some explanation of Alverno's approach to outcome-based education with examples of how we pursue program and institutional assessment, albeit we have many remaining questions, which often seem to spawn new ones. Collaboratively discussing challenges and questions with our colleagues at other institutions creates opportunities for those engaged to see new approaches and possibilities. We look forward to the conversation.

NOTES

[1] For additional historical information, refer to Meehan (2011), Archives (2011), and Alverno College Faculty (1976; 2005).

[2] For more information about Joel Read, refer to Dictionary of Wisconsin History, (2012).

REFERENCES

Ability-Based Learning Program. 1973 (revised 1980, 1083, 1985, 1988, 1991, 1992, 1993, 1994, 1996, 2000, 2002, 2005, 2010). Milwaukee: Alverno College Institute.

Archives—A Trip Through Alverno History. 2011. *Alverno College*. At http://depts.alverno.edu/archives/archome/exhibits.html.

Alverno College Faculty. 1976 (revised 1981, 1985, 1989, 1992, and 2005). *Ability-Based Learning Outcomes: Teaching and Assessment at Alverno College*. Milwaukee: Alverno College Institute.

———. 1979 (revised 1985, 1994). *Student Assessment-As-Learning at Alverno College*. Milwaukee: Alverno College Institute.

Arenson, K.W. 1996. 6 Colleges With Bit of Genius Are Given $750,000 Rewards. *The New York Times*. At http://www.nytimes.com/1996/06/26/us/6-colleges-with-bit-of-genius-are-given-750000-rewards.html.

Banta, T.W., K.E. Black, and E.A. Jones. 2009. *Designing Effective Assessment: Principles and Profiles of Good Practice*. San Francisco: Jossey-Bass.

Colby, A., E. Beaumont, T. Ehrlich, and J. Stephens. 2010. *Educating Citizens: Preparing America's Undergraduates for Lives of Moral and Civic Responsibility*. San Francisco: Jossey-Bass/Carnegie Foundation for the Advancement of Teaching.

Consortium for Innovative Environments for Learning. 2011. At http://www.cielearn.org/.

Dictionary of Wisconsin History. 2012. *Wisconsin Historical Society*. At http://www.wisconsinhistory.org/dictionary/index.asp?action=view&term_id=15570&keyword=marquette.

Hutchings, P. and T. Marchese. 1990. Watching Assessment: Questions, Stories, Prospects. *Change* 22 (5): 12-38.

Jennings, P.K., L. Lyda, and B. Rienzi. 2006. Assessing Student Learning: A Case Study. *Teaching Sociology* 34 (3): 286-295.

Kuh, G.D., J. Kinzie, J.H. Schuh, and E.J. Whitt. 2010. *Student Success in College: Creating Conditions That Matter*. San Francisco: Jossey-Bass.

Loacker, G. and G. Rogers. 2005. *Assessment at Alverno College: Student, Program, Institutional*. Milwaukee: Alverno College Institute.

Maki, P.L. 2010. Assessing for Learning: Building a Sustainable Commitment across the Institution, 2nd ed. Sterling: Stylus Publishing.

Manning, M.M. 2005. Creating Conversations of Consequence. *NovaLearning*. At http://www.nhcc.edu/main/AboutNorthHennepin/Accreditation/AQIP/~/media/FacultyResources/Manning.ashx (accessed 4 July 2012).

Meehan, M. 2011. Celebrating 125 Years of Great Beginnings. *Alverno College*. At http://www.alverno.edu/125/.

Mentkowski, M. et al. 2000. *Learning That Lasts: Integrating Learning, Development, and Performance in College and Beyond*. San Francisco: Jossey-Bass.

Time Line of Alverno College History. 2009. *Alverno College*. At http://depts.alverno.edu/archives/archome/timeline.html.

Wabash National Study of the Liberal Arts. 2006-2009. 2011. *Center of Inquiry, Wabash College*. At http://www.liberalarts.wabash.edu/study-institutions/#2008.

APPENDIX 1. Relationships among Outcomes: Alverno College Social Science Example
FROM JEANA ABROMEIT – SSC 101, INTRODUCTION TO SOCIAL SCIENCE (1st Year, General Education Course)

MISSION

Alverno College is an institution of higher education dedicated to the undergraduate education of women and the graduate education of women and men. The students—their learning and personal and professional development—are the central focus of everyone associated with Alverno.

INSTITUTIONAL OUTCOMES

1. Communication
2. Analysis
3. Problem solving
4. Valuing in decision making
5. Social interaction
6. Developing a global perspective
7. Effective citizenship
8. Aesthetic engagement

PROGRAM OUTCOMES

1. *Use sociological perspectives:* You effectively use sociological concepts and theories to analyze, explain, and address significant social problems and public issues.

2. *Conduct social scientific research:* You effectively develop and use quantitative & qualitative research to investigate sociological questions and issues.

3. *Interact and communicate effectively in academic and community settings:* Apply sociological and communication expertise to express yourself and interact effectively with people from diverse backgrounds in a variety of academic and community contexts.

4. *Articulate your social philosophy:* You articulate your social philosophy and refine it in dialogue with others.

5. *Conduct meaningful self-assessment:* You demonstrate insight into your individual style and accurately judge the quality of your performance in your major using specific criteria in order to continually strengthen your knowledge and abilities.

*Program Outcomes 1–4 are in Course Outcome #1; Program Outcomes 1, 2, & 3 are in Course Outcome #2

COURSE OUTCOMES

Faculty introduce students to the perspectives, methods, & content of the social sciences. Students develop skill in analyzing social processes and structures and examining various social groups from sociological, anthropological, demographic, economic, & political perspectives. They also work at identifying their own values and learn how values originate in and shape the environment in which we live.

*Course Outcomes:

1. Make systematic observations of and inferences about social life.

2. Accurately use social scientific concepts to describe and analyze what you observe.

3. At a beginning level, identify diverse patterns in social life and explain how social, political, economic, and cultural forces contribute to patterns' emergence.

4. Describe influences of culture and existing political, social and economic organizations on your values, opinions and behaviors, and those of others.

5. Practice basic skills of research.

6. Apply social scientific abilities listed above to explore & compare diverse societies, & analyze how they might be interconnected.

7. Prepare to better address important public issues in your own community by describing what you already know and can do about these issues.

ASSESSMENT PROMPT

In the first major assessment, students choose between 2 options. In Option #1, they make participant observations of a micro-culture that is "new" to them, and they interview a cultural informant. They write a 4-6 page mini-ethnography using social scientific concepts to analyze the micro-culture.

Related Course Outcomes: 1 to 6

Criteria (Abbreviated)

1. Make numerous, accurate & detailed observations while conducting interviews and participant observations. (Analysis & Problem Solving L1 & L2)

2. Provide sufficient evidence from your observations to make well-supported inferences. (Analysis & Problem Solving L2)

3. Accurately use a variety of social scientific concepts in your analyses. (Analysis L2 & Possibly L3)

4. Optional: Correctly use a sociological theory to interpret and analyze the micro-culture. (Analysis L3)

5. Identify values in micro-culture & compare them to own values; describe your emotional responses and explain how they are connected to your values. (Valuing L1)

6. Demonstrate beginning-level skill in using ethical guidelines for research by obtaining written consent from the cultural informant, protecting confidentiality, & causing no harm to research participants. (Analysis & Problem Solving Level 2)

APPENDIX 1 (Continued)

SELF ASSESSMENT PROMPT

1. Examine your field notes/interview notes in terms of **how many** observations you made and how **accurate** and **detailed** they are. What do you notice?

2. In your research report, examine the extent to which **you used concepts in accurate and meaningful ways** as you analyzed the micro-culture or ethnocentrism.
   - Which concepts did you use accurately and meaningfully?
   - Which concepts, if any, did you use inaccurately/poorly?

3. Look at the "Observation Model." How well did you use it?

4. What one or two things will you do differently in the future to further strengthen your work in SSC 101? Be specific.

FEEDBACK (Excerpts)
Regarding Criterion #3:
In your self assessment, you indicated that you thought you used nonmaterial culture and symbols accurately, but not material culture. I agree. However, you used more than just the 2 concepts accurately and meaningfully at least once in your research report. Therefore, you demonstrated Level 2 in Analysis in Social Science.

To further strengthen your analytic ability, use concepts more frequently in your work. See my comments in your paper for suggestions.

Congratulations on your success in this assessment!

INVITED
ADDRESS

10

EDUCATION, LEARNING, AND MEASURING THE RIGHT THINGS

Ken Dryden

Leaders in Canadian higher education have a tough job. They are being asked to measure and justify what they never had to measure and justify before. My parents and most parents until recently had just assumed their kids were learning at university or college, and learning what they needed to learn.

Some were like my dad. When I was in university and I'd do something he thought was stupid, he'd say—"University? What we need for our kids is a practical education." But he was joking (mostly). Like most other parents he hadn't gone to university and had never had the chance. Now, here were all these kids surrounded by the best of everything—classrooms, labs, equipment, and facilities of all kinds, as well as teachers who hadn't just one degree but three or four. For their kids, university was sheer opportunity. And if their kids didn't learn, it was their own fault. The evidence of that learning, if ever they needed it, came later. Parents knew that university graduates earned more, and far more than high school-only graduates. They got better jobs. They lived better lives.

Cost wasn't much of an issue either. It wasn't just that tuition was lower but that most kids who went to university came from families where they could afford it. Kids whose families couldn't afford it didn't go. But that wasn't the end of the world either. Not every job, it seemed to people then, required a university education.

The job experience was also different. Companies hired their employees to work with that company forever. Not only did an employee have the chance to work his—and it was usually "his"—way up, he also learned his way up. There didn't need to be government loans to help those who couldn't afford university or college, so there also weren't big debts for

Measuring the Value of a Postsecondary Education, ed. K. Norrie and M.C. Lennon. Montreal and Kingston: Queen's Policy Studies Series, McGill-Queen's University Press. © 2013 All rights reserved.

them to pay off later. There also weren't big debates about whether higher education was really worth it. Of course, it was worth it. Everyone knew that!

But now institutions *are* expected to justify and measure because the cost of university and college is higher and can generate big debts for the many who now attend; because a postsecondary education now seems a necessity in everyone's life; because more people are graduating and not getting a job right away; and because—simply—more things *are* now being measured.

There's also pressure to measure because of what else is being measured—by *U.S. News & World Report*, by *Maclean's* and a host of other publications—many things that have little to do with real learning and what higher education is for—many things that you know aren't a big deal but because they are easy to measure and put in print, they become a big deal. So if you *are* going to measure—and now you need to—you feel the pressure at least to measure the right things.

All this reminds me of a conversation I once had with a former scout for the Montreal Canadiens. He said he'd developed a new formula for evaluating players and, excitedly, he took me through it. He had assigned a certain number of points to different categories—skating, size, competitiveness, etc.—which, as he was talking, seemed to me a little arbitrary—and then, even more excitedly, he announced that easily the best player of the time—Bobby Orr—got the highest number of points. *Eureka!* Then I got it. He hadn't used his categories and points as a way to reveal some heretofore invisible truths; in fact, he'd worked in the reverse. He'd identified the best player and from that decided on the most important things to measure. His formula didn't offer objective insight; he'd used it to confirm subjective opinion. To me that's the problem with many of the university ranking exercises that often make headlines today.

But there's another problem. It's a variation on one of the clichés of management—if you don't measure it, you don't do it. But in this case, if you do measure something, you know you will do it because you can't resist trying to make things better even if many of these things don't matter much. So if you measure the *wrong* thing, you'll do the *wrong* thing. You have to measure the right things and not measure the wrong things—even if you can.

What are the right things to measure?

My own experience, and the experience of our kids, are with universities, but much of what I say is relevant to the entire postsecondary system. I have a confession to make: I'm a university junkie. I travel a lot and whenever I can I rent a car, take an extra day or part-day, and discover the area. And when I do, no matter what roundabout route is required, I seek out the local universities and wander around their campuses. I've been to hundreds of campuses and I love the exciting feeling of learning and importance they give me.

Let me tell you what I think university does, what I think its value is.

To me, university is an incredible gathering place—a candy store of people and experiences like no other. It is a place where you're surrounded by students from many different backgrounds and countless different countries; by teachers who've given their lives to a field of study; by libraries, labs, and gyms that are bigger and better than you've ever seen in your life. It's a place where the learning is everywhere—in the classroom, where discussion can take you deeper and deeper into a course or a topic that is of *your* own choice, that builds on *your* interest, that may well become part of *your* future. It's a place of wonderful experiential learning; of music, dance, drama, visual arts, sports; and lots more.

A few years ago, I was helping a design company to imagine all that a redeveloped Varsity Stadium at the University of Toronto might be. I saw it as a contemporary Hart House, that historic but remarkably visionary place, where different facilities reflecting different learning experiences would be piled on top of each other. There would be classrooms, minilibraries, sports facilities, fitness areas, a large lecture hall, cafes, music rooms—all together in one place—with lots of windows so that those with a few primary interests but many curiosities, could be drawn to and fulfill those curiosities.

University is also about getting things wrong, as one does all the time and developing ways of coping with wrong and finding ways of making things better, if not getting them right. It's a 24-hour place where work is play and play is work; where you learn about others and you learn about yourself, living on your own perhaps for the first time, making your own decisions; where you really begin to imagine your own future, your path, your life, how you fit in, and what you will do.

University is where, maybe for the first time in your life, it's clear to you that learning matters and where you come to believe that you *can* learn. This is so critical in a world that's not only changing rapidly, but is transforming. In this transforming world, you need to adapt and to adapt you need to believe you can learn new things. And to believe you can learn new things, you need to have had good learning experiences. You need to feel you *can* learn.

And one more thing—this wasn't part of my university experience, and it's not part of the experience of many students now, but it should be. University needs to be a place where students learn and develop the capacity, the attitude, and the instinct to *think the future*. Today's students have more than 60 years of their lives ahead of them. During this lifetime, the world will change more and faster than it has ever changed through history. Will today's students be spectators to these changes, or will they also be participants in making and driving them?

We talk about the importance of "entrepreneurs" and most often we associate entrepreneurship with business. But, entrepreneurship is a way of thinking; it's an attitude and an approach. It's seeing something that needs to be done and doing it. Students need to do this same kind of thinking about their own lives, about their country, and about their world. They need to think the future in order to make the future.

Universities may be about learning the past and the present, but they are mostly about creating the future. Universities need to think this way even more consciously and start asking their faculty members and their students to think this way. We need to make universities and learning even more important to the future.

To me, all this is what a university is. As a student, this is what your grades earn you access to. This is what your money buys. Academic learning, experiential learning, learning about yourself and about others, learning that you can learn, learning to think the future—this is why a university matters so much.

As university researchers and administrators, this is what you need to measure. If you can measure this, if you can measure the differences over time in one university, if you can measure the differences between one university and another, measure them. Because if you can measure them, you'll do it. But, if you can't, if all you can measure are the wrong things, don't bother.

Queen's Policy Studies
Recent Publications

The Queen's Policy Studies Series is dedicated to the exploration of major public policy issues that confront governments and society in Canada and other nations.

Manuscript submission. We are pleased to consider new book proposals and manuscripts. Preliminary inquiries are welcome. A subvention is normally required for the publication of an academic book. Please direct questions or proposals to the Publications Unit by email at spspress@queensu.ca, or visit our website at: www.queensu.ca/sps/books, or contact us by phone at (613) 533-2192.

Our books are available from good bookstores everywhere, including the Queen's University bookstore (http://www.campusbookstore.com/). McGill-Queen's University Press is the exclusive world representative and distributor of books in the series. A full catalogue and ordering information may be found on their web site (http://mqup.mcgill.ca/).

School of Policy Studies

Measuring the Value of a Postsecondary Education, Ken Norrie and Mary Catharine Lennon (eds.) 2013. ISBN 978-1-55339-325-2

Immigration, Integration, and Inclusion in Ontario Cities, Caroline Andrew, John Biles, Meyer Burstein, Victoria M. Esses, and Erin Tolley (eds.) 2012. ISBN 978-1-55339-292-7

Diverse Nations, Diverse Responses: Approaches to Social Cohesion in Immigrant Societies, Paul Spoonley and Erin Tolley (eds.) 2012. ISBN 978-1-55339-309-2

Making EI Work: Research from the Mowat Centre Employment Insurance Task Force, Keith Banting and Jon Medow (eds.) 2012. ISBN 978-1-55339-323-8

Managing Immigration and Diversity in Canada: A Transatlantic Dialogue in the New Age of Migration, Dan Rodríguez-García (ed.) 2012. ISBN 978-1-55339-289-7

International Perspectives: Integration and Inclusion, James Frideres and John Biles (eds.) 2012. ISBN 978-1-55339-317-7

Dynamic Negotiations: Teacher Labour Relations in Canadian Elementary and Secondary Education, Sara Slinn and Arthur Sweetman (eds.) 2012. ISBN 978-1-55339-304-7

Where to from Here? Keeping Medicare Sustainable, Stephen Duckett 2012. ISBN 978-1-55339-318-4

International Migration in Uncertain Times, John Nieuwenhuysen, Howard Duncan, and Stine Neerup (eds.) 2012. ISBN 978-1-55339-308-5

Life After Forty: Official Languages Policy in Canada/Après quarante ans, les politiques de langue officielle au Canada, Jack Jedwab and Rodrigue Landry (eds.) 2011. ISBN 978-1-55339-279-8

From Innovation to Transformation: Moving up the Curve in Ontario Healthcare, Hon. Elinor Caplan, Dr. Tom Bigda-Peyton, Maia MacNiven, and Sandy Sheahan 2011. ISBN 978-1-55339-315-3

Academic Reform: Policy Options for Improving the Quality and Cost-Effectiveness of Undergraduate Education in Ontario, Ian D. Clark, David Trick, and Richard Van Loon 2011. ISBN 978-1-55339-310-8

Integration and Inclusion of Newcomers and Minorities across Canada, John Biles, Meyer Burstein, James Frideres, Erin Tolley, and Robert Vineberg (eds.) 2011. ISBN 978-1-55339-290-3

A New Synthesis of Public Administration: Serving in the 21ˢᵗ Century, Jocelyne Bourgon, 2011. Paper ISBN 978-1-55339-312-2 Cloth ISBN 978-1-55339-313-9

Recreating Canada: Essays in Honour of Paul Weiler, Randall Morck (ed.), 2011. ISBN 978-1-55339-273-6

Data Data Everywhere: Access and Accountability? Colleen M. Flood (ed.), 2011. ISBN 978-1-55339-236-1

Making the Case: Using Case Studies for Teaching and Knowledge Management in Public Administration, Andrew Graham, 2011. ISBN 978-1-55339-302-3

Centre for International and Defence Policy

Afghanistan in the Balance: Counterinsurgency, Comprehensive Approach, and Political Order, Hans-Georg Ehrhart, Sven Bernhard Gareis, and Charles Pentland (eds.), 2012. ISBN 978-1-55339-353-5

Security Operations in the 21st Century: Canadian Perspectives on the Comprehensive Approach, Michael Rostek and Peter Gizewski (eds.), 2011. ISBN 978-1-55339-351-1

Institute of Intergovernmental Relations

The Evolving Canadian Crown, Jennifer Smith and D. Michael Jackson (eds.), 2011. ISBN 978-1-55339-202-6

The Federal Idea: Essays in Honour of Ronald L. Watts, Thomas J. Courchene, John R. Allan, Christian Leuprecht, and Nadia Verrelli (eds.), 2011. Paper ISBN 978-1-55339-198-2 Cloth ISBN 978-1-55339-199-9

Our publications may be purchased at leading bookstores, including the Queen's University Bookstore (http://www.campusbookstore.com/) or can be ordered online from: McGill-Queen's University Press, at **http://mqup.mcgill.ca/ordering.php**

For more information about new and backlist titles from Queen's Policy Studies, visit http://www.queensu.ca/sps/books or visit the McGill-Queen's University Press web site at: **http://mqup.mcgill.ca/**